THE **TRIUMPH** *STORY*

THE *TRIUMPH* STORY

Racing and production models from 1902 to the present day

DAVID MINTON

Haynes Publishing

First published in 2002

A catalogue record for this book is available from the British Library

ISBN 1 85960 413 7

Library of Congress catalog card no. 2001-131350

Published by Haynes Publishing, Sparkford, Yeovil, Somerset, BA22 7JJ, UK

Tel: 01963 442030 Fax: 01963 440001
Int. tel: +44 1963 442030 Int. fax: +44 1963 440001
E-mail: sales@haynes-manuals.co.uk
Web site: www.haynes.co.uk

Haynes North America, Inc.,
861 Lawrence Drive, Newbury Park,
California 91320, USA

Printed and bound in England by
J. H. Haynes & Co. Ltd, Sparkford

Contents

Foreword by Percy Tait

The best days of my life were spent at Triumph. I don't mean that in any schoolboy sense, but the atmosphere at Meriden was wonderful. Looking back, I feel very proud to have been part of a team that was without doubt the best in the business. I visited some of the other factories and even worked here and there sometimes when it was necessary, but there really was nothing like Meriden.

What nobody now seems to know is that all racing was done on a shoestring. There were only five fitters in the Experimental Shop, although there was the test bed (department) as well with Doug Hele in charge. Jack Shemmings worked with him, and Jack was absolutely brilliant. I should explain that Triumph did not have a proper race department, so the Experimental Shop was where nearly all the race work was carried out, as well as the production development work. So it was a very busy place. If any testing had to be carried out at MIRA (Motor Industry Research Association test track), all the lads would go there after work if necessary no question at all.

I wonder how many people realised that the Daytona triples were race developed almost completely with the Daytona twins technology? I don't say it was done for nothing, but because everyone was dedicated and worked so hard in their own time using 'borrowed' race know-how, it must have cost very little.

Half the trouble was that Turner (Edward) did not approve of racing, especially in the early days, so when we began work on the 5TA (490cc twin) racers back in the mid-Sixties they had to be hidden from him. It was all done

in secret in a half-disused machine shed behind the Experimental Shop. Turner often said there was no point in spending lots of money going racing because it did not benefit production bikes. He began to change his mind when his bikes started doing well, especially in America, but he would never admit it. In fact an enormous amount of racing know-how was put into the production bikes. I know it was, because I had a hand in it.

A lot of people got the wrong impression of Turner and were frightened of him, but I always found that if you knew your job and did it properly, and were honest and direct with him, he respected you. We seemed to get on well. For instance, when we were putting the pre-unit construction 500cc twins together he came to MIRA. When I came in he asked me how the bike went. I told him that the teles were walking around the banking, and they were, you could see it! He said, 'Well, what do we do?' I told him we had to fit heavier bottom yoke clamp bolts and a slider bridge-piece, or we'd never get anywhere. He said, 'Can we do it?' He meant cheaply of course. I said 'Yes, easily.' And he said, 'Well, do it then.'

I liked Turner. He could be very kind and he had a sense of humour. When I got married back in the Fifties he sent to Holbrooks (furnishers) of Coventry and had my entire house fitted out with carpets. That was when he was still with his first wife. He was never the same once she died. He became a different man. Another time he and I went into the Experimental Shop and he nudged me and said, 'Watch this', and began patting around his pockets

as though searching for his cigarettes, because he was a heavy smoker. Almost immediately half-a-dozen arms holding packets of cigarettes and lighters whipped out towards him and he turned and winked at me.

Turner could ride pretty well, too. He used to test all the new models himself, but it could look funny. I've seen him jam his bowler hat down low on his head and take a Grand Prix out for some very fast mileage. What a picture!

I know very little about the really early days. I liked the old Tiger singles and was very sorry they were never developed, because they were the best of their time by a long way. Of the time before that, though, I know nothing, or very little. To have that early history, which I have never seen before, in a book like this gives me a lot of pleasure. I thought I knew most of the inside story of Triumph, but now I know there's another story as well.

I still grieve over Meriden. It was all so unnecessary because right up to the end Triumph was profitable. When NVT took over I was offered a job. I met Dennis Poore, who asked a lot of questions. I explained to him that I had covered 30,000 miles on one Trident during development without the slightest trouble. He asked me to do the same on a Commando. The NVT rescue crew picked me up in their van that lunchtime.

This was the beginning of the end of my time with both Triumph and Norton. My next challenge came from Yamaha, when I was asked to sort out the bad handling of its 650cc twins. But that's another story entirely.

Percy Tait pictured at the 1975 Isle of Man TT. (Elwyn Roberts)

Percy Tait aboard the 750 Trident racer during the 1974 Isle of Man TT. (Elwyn Roberts)

Introduction

The author makes no apologies over his admiration of Triumphs. Coventry and Meriden may not always have built the best motorcycles ever, and probably Hinckley never will either, but the marque has always been greater than its metal. This is truer now than ever it was because among more than motorcyclists alone the familiarly scripted 'Triumph' logo is increasingly becoming a British standard bearer. Paradoxically, in a world of nations grasping symbols of indigenous culture ever closer to their nationalistic hearts, it is also publicly hailed in both Continental Europe and North America – not merely as a standard of British engineering excellence but as a symbol linking all that was fine in the lost 'Golden Age' of motoring and motorcycling when the world was young with the white heat of new technology. Whatever may be the excellence of British leads in, for example, cancer research or software security, they rarely excite public imagination.

As with Harley-Davidson, Moto Guzzi and BMW, Triumphs have become more than motorcycles. This transformation, from general perceptions of utility transport with half-crazed occasional ventures into racing, into dynamic folk art is pretty recent. These four makes in particular, with the possible addition of Ducati, are motorcycling's living icons. At a time when stylists (curse them and their superficiality) tempt buyers of practicalities (from recipe books to shavers) to guillotine the past in favour of something new and therefore by definition better, and thus rupturing tradition, there is a growing fascination with the past which is now part of modern life.

Why are these four such icons? Because they reflect the soul of their nations or, rather, the perceived soul. A modern Harley-Davidson, so meticulously designed to an antiquated format, is the quarter horse on an early Mid-Western highway. A 'Boxer' BMW is the archetypal Teuton in perfect balance with his streaming autobahn. A Moto Guzzi is the vital statement of radical Italian individualism. And a Triumph, a Hinckley Triumph, reflects the British love of triumphing against all odds, because by all that's right it simply should not be. This, the Japanese cannot match, not even Honda the greatest manufacturer that has ever been. They, the Japanese, are seen as modern, as is everything post Second World War.

That this impression is inaccurate matters little of course. As far back as the 1930s, the British magazine *Motor Cycling* identified Triumph as being 'Not one of the pioneers', because Triumph was not established as a manufacturer until 1902. This date placed it among the second wave of manufacturers. Harley-Davidson in the same period, followed a year later. Not until two decades later, in 1921, did Moto Guzzi appear and BMW shortly after, in 1923. Yet all now are members of that exclusive club – national originals remaining true to the old values. As BMW discovered to its cost in the 1980s, when it attempted to break with its boxer engines, woe betide the Western manufacturer who scorns his origins for it is these we cherish.

When someone buys a modern Triumph he or she, consciously or not, is buying a pretty horny handed pedigree harking back to a time when bikes were built by calloused-thumb engineers in flat caps who brooked no nonsense about styling: 'If it looks right it must *be* right and that's all there is to it lad.' The fact that Edward Turner was much, much more of a stylist than an engineer and by being so was laying the foundations of the future, is something we conveniently overlook. His Speed Twin, after all, *looked* so right it *had* to be right and so it was, as precious little else on two wheels had ever been.

Now, of course, he or she who buys a Meriden 'Trumpet' rightly treasures it as a classic and basks in the reflected glory of times past when functionality ruled the roost, when development was indebted to racing, when designers rode their products to and from work. Besides, didn't our Trumpets then blow such clear clarion calls of victory against Harley-Davidson and BMW and Moto Guzzi? Well, not quite, but read on and revel in a story of such high adventure and romance that if it was offered as a novel you would never believe it.

1

Foundation

*Horses, the bicycle, a highway and social revolution; Triumph –
premier British motorcycle manufacturer, Bosch's HT magneto – a
technical revolution*

In 1884, Germany had been unified into a single nation for no more than 13 years. The US cavalry was two years away from its final campaigns against North America's indigenous people. Britain was still three years from the last of its colonial military actions – the Boer War. This was the old world, more closely related in the materially advancing West to that of Napoleon and Nelson than it is to us now. Yet the internal combustion engine, however slow and unsure, had been stuttering away in Germany (Dr N. A. Otto) and in England (Edward Butler) quite independently of each other, for eight years.

Although it was in most senses an old world, where horse transport was the highway norm, science was beginning to accelerate progress at a previously unimaginable rate. Steam-powered ships were replacing sail and the practice of machine-tooled mass production techniques had been adopted, largely as a consequence of Samuel Colt's (USA) introduction of his volume-produced 0.45 revolver in 1873. James K. Starley (GB) was about to produce his 'Safety' bicycle, which was to provide the skeleton for all two-wheelers throughout the next century.

Then, in the final decade of the 19th century, a revolution occurred, one which is rarely acknowledged by historians. The western world went bicycle crazy. Hundreds of thousands, millions, multitudes of men and women, mainly from the semi-skilled and artisan classes, discovered in the bicycle a uniquely satisfying and affordable form of cheap travel. For the first time in the history of the world, the great mass of its people had at their disposal a method of fast and convenient personal transport. Unlike the horse, the bicycle was clean and handy in towns and, in normal use, faster than four legs over empty highways.

In fact, the bicycle in the hands of committed enthusiasts was faster between towns than even the first cars, and certainly more reliable. So numerous were cyclists and so influential were cycling clubs that it was they who pioneered the first worth-while road maps in Britain. It was also they, not the rare, affluent and usually aristocratic motorists in the declining Victorian period, who, by-and-large were responsible for the improvement of the appalling old roads into reasonably graded highways.

This new means to travel at will fired the population as precious little before ever had. Cyclists discovered a thrilling new freedom of spirit within their freedom of movement. It was a wonderfully contagious 'virus' which infected, penetrated then stimulated immense changes. Without the slightest doubt the bicycle has contributed as much to social and political reform in Britain as has any other factor. Practically and figuratively it provided

Racing what appears to be a 3½HP model, c1907. VMCC

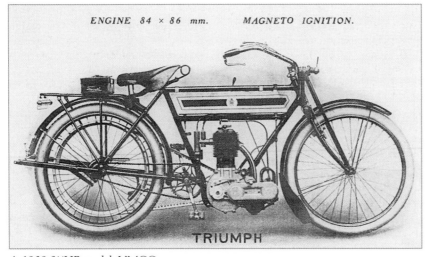

ENGINE 84 × 86 mm.   MAGNETO IGNITION.

TRIUMPH

A 1909 3½HP model. VMCC

the early Women's Movement (now feminism) with a vehicle of unparalleled power, providing as well as symbolising personal freedom. Any study of the posters of the period quickly reveals the bicycle's strong metaphysical elements.

Into this maelstrom of change, wherein the old world and the new clashed, often bitterly as hooves gave way to wheels, in November 1884 came Siegfried Bettman. He was a very well educated young German from an established professional family in Bavaria. At this time in history Britain was by far the world's greatest commercial power, thanks to a globally administered empire, which in turn had led to the City of London's domination of world banking and thus enterprise. Young Siegfried recognised London as a place of opportunity. With financial help from his father, and fluent in French and English, he found a position with Kelly's Directories selling space to Continental European companies. Dissatisfied, but with excellent contacts, over the next 18 months the ambitious young man moved from job to job, one of which was as a sales representative for the White Sewing Machine Company of America, throughout Europe and North Africa.

This gave him the experience to start his own business as the British importer of German sewing machines. He also recognised a boom industry when he saw one and decided to capitalise on the unprecedented bicycling craze of the period. There can be little

doubt that his familiarity with the lightweight machinery of sewing machines encouraged him into the bicycle business.

London may well have been the trading centre but Birmingham, with good reason, claimed to be the 'Workshop of the World'. Bettman had his bicycles made for him by William Andrews, a Birmingham contract engineer. British bicycles were then especially highly prized but to Bettman's dismay his exports were poor, probably because the name was not identifiably British, and his home sales were also unsatisfactory. By this time, Otto von Bismarck, young Germany's first chancellor, was voicing bellicose ambitions for an empire to rival the British, and Bettman must have appreciated the dislike in Britain for Germany because of the challenge it represented. Certainly the British had begun to resist buying German goods, often under a false pretext that they were shoddily made.

The name Triumph for his new company was a masterstroke, because while British it was also shared, or at least recognised, by most of Europe. The rebranded bicycles sold well enough through 1876 and 1877 for Bettman to need an assistant. How he met Mauritz Johann Schulte is a mystery, but as the two were both from Nuremberg, Bavaria, it could have only been through family connections. Bettman chose his partner shrewdly, for Schulte was a trained metallurgical engineer and by 1899 demand for the by now greatly improved bicycles had

increased to the stage whereby a strategic move had become necessary. Some modern authorities doubt Schulte's engineering background, but as it has been noted by a variety of reputable historians, and as the man evidenced such undeniable qualities, it seems churlish to deny his talents.

Schulte persuaded Bettman that to maintain the high production standards necessary to improve the new Triumph Cycle Company's sales they would have to build their own bicycles. Bettman agreed and Schulte located some premises in Coventry, which had become the bicycle manufacturing centre of Britain by exploiting neighbouring Birmingham's mighty industrial resources. Two incidents concerning the change were to have long-term effects. The property found by Schulte in Much Park was leased to Triumph by a local politician, Albert Thomson. He was sufficiently impressed by the two partners to invest in their company to the tune of £2,000 in partnership with Alfred Friedlander, a powerful Coventry financier. This not merely boosted the funds of the capital-starved new company, but of far greater significance it introduced Bettman into the ranks of the West Midlands industro-political Establishment. Equally decisively, of the capital the two men raised for the new business, Bettman obtained £500 from his family and Schulte just £150, giving the founder a useful 70 per cent shareholding advantage over his partner.

Triumph may have been small but it was highly profitable and even before the move to Coventry Schulte had been experimenting with motorcycles. Namely with the Hildebrand and Wolfmuller, which was imported from Germany with half an eye on Triumph becoming the British distributor, and half an eye on technical research, for Schulte was looking to his company's future. Motorcycles then were so rare that in company with intrepid representatives of other pioneer marques in 1895 Schulte demonstrated a few laps at Coventry Cycle Stadium, a racing circuit, but he was unimpressed with the German four-stroke twin. From reports at the time it appears that the demonstration was no sudden novelty, because Schulte rode with skill and

The old logo, or trademark, as used on the first 2hp, sometimes 2¼hp Minerva engined model of 1902. VMCC

experience. Nor did the diligent engineer find much merit with other motorcycles he rode.

Thanks to Schulte's single-minded pursuance of high quality and Bettman's flare for management, at the turn of the century Dunlop, impressed by the success of the Triumph Cycle Company, and probably following some sort of mutual agreement by Triumph to fit Dunlop tyres, persuaded Harvey du Cros, an Anglo-Irish businessman, to invest the then extraordinary amount of £45,000 in the company.

Using some of that money, Schulte began serious motorcycle research and in November 1902 a small, simple advertisement for a Triumph motorcycle appeared in *Motor Cycling* magazine's guide to London's Stanley Show. The magazine also enthused: 'The Triumph Cycle Co. Ltd (will) show their latest specially built frame fitted with the latest pattern Minerva engine (and) they have fitted a very clever arrangement for regulating the throttle valve. A rod is fitted to the top rail of the throttle valve, the top end being serrated with a number of notches into which engages a small spring governing the amount of lifting.' Smile if you like, but this was serious stuff at a time when little but innocent comment could be expected or even understood by writers in the thrall of combustion engine mecha-

nisms as alien to them as induction and exhaust harmonics are to us now.

As a consequence, solely of the stiff-necked, bloody-minded traditionalism of the horse-besotted, landed aristocracy who then owned and/or ran Britain – often both – and who perversely resisted progress, Britain had no engines to compare with Europe's best. Hence Schulte's choice in 1902 of the 2¼hp (rated) Belgian Minerva engine. Adopted by Triumph after what must have been painstaking research, the Minerva was greatly respected for its advanced specification, especially its patented mechanically operated inlet valve at a time when most were activated somewhat haphazardly by induction depression, and would remain so for some years. It sold well enough for Triumph to advertise in *The Motor Cycle* magazine for agents (retailers) in London, Manchester and Leeds. By this time the wretched Road Acts of 1861 and 1865 in Britain, that had been the prime cause of stagnation amongst British potential auto-engineers, had been repealed. From 1896, no longer was a pedestrian waving a red flag required to walk ahead of a self-propelled vehicle, thanks to the Locomotives on Highways Act. Because of men like Schulte, Britain began to catch up fast.

No material records remain of either the appearance or the performance of the embryonic Minerva-powered Triumph but one can only surmise a similarity with the following 1903 model, which employed a 293cc JAP engine. This was technically very similar to the Minerva, which as it was John A. Prestwich's first production unit is perhaps unsurprising. Announced at London's Stanley Show in March it appears to have dissatisfied the demanding Schulte, and by November that year a more powerful 3hp Fafnir-powered bike was on offer at £43. It was highly regarded by the press of the period, which reported in almost lyrical terms its magnificent speed and climbing ability. This was thanks to an engine which reportedly developed 3bhp at 1,800rpm, although one has to query the availability of accurate dynamometers at such an early age. By this time Schulte had decided that if Triumph was to establish itself firmly, it would have to do so on its own terms, as it had so successfully with bicycles, and achieve maximum control of its own destiny by manufacturing all it could of its own final product.

By this time, the British industry had reached a difficult stage. The glamour of truly original pioneering,

The milestone 3HP model equipped with Triumph's first, supremely successful, sv engine. VMCC

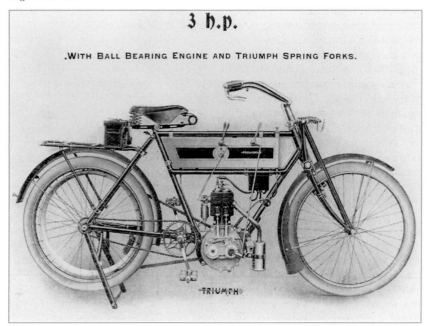

In 1906, Triumph offered the huge advantage of improved starting and reliability of Bosch's new HT magneto. VMCC

when rich young men regarded mechanical defects as personal challenges to be overcome through strength of leg, wallet or character, had disappeared. Ironically, motorcyclists had accepted the often previously unrealistic claims of manufacturers and were beginning to expect the sort of functional qualities that would at least allow the completion of a planned journey. Schulte's wisdom may well have saved Triumph, because although in 1904, towards the end of a boom, almost 23,000 motorcycles from 376 manufacturers were in use in Britain, a sales slump was about to appear. This was probably because the majority opinion held such a pessimistic view of the motorcycle's future, thanks to its notorious unreliability.

In 1905, after what must have been a period of the most intense design and development, Triumph announced its first all in-house motorcycle. This was the incomparable Model 3HP, which enforced on other manufacturers the same sort of high standards that Honda would 60 years later. As Honda, with its 305cc CB77 and 750cc CB750 almost single-handedly lifted motorcycling in Europe, if not the USA, from apparently irreversible decline as the 1960s gave way to the 1970s, so Triumph on the strength of its robustly dependable Model 3HP saved motorcycling from what may well have become a major depression.

Motorcycling has its milestone models – 1995 BMW R1100 R for its break with the steering head, 1977 BMW R100 RS for its aerodynamic stability; 1968 Honda CB750 for its glamorous practicality; 1936 Triumph Speed Twin for its potent civility; 1927 Velocette KTT for its positive stop foot-change, and the 1904 Triumph Model 3HP for its dependability. Make no mistake, this machine, above and beyond any other, formed the first evolutionary step in Britain towards the motorcycle as reliable transport. At its appearance, pioneering ceased and research and development followed in the wake of design based on applied knowledge.

Two men deserve credit for the 3HP – Mauritz Schulte, Triumph's technical director, and a new name in Triumph, Works Manager Charles Hathaway. Records are vague but it seems that he must have been engaged shortly after Triumph diversified into motorcycles. He is not often given the credit he deserves, but he was a motorcyclist of immense experience and a mechanic, if not an engineer, of rare application.

Motorcyclists then were plagued by a variety of ills. Quite apart from the social evils of drovers' whips, vindictive judiciary, mud and horse droppings, dust and rocks, and rashly unsuitable clothing, their machines

broke down. Punctures were a problem, although much less so to them than to their four-wheeled brethren's heavier and more highly stressed machinery. Ignition systems, of the low-tension variety with their delicate trembler coils and rickety contact breaker points, were gremlin-infested; spark plugs cooked, coked-up and literally fell apart; frames snapped; wheels collapsed and engines broke into their constituent parts, although rarely as originally fastened. Hathaway, the practical engineer-mechanic, with Schulte's executive lead developed the 3HP to counter this. As an example, the ignition system, while familiarly a low-tension coil, battery and contact-breaker type was sufficiently robust to operate for long periods without undue attention. The frame, although still little more than that of a delivery-boy's bicycle, was just about adequate.

Of greatest significance, the crankshaft ran on ball-bearings. At a time when hydrocarbon lubricants were more closely related to bitumen than they are to modern oils, it is not much exaggerating the case to state that if a rider managed to raise his machine's engine heat sufficient to burn off tar and clinker from the spark plug, the crude oil would through consequential loss of overheated lubricity eventually bring the crankshaft and/or its

The last of the non-Triumph-powered models, the 1905 2½HP, probably a Fafnir engine. VMCC

plain bearings to ruin. Besides, the only oil supply then was via a somewhat inconsistent flow from a hand-pump on the petrol tank. Triumph revolutionised durability with its ball bearing crankshaft. Ball bearings can whiz around with near impunity on little more than cooking oil.

One may get an idea of the standards of the time from a period advertisement, in which Triumph proudly claims that owners may anticipate 10,000 trouble-free miles from the ball bearing mains!

The twin demands of low engine speeds (to avoid engine stress) and thus high gearing for a reasonable pace, yet low road speed in town without a clutch, conflicted, often horribly. Hathaway – it must have been him – overcame this with his 3HP's massive 23lb (10.4kg) flywheels. They smoothed his engine's combustion strokes into a fluid series of utterly vibrationless and wholly charming pulses which seemed able to plod along at walking pace through town and tackle severe gradients with equanimity.

As far as performance is concerned, the 125lb (56.74kg) machine's 3bhp at 1,500rpm was enough for a top speed of about 45mph (72km/h), cruising at 30mph (48km/h) and petrol consumption of perhaps 90mpg (3.1 litre/100km). Other makes could rival this of course. Indian, Sunbeam, Rex and Peugeot were selling fine machines but few, if any, could equal the painstakingly developed and immensely satisfying well-rounded attributes of the 3HP. By the standards of the day its performance was vice free and trustworthy in all respects, it was innocent of rare maintenance trickery, the engine was durable, its finish was truly magnificent yet the supreme attraction of the model was its utter simplicity of operation. At a time when 90 per cent of all motorcycles made were bought on faith, ran on hope and maintained on charity, those such as the 3HP, on which an owner could more-or-less expect to

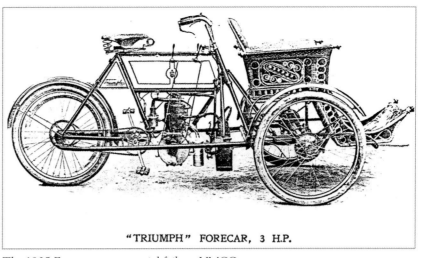

"TRIUMPH" FORECAR, 3 H.P.

The 1905 Forecar, a commercial failure. VMCC

start and finish a journey, were rare treasures.

Before the 3HP's first year's production had been completed, Lady Luck (who smiles on the virtuous), positively beamed at Triumph, as well as motorcycling in general, in the form of Bosch's invention of the high-tension (HT) magneto. Although the name of Simms is usually partnered with Bosch, in fact the technical development of the instrument was

wholly Bosch's, Simms being an English auto-industry entrepreneur of extraordinary investment wit.

For an extra £7 an owner could enjoy the huge benefits of truly reliable ignition on one of the few machines then in production with the potential to fully exploit the reliable and powerful ignition spark.

Reliability was rapidly becoming a partner in the adventure of motorcycling.

A 3HP model of 1905, but before the well-known for-and-aft front fork was employed. VMCC

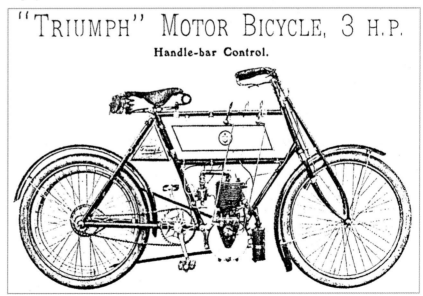

"TRIUMPH" MOTOR BICYCLE, 3 H.P.
Handle-bar Control.

2

Light pedal assistance

*Long-distance record breaking, racing begins in the Isle of Man,
the introduction of the clutch, pioneer running costs*

Anyone who has ever attempted to pedal more than a few yards on a 1970s 50cc moped will all-too-well appreciate, there's a lie hiding in the reassuring term light pedal assistance (LPA). Amongst pioneer manufacturers without the means to otherwise build hill-climbing motorcycles, LPA was intended to indicate gentle persuasion, but buyers quickly learned that it actually warned of a need for massive, often totally overwhelming, physical effort.

Admittedly, a 1905 3HP Model Triumph was claimed to weigh a mere 125lb (56.7kg), but that was its dry

weight. Include another approximate 40lb (18kg) for petrol, oil, tools and spares, a horn, lighting and then consider the additional weight of the rider's weatherproof clothing, say 20lb (9kg). Finally aim the whole sulking plot up a hill of rutted mud and stones and feel the Grim Reaper's presence in the leg-paralysing, chest-straining, sweat-drenching effort needed to get up. In theory, of course, a rider was expected to provide a little LPA up hills, but in practice, once engine speed had fallen far enough for the rider's legs to keep up with engine revs, he, rather than the labouring

machinery, would be contributing most to roadspeed.

As a consequence of the mixture of longish periods of comparatively undemanding riding punctuated by short bursts of huge physical effort combined with exposure from poor clothing, pioneer motorcyclists commonly suffered from rheumatic and bronchial ailments. Starting the clutchless, fixed-gear machines required strength, stamina and great co-ordination, while slowing them on a descent, let alone actually stopping them, demanded the forward planning strategies of a modern hot-air balloonist. Thus, the Victorian motorcyclist was of necessity male and young: riding motorcycles then had no practical value yet required strength and stamina combined with irrational boldness, so women in general remained aloof.

When, in January 1903, *The Motor Cycle* magazine published a report of the new 3HP model with its Triumph engine, although unappreciated at the time, it was heralding a new age. By this time there were 29,606 motorcycles in Britain and sales had begun to increase by approximately 7,500 per month. *The Motor Cycle* praised the new Triumph for its handling and stability, which it attributed to its long wheelbase, but was most impressed with the engine's 'elasticity' and smooth flexibility. Shortly after this the same magazine's Stanley Show review stated: 'Needless to say, the

The world's first purpose-built grand prix machine? This is a 1912 version of the 3½HP TT model with fixed gear and no pedals. VMCC

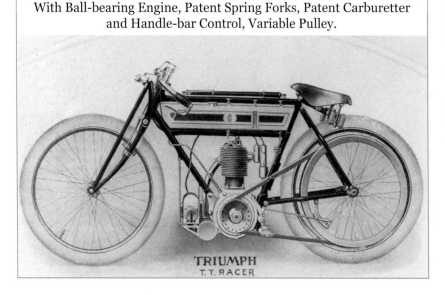

With Ball-bearing Engine, Patent Spring Forks, Patent Carburetter
and Handle-bar Control, Variable Pulley.

TRIUMPH
T.T. RACER

finish of these machines is beyond compare and their general excellence [of performance] is shown by the manner in which they performed in the hands of professionals and amateurs during last season.' In short, Triumph had not only won a place in the commercial stewpot, it was impressing experts and beginning to set standards.

Progress continued through 1905 but, thanks to Schulte's insistence upon rigorous testing before incorporating anything new, it seemed slow compared with other more ambitious manufacturers, such as Bitton & Harley which proudly offered for sale their now forgotten hub-centre steered model. By 1906 the working partnership of Schulte and Hathaway was paying dividends, as exemplified in the stronger frame now cradling the 3HP and a set of fore-and-aft sprung front forks.

Precisely why Hathaway, who as he shared patent rights with his employers must have been the fork's designer, did this at a time when almost everyone else recognised the need for up-and-down action, is hard to understand. A clue lies in some stability experiments carried out by NSU in the late 1930s, when this most progressive of German manufacturers' research and development programme revealed a considerable improvement in stability over bumpy surfaces once a fore-and-aft front fork action had been adopted. Despite their low power, motorcycles in the early years of the 20th century suffered badly from instability. As much as anything this was a consequence of their reliance on bicycle frames, however strengthened. Schulte, ahead of most, recognised the need for motorcycles to develop independently of bicycles if they were to properly mature, so it seems reasonable to assume that stability took precedence over comfort in the 1903 3HP's fork type.

Highly regarded Triumphs may have been, but an indication of even their fragile durability was revealed by an endurance test carried out by 'Ixion' (Rev, later Canon, Basil H. Davies), the erudite, tough, highly respected regular columnist to *The Motor Cycle*. Halfway through 1906 he rode a 3HP for 200 miles (321km)

daily for six days over Oxfordshire's broken byways. By the fifth day his machine's piston rings, bore, and exhaust valves had almost worn out. The valves were reground for the sixth day and the robust Ixion's tortured calf muscles had to make up for the worn piston rings and cylinder bore on hills; 1,200 miles (1,931km) in six days was then a example of rare reliability. However superior such proof of machine stamina (to say nothing of the long suffering Ixion) may have been, Schulte was sufficiently dismayed to engage a metallurgist to research further into improved engine component materials.

By this time Triumphs were proving popular with competitors in various events, mostly road based endurance-come-time trials, and hill-climbs. One of the greatest of these was Frank Hulbert, Triumph's works rider, who won so many events on his 3HP that he was close to dominating one and

all. A good many of these had been organised by the newly formed ACC (Auto Cycle Club) and which was to become the ACU (Auto Cycle Union). Perhaps the greatest of these was the ACC Six Days Trial, but this was merely the start of what was to become Triumph's first age of greatness.

Towards the end of 1906, Frank Hulbert knocked a stupendous seven seconds off the ACC's Dashwood Hill Climb with what was in reality a prototype 3½HP model. Now, while the 298cc 3HP is rightfully hailed as the one which earned Triumph national fame, and the 499cc 1911 free engine 3½HP model as that which won it global fame, in fact it was this new 453cc 3½HP model that technologically speaking was the real ground breaker. Its claimed power was up from its predecessors' 3bhp at 1,500rpm to a claimed 3.5bhp, although still at the same 1500 revs

J. R. Haswell fills up his 3½HP Triumph at Ramsey. He finished second and was the first amateur and the first single-cylinder home in the Isle of Man TT. VMCC

Jack Marshall, who was to feature so largely and influentially as a pioneer Triumph road racer. VMCC

and using the same 4.5:1 single gear ratio.

The original 298cc 3hp engine measured 78 x 76mm (oversquaring in its infancy), which in 1906 was enlarged to 453cc thanks to new dimensions of 82 x 86mm. Although fundamentally from the same blueprint as the 3HP, this new engine incorporated the sort of advanced specification that could have only originated from the type of painstaking development that was to make the name Triumph a symbol of two-wheeled virtue.

The 3½HP's frame had been strengthened to eliminate the occasional breakage, its height had been lowered an inch (25mm) to facilitate rider comfort and control, and a Bosch-Simms HT magneto was fitted as standard. It was chain driven from a crankshaft-driven sprocket mounted ahead of the crankcase. Internally, however, were more significant improvements, mainly in the form of forged-steel flywheels, the strength of which resisted the enlargement under stress of the sockets of the interference-fit crankpins, a common cause of failure in the early days of low-cost, high-volume iron casting. And around the steel wheels was the vital rim of extra-heavy cast iron whose inertia contributed so much to Triumph's high reputation. Another of Triumph's features could be recognised in the longevity of its cams and followers. Finely machined from top grade hard steel billets, which demanded the very best and therefore expensive machine tools, when so many others relied on cheaper, inferior materials, and despite their minimal lubrication these highly stressed parts wore well.

For £47 10s (£47.50) a motorcyclist could buy a 3½HP and enjoy ownership of a machine which he could be reasonably sure would provide him with faithful service over a few years of regular use. Even though the motorcycle had yet to blossom into the practical vehicle it was set to become, its performance had increased sufficiently for it to climb most main road hills without the need for LPA. In Triumph's case, while pedals were far from superfluous – being necessary for starting as the rider heaved the engine around – the 3½HP's addi-

tional 155cc and ½bhp was just about enough extra to attract the interest of serious racers. Remember, while approximately 30mph (48km/h) was generally considered to be an excellent travelling speed (approximate because speedometers barely existed then) a well fettled 3½HP over a flat road would eventually achieve a maximum of up to 50mph (80km/h).

Up to this point, most competitions had concentrated on reliability, but now that this was no longer a novelty, speed was the natural target. While most British county or town councils were agreeable at the time to licensing short duration events, like hill-climbs, on closed public highways, they inevitably refused to agree the same for the long distance road races then becoming popular.

Fortunately, the Isle of Man, while part of the United Kingdom enjoyed then as it still does, the freedom of law-making under its own parliament, or Tynwald. In 1904, its Governor, Lord Raglan, a motoring enthusiast fired by the Continent's famous International Gordon Bennett Cup car races, suggested to the Royal Automobile Club (RAC) that a request to hold the races in the IoM would be warmly considered. One year later when the ACC, which had been formed by the British motorcycle trade as a means of promoting their interests in the face of often strong

Establishment disapproval, needed a team trial venue for the poorly administered and short-lived International Cup Races, the IoM was the natural choice. They arranged what became known as the St John's Circuit, a 15.8-mile (25.4km) route. Following a proposal made by motorsport journalist, Etienne Boileau, at an ACC function in January 1907, the ACC made arrangements with the IoM Tynwald for a motorcycle race to be held in May of the same year over the St John's Circuit.

Because the race was intended to be a test of production models, regulations were drawn up and two classes adopted: one for single and another for twin-cylinder machines with 10 laps totalling 158 miles (254km) and a 10-minute rest halfway comprised the event. It was named the Tourist Trophy because, like the similarly named car races before it and which had their origins in the first Gordon Bennett race, it was intended for touring motorcycles. For this reason petrol was restricted for the singles to a consumption of 90mpg (3.1 litre/100km) and for the twins to 75mpg (3.8l/100km). Tool kits, spares and spare tyres, were required equipment. But, curiously, considering the time, the place and the inclination, pedals were not.

The world and his wife knows by now that Rem Fowler on a V-twin

The free engine 3½HP model of 1913 made all the difference to starting and stopping. VMCC

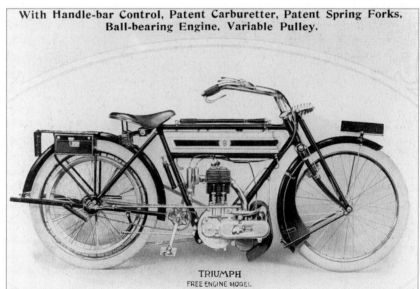

With Handle-bar Control, Patent Carburetter, Patent Spring Forks, Ball-bearing Engine, Variable Pulley.

TRIUMPH
FREE ENGINE MODEL

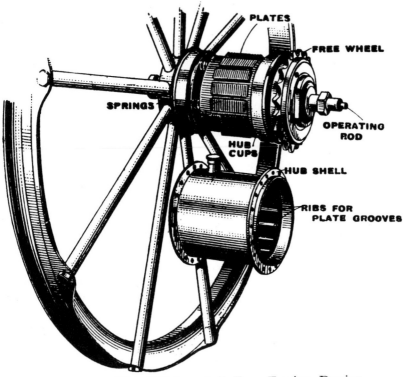

The " Triumph " Free Engine Device.

This is the free engine device, in reality a tiny hub-located multi-plate clutch. Its nature was erratic and somewhat fragile, but that has to be the way of progress. VMCC

Peugeot-engined Norton won. He did so at an average speed of 38.22mph (61.5km/h), including a fastest lap of 43mph (69km/h), thanks to Norton's crafty race-tuning trick of employing stronger inlet valve springs than standard. Inlet valves then were commonly 'automatic', which means they were opened against light spring pressure by cylinder depression on the idle stroke's piston descent. James Norton, founder of that company, race tuned his V-twin's engine by increasing the light seating spring pressure from 4 to 8lb (1.8–3.6kg), which ensured less fresh mixture was lost as the valve seated faster and more securely as cylinder depression was lost. Much less remembered are Jack Marshall's (37.11mph/59.7km/h) and Frank Hulbert's (35.89mph/57.78km/h) second and third places to Charlie Collier, who on a Matchless (possibly Triumph's greatest rival at the time) won the single-cylinder class. Marshall and Hulbert rode Triumph singles.

The ambitious Schulte was not best pleased, because by this time he, or perhaps Hathaway, had improved the

3½HP still further by overboring it by 2mm and so increasing displacement to 475cc. At the same time iron-casting technique had improved to ensure minimal cylinder distortion when hot, and Triumph had equipped the machine with its new and supremely efficient tandem-barrel carburettor, which was a great improvement over the old Brown & Barlow instrument. Unsurprisingly Marshal, like Hulbert, had stripped his machine to its limit, which included the removal of its pedals. Collier had retained his.

Triumph, presumably through the influential Bettman, protested that this was, after all, a race for motorcycles (as opposed to motorised pedal cycles), and that had Triumph fitted its machines with pedals, like Matchless, then it would have won. Pedals, Triumph insisted, should actually be banned. Against the odds this was accepted as the rule for all subsequent races, despite the fact that in this first TT, Marshal had been forced to run beside his stripped down and pedal-less Triumph up Creg Willy's Hill steep ascent! Collier pedalled,

while on his 690cc Norton twin, Fowler did not.

The consequences of all this were far-reaching because for the following year, 1908, Triumph constructed what should be regarded as the world's first pure grand prix racer. This time Jack Marshal won the singles class from Matchless's Charlie Collier at an average speed of 40.49mph (65km/h) and a fastest lap of 42.48mph (68.36km/h). Collier achieved a race average of 40.01mph (64.3km/h). H. Reed on a V-twin DOT won the twin-cylinder class at 38.5mph (62km/h). Eight of these special racing 3½HPs entered the 1910 IoM TT and eight finished. From thereon British motorcyclists adopted four new lore. 1: Triumphs were the undisputed lords of two-wheeled creation. 2: pedals were primitive. 3: the IoM TT would be the sole hunting ground of big singles, save for a few briefly amusing aberrations. 4: European road-racing machines would evolve into razor-edged specialised exotica.

These TT racers were closely based on the standard 3½HP but with numerous modifications. The frame was lowered, as was the saddle and handlebars, the wheelbase lost a couple of inches to quicken steering, there was provision for neither pedals nor lighting, and engine power was raised by recarburation and an open racing exhaust system. No great power tuning method was adopted within the engine, apart from the preference of some riders for slightly stronger valve springs. Considering their primitive design these machines had a surprising turn of speed, although their acceleration was by modern standards minimal. For all that, a well prepared racer in good hands could manage anything up to a maximum of 70mph (113km/h).

From a modern perspective, the difficulties of racing over roads that now would be regarded as a forest track ideal for enduros are hard to image. So consider this. Vital items specified by Triumph for its racer were high tensile steel wheel rims, because the mild steel rims of the roadsters were insufficiently robust. In those days tyres were bead-edged. Without the wire universal now through the periphery of their edges, tyres could only be held on their rims by the most stupendous pressures, which forced the bead-edge under an inner lip on the wheel rim. Tyre pressure could be anything up to 90psi (6.2 bar) and 70psi (4.83 bar) was normal on these 2.25 tyres. Yet still this was inadequate. The effect on riders of hurtling over bad roads on these effectively suspension-less machines on wood-hard tyres was brutal.

By 1910, the second technological step in the evolution of the motorcycle was under way. The first had been the adoption of the HT magneto, which provided previously unimaginable reliability. The second step towards social acceptability was Triumph's 'free engine' device. This took the form of a miniature wet drum 'clutch' within the rear wheel hub. It was foot operated and while far from flawless, for it tended to stick, it transformed starting especially.

Until its introduction, a rider could in practice only fire his machine's engine either by push or pedal starting, which with a fixed gear required an open road, an agile body and nimble fingers on the controls. With the new device an engine could be started up by placing the bike on the stand and pedalling. Once the engine was running the clutch could be disengaged, the machine rolled off the stand and then, when the rider was seated securely, the rear-hub clutch engaged for a rolling start. Although in truth this could often prove a little sudden, for the first time motorcycling was reliably available to the average woman.

Since 1908 two gears of 4 and 6:1 had been offered, but while the new low ratio guaranteed the successful climb of almost any hill, to engage it the rider was forced to dismount and with his tool kit adjust the engine pulley to its new setting and remove a few inches of sections from the drive belt to take up the slack. However inconvenient it may seem now, when coupled to the stupendous low speed torque of the 3½hp engine, it endowed a Triumph with enough energy to climb any main road hill in Britain. To demonstrate this in January 1910, Triumph's chief tester and two pillion passengers ascended Worcester's

notoriously steep Stoneleigh Hill in top gear on one of the experimental 499cc (86 x 88mm) free engine models, stopped half way up, and restarted. As a matter of interest, every Triumph was tested for 15 miles (24km) by one of a team of eight test riders before it left the factory.

Largely on the strength of its free engine models, these were momentous times for Triumph. During 1910, its machines made headlines time after time. In June they came home third (W. Creyton at 46.28mph/74.5km/h behind vengeful Matchless's Charlie Collier's win at 50.63mph/81.5km/h), fourth, fifth, sixth, seventh, eighth, 11th, 13th, and 15th in the last of the old-time IoM TT races around the St John's Circuit. From 1911 on, it was to be the arduous 37½-mile (60.3km) Mountain circuit with racing divided into the familiar Senior and Junior classes. Even so, Triumph riders finished high up, although none was on a leader board filled by what was possibly their second greatest rival – Indian.

In August, an extraordinary individual, insurance broker Ivan Hart-Davies, described in *Motor Cycling* how the purchase of a Triumph had allowed him for the first time to rely on a motorcycle for business purposes. 'In two days I can do one previous week's work.' The same man also claimed the record for the 900-mile (1,448km) Land's End–John O'Groat's route the length of Britain, at 33 hours and 22 minutes on his Triumph. He claimed, hopefully with some veracity, that he used the same machine for work and racing and that he covered 12,000 miles (19,311km) annually. The following year, 1911, Triumph supplied him with a specially prepared model equipped with an exceptionally large petrol tank, with which he reduced the record to 29 hours 12 minutes. Even now, a 30mph (50km/h) average speed over unmetalled roads and tracks would be a remarkable achievement; then it was downright superhuman, considering the iron-hard tyre pressures the old bead-edge tyres needed to remain in place; that and the lack of worthwhile suspension and brakes. Although admittedly Triumph and

Davies had stationed route marshals and fuel and service depots at strategic points along the way. Tragically, brave Hart-Davies, who displayed all the characteristics of a modern pentathlon athlete, was killed in an aeroplane crash during another of his endurance attempts.

The other great Triumph endurance rider was, of course, Albert Catt. This remarkable man decided in 1911, following a similar attempt the year previous, to double the distance set by Ixion in 1906. Using Northampton as his base, he rode his 3½HP free engine model the length and breadth of the country's appalling roads to cover 2,000 miles (3,218km) in six days. Without exaggeration the sustained effort almost killed him and left him in such poor physical condition that at the outset of the Great War in 1914 he was rejected by the Army as unfit.

That with the free engine model Triumph had cracked the practicability nut for good may be gauged by a report published in *The Motor Cycle*, June 1912. Without particular note it listed a helpful reader's running costs over one year and 7,007 miles (11,276km). Petrol consumption: 53.44mpg (5.28 litre/100km) £151 1s; drive belts £77 0s 9d; tyres £270 0s 5d; oil £11 0s 5d; repairs £51 0s 5d; extras £48; licence and insurance £93 4s; sundries £12 5s. Total: £716 4s at 1.2d (½p) per mile. Depreciation: £16 16s 3d. Grand total: 1¾d per mile.

As the new Triumphs established themselves, *The Motor Cycle* in March 1911 reviewed the range, commenting from a perspective difficult to perceive now, that it did not regard Triumph as a pioneer because: 'Triumph entered the industry comparatively late.' (!) It reflected that the first 3HP model of 1905 was: 'Inspired (with a) positively enthralling performance, excellent ignition . . . sturdy and reliable. The ordinary was not good enough for Mr Schulte. Triumph never stinted their customers.'

Shortly after Triumph got into its industrial stride, an event occurred which in the car world was of great consequence, although its effect on motorcycling was in general minimal. Brooklands opened in 1907.

3

Mud and blood

Don Rs, the immortal Trusty, kick-starts and foot-changes, proto-alternators, the remarkable 3TW, the Coventry Blitz, the unremarkable TRW

Triumph's fame lay in the incomparable reliability of its motorcycles. The two men responsible, Schulte, the idealist executive engineer, and Hathaway, his mechanically talented practical engineer, were methodical men. Nothing new was adopted unless its performance had been amply proved. Both were expert riders, especially Hathaway who annually logged a huge test mileage, so they knew their motorcycles intimately.

When the Great War of 1914–18 began, Triumph was one of the factories the British Government turned to for its supply of military motorcycles. The Model H, which was developed at the end of 1914 specifically for the Army, was in one outstanding respect – its belt-driven rear wheel – an old fashioned machine. More progressive manufacturers, such as Phelon & Moore, Indian and Royal Enfield, had by this time staked their futures

A squad of Trusty-equipped 'Tommies' of the First World War, pipes fully loaded and ready for action. VMCC

on the superiority of chain drive. Why not Triumph, whose Model H's reputation amongst despatch riders would surely have risen to mythological heights (it became legendary) with the advantages of chain drive? In fact, the Army had specified belt drive for the majority of its motorcycles, because it felt, with some justification, that belts were more reliable in the field than chains.

By far the majority of motorcyclists then relied on the good nature of belts to absorb their often simplistic riding methods, for mechanical sympathy was a rare commodity in those pioneering days. No less did manufacturers rely on the performance-enhancing nature of belt drive for reliability. Doubtless aware of all this, wise Schulte and Hathaway presented the army with a model which depended on tried and trusted technology, so in the hands of the average hard riding 'Tommy' it would, and did, resist abuse and keep going almost regardless.

Chain drive experiments had been carried out by Ixion in 1905 or so on his 3HP Model Triumph of which Triumph must have been aware and in all probability fully co-operated. Phelon and Moore's (Panther) all-chain twin-countershaft transmission was adapted, and to quote from Ixion's immortal motorcycling history, *Motor Cycle Cavalcade*, 'The additional vibration bred by the rigid drive literally shook both machines [there was another] to pieces. Every minor component either broke or fell off.' The experience made a profound impression on all concerned.

The 499cc 3½hp Type A Roadster first appeared in 1912 for £48 15s (£48.75) with a variable pulley affording two ratio steps of 4.25:1 and 6.25:1 following, of course, obligatory spanner work at the bottom of the hill. One year later the 550cc 4hp (85 x 97mm) Type A Roadster Free Engine Model appeared at £55 10s (£55. 50). If previous Triumphs had been torquey, the slogging ability of this model at low revs was stupendous. Few modern enthusiasts can begin to imagine what seems to be the sheer unstoppability of that mighty single at low revs. If ever a road-going internal combustion engine's power

It was not only the British Army that used 4hp Trusties. This military gentleman is a member of the Indian Army. VMCC

development resembled steam motivation, this was it. Also available at an extra £10 was either a Sturmey-Archer three-speed hub or Triumph's own hub-located free engine device (hub clutch). The free engine speed hub was not as good as it implied, because its plates often stuck together under the influence of the gluey engine oil available then. It could only be freed with a squirt of petrol, then needed further lubricating every 250 miles with more engine oil, and it often engaged with the sudden characteristics of a dog-clutch. As a consequence, when a rider incautiously let in his heel-and-toe pedal, it could, and sometimes did, break the drive belt.

The Sturmey-Archer device was actually little more than a heavy bicycle hub three-speed and was not overly successful because it was too fragile and quirky. Schulte, it is claimed, but most probably it was the self-effacing Hathaway, experimented with the free engine device on the engine shaft. Thus must have been born Triumph's notion of a multi-plate clutch.

Although the first military machines supplied by Triumph were

lightly modified Type A models, by far the majority from the final days of 1914 onward were the new Type H, which officially started production in 1915. Larger valves, lifted by more efficient gears and cams, increased engine power, and the old plain bronze-bushed big end was replaced by twin rows of caged roller bearings, which greatly improved longevity. However, the greatest improvement was to the Type H's transmission. It utilised a brand new system – chain-driven primary drive and spring-loaded face cam shock absorber sealed inside a cast aluminium oil bath, a multi-plate clutch and a three-speed Sturmey-Archer gearbox. Yet it retained belt drive. This, now an inch wide and of V section, was made of heavy rubberised canvas. It slipped much less over the engine pulley when wet than its predecessors. Perhaps best of all was the adoption of a kick-starter crank, which was allowed by the proper clutch. Gear ratios of 13.5, 8.25 and a top of 5.0:1 were standard.

Apart from the tiny two-stroke 'Baby', it was Triumph's first model without pedals – a curious mix of pioneering and progressive technology.

A 'Don R' at the outset of the Second World War, on what appears to be a 3HW.
VMCC

UK as essential equipment for the bad conditions of Egypt and Gallipoli. The plainly ingenious NCO rider-mechanic added: 'Our praise cannot be to high for the "Trusty" Triumph. Its durability is miraculous.'

These DRs had through trial and error modified the hand-change lever by shortening it and bending the end outward. A foot change improved a DR's machine control beyond that of a hand change, which could prove next-to-impossible in severe conditions, whether rock, ruts, mud or sand. Cog-swapping was not a simple operation, for the gear selectors contained no modern-style positive stop, but relied on steps in the hand lever gate guide. *The Motor Cycle* consulted Sturmey-Archer, then world leaders in motorcycle transmission who would eventually inspire Norton's unparalleled four-speeder. SA observed cautiously that: 'While possible, foot *and knee* (!) changes are familiar [to us] but [we] suspect they are not as simple as reports suggest. We propose to experiment.' One can only infer from this that gear changing with this modified system demanded considerable skill. Certainly the repositioning downwards of the wooden knob-ended hand-change lever, so it could be moved by the right foot, proved popular amongst Norton racers immediately following the First World War.

The claim that war stimulates material progress appears amply proven by the appearance of the Type H within a few weeks. Although the Great War broke out in August 1914, not until November of that year did the British Government wake up to the fact that this time active military communications would need more than an aristocratic young cornet fizzing with heroism on horseback. Once such radical information had been digested, the War Office panicked and at 13.00 Saturday, 3 November 1914 it telegraphed Triumph for 100 motorcycles for immediate despatch. In fact, because it was a weekend, the War Office had first to track down Charles Hathaway, Works Manager. By dint of astonishing effort Hathaway managed to locate a handful of the essential workforce and obtain the co-operation of vital subcontractors and 36 hours

Despatch riders loved it, although the 350cc fore-and-aft Douglas was also held in great respect. But in comparison with others, the Type H was light, handled easily, had near-miraculous tractability and, above and beyond all other considerations in that terrible place of mud, blood, shrapnel and death, it was utterly dependable. For this the Type H won the greatest accolade soldiers can give, a nickname. They called it after Triumph's own telegraphic address name – 'Trusty'. Its fame spread worldwide, at a time when the British Empire covered the globe and vehicles tough enough to

withstand the hammering of colonial conditions were in demand.

While to Velocette must go the prize for commercially manufacturing the world's first foot-operated, positive-stop efficient gear change, it is the Type H which deserves credit as manifesting the first foot-change modifications. Rumours of a popular Army foot-change modification to the Type H had been circulating in Britain. Not until February 1916 however, did *The Motor Cycle* report that Corporal Beck of the Royal Signals Division claimed his DR's (Despatch Riders) did it first in March 1915 prior to leaving the

later, the contract had been fulfilled with Type A models produced to military specification. The transmission system of this first batch is unknown but a few later Type As were supplied to the military in both free engine and three-speed specification.

The great bulk however, were Type Hs. They were in full-scale production by the very end of 1914 and were delivered early in 1915. Whether Triumph would have produced such a model, at least in such haste, without war stimulus, is conjectural. By good fortune for everyone concerned, Sturmey-Archer had its recently developed three-speed transmission package to hand and it, along with Triumph's own engine improvements, was fitted to the Type A basic rolling chassis. In total, 30,000 Triumphs were supplied to the military: 20,000 to the British Army and 10,000 to its allies.

Their civilian price in 1915, when the Type H appeared, was £63 cash or £68 on Triumph's own instalment plan. It was to be the last of the first generation, or belt-drive, Triumphs. Although recognisably a close relative of the 1905 3HP model, through the diligence of Schulte and Hathaway, within a single decade it had matured into a thoroughly dependable motorcycle with a reliability record equalling that of the best cars, and exceeding most. Probably no other belt-driven machine would ever be its equal.

Between the First and Second World Wars, Triumph, in concordance with other British manufacturers, supplied the War Office with a wide variety of military motorcycles for evaluation. Most were adaptations of existing civilian models and Triumph was never a major contractor. Then, in 1938, the War Office contracted Triumph for 10,000 of its specifically military designed 343cc sv 3SW.

By 1939 and the outbreak of the war, the War Office with Army experience, had decided what it required in a motorcycle after close consultation with leading British industrialists, journalists and competition riders of the period. It amounted to what we would now call a trail bike – a motorcycle combining a high standard of off-road capability with highway performance. By this time Edward Turner was running Triumph. Full of wartime vim and

Light weight and excellent torque have given TRWs a second lease of life in British pre-1965 trials. VMCC

ably assisted by a talented young engineer, Bert Hopwood, he was forcing the startlingly new 350cc 3TW parallel twin into advanced development. The prototype exceeded the performance brief of the War Office's proposed machine so terrifically during evaluation tests that it was planned that the design would be adopted as standard by all other manufacturers and built in large numbers under licence, as aircraft were.

A highway-equipped TRW with an Avon fairing, auxiliary headlamp and a dual seat. It would not have matched the 5T behind it. Cyril Ayton

The registration plate is the give-away. This is that rare Cub, a British Army T20WD. John Nelson

Its radical departure from normal was ac electrics, although the puny 20w alternator on this prototype was strangely within the timing chest. Its frame was wholly welded and the tank was a stress member. In 1940 an improved model was submitted for approval. A more powerful alternator was mounted on the crankshaft but outside the engine sprocket where its vulnerability to the hazards of ordinary motorcycling, let alone warfare, was plain. Significantly, a BTH magneto supplied the sparks. The redeveloped engine developed considerably more bottom end torque thanks to a milder camshaft and recarburation, heavier flywheels improved its slogging ability, the engine ran a built-up crankshaft on ball-and-roller-bearings, and a four-speed gearbox was fitted with a top gear ratio of 5.89:1. A set of tele-forks was fitted, but these, apparently, were of Matchless extraction, which in turn were of patent-busting BMW inspiration, so presumably would eventually have been licence built by Triumph.

The War Office had demanded a machine capable of 60–70mph (96–113km/h), averaging 80mpg (3.53 litre/100km), weighing no more than 300lb (136.2kg), stopping in 35ft (10m) from 30mph (48km/h), with a ground clearance of no less than 6in (152mm) and to be wholly inaudible under acceleration from half a mile (0.8km). What it got was a revelation in advanced design and performance.

The production 3TW had a top speed of 75mph (121km/h), averaged 75mpg (3.8 litre/100km), weighed a mere 259lb (117.6kg), stopped on a sixpence, was practically inaudible, was stupendously tractable and cost less to build than the £39 7s (£39.35) to £47 18s 11d (£47.94) – depending on specification – 3SW single. Had the aluminium alloys been available that Triumph had intended, it would have weighed a mere 235lb (106.7kg).

To sob, like a blister-fingered angler, into one's beer over the one that got away, achieves nothing but a briny pint. There are, however, real tragedies and the destruction of the Triumph factory in Coventry on that fateful night of 14 November 1940 when the city heart was obliterated was one. The human tragedy was plainly of the first magnitude. Further down the scale, however, is the secondary one to Triumph and to motorcycling in general, because Triumph that night lost what may have become one of the great motorcycles of history. Of the 50 produced, all save one model now thankfully with the National Motorcycle Museum near Birmingham, were lost along with all blueprints and machine tools. Had this not occurred then in all probability the magnificent 3TW, rather than the 5T, would have provided Triumph with its foundations for post-Second World War production.

In March 1941, *The Motor Cycle* published a test report on the new Army Triumph. The journalist, Arthur Bourne, was undisguisedly impressed beyond any previous experience and enthused liberally, as that austere journal rarely allowed. He claimed that its speed was superior to almost all other bike's, yet its tractability was too. It handled like a trials bike, held the road like a racer, accelerated in top between 20 and 50mph (32 and 80km/h) in just 12.6 seconds and, the journalist proposed, exceeded the highly regarded Tiger 85's performance all round. The price to the War Office of the two experimental versions was £250 for the first and £238 10s (£238.50) for the second.

Although the press was wildly enthusiastic about the proposed new Army twin, not everyone in the industry was. Neither Bert Hopwood, in a subordinate position to Turner, nor Freddie Clarke, Triumph's singularly talented development rider-cum-engineer in charge of Triumph's Experimental Department, much liked the ultra-lightweight 3TW. In their opinion sound engineering principles had been sacrificed as a means of achieving the necessary low mass and high performance. The fragility of its frame, the puny construction of its wheels and brakes and the delicacy of its undersized gearbox promised long-term notoriety.

Why, with one 3TW left to work back from and a wealth of intellectual capital, did Triumph not remake the project after bombing? Because its primary objective was to relocate to a new factory at Meriden village outside Coventry and then to produce in double-quick time what it did have to hand for the War Office. And that came in the shape of the 3SW and 5SW. They were military incarnations of the company's civilian utility 1935 sv single, and the 3HW, which was actually little other than a budget-built Tiger 80. In reality it was one of the liveliest of British Army bikes, but the irony of its enforced adoption is bitter indeed. If proof was needed of the 3HW's smashing performance, of all the tens of thousands of ex-military motorcycles sold into 'Civvy Street' after the war, none were in greater demand by British competitors than the khaki-coated 'Tiger 80s', but so very few have survived.

In the days before the Royal Corps of Signals had become famous as the White Helmets display team, and before they rode T140 Trophies, they collect their new TRWs. No khaki paint, lots of chrome, strengthened rear carriers and some with front-mudguard pillion pads! John Nelson

By that time the War Office, presumably influenced two-fold, by the reports that common sense suggests, must have been concerned with the unreliability of the planned new super-350s, as well as the rugged reliability of existing big singles, so changed its mind. The Army wanted strength and stamina much more than mere speed, and these it got in full from the tens of thousands of Norton 16Hs, BSA M20s and Royal Enfield WD/C 350s it received.

Approximately 1,476 5SWs, 13,420 3SWs and 30,720 3HWs were supplied to the War Office, the latter model costing £63 9s 8d.

There had also been a side-by-side development by Bert Hopwood of a 500cc sv twin, the 5TW, also specifically military, because of an Army demand for a heavy duty machine, combined with a War Office distrust

of ohv engines. They were probably regarded as over-complicated therefore potentially unreliable. By the middle of 1942 Hopwood's new machine was up and running and was planned for production for 1943, but by then Triumph was largely committed to its existing military commitments with its 3HW.

The 5TW may have reached production but by this time the War Office favoured big singles, so it was shelved. This was a shame because unlike all the other factories' Army bikes, which were adapted civilians, the 5TW, like the 3TW, was designed and built to meet a particular military brief. Slightly larger and heavier than the 3TW, the 5TW weighed 350lb (159kg), and the wheelbase was an inch longer at 52.5in (1,333mm), but it was also equipped with wholly alternator electrics of greater power. It

shared the 3TW's gearbox, although via a larger engine sprocket and top gear ratio had risen to 5.2:1. This was sufficient for unstressed cruising at a constant 60mph (96km/h), a top speed of 75mph (121km/h) and operational silencing exceeding even that of its smaller brother. A unique design feature by Hopwood was the routing of its inlet tracts internally between the barrels to improve cooling, which on hard driven, air-cooled sv engines is traditionally inadequate and the cause of countless breakdowns from blown head gaskets.

For reasons best known only to the inner workings of the British military, the 5TW was hauled off its dusty shelf at the end of the Second World War. Hopwood had left Triumph and Turner, ever a man to use what he had to hand, redesigned the engine to conform much more closely to his own 5T format: a sort of Speed Twin hobbled by a technically retrograde sv conversion and unsprung rear wheel. A very prosaic motorcycle, even by the military standards of the 1950s, its one and only claim to fame was its pioneering use of all-round ac electrics on a production machine. The author remembers riding them during his service with the RAF and wondering at the time, the early 1960s, why they were so popular with the world's military, which bought them in their thousands. Only years later, as a motorcycle journalist, did he discover that the design had been adopted by NATO as its approved standard military motorcycle. But they were reliable and tractable, and the flat purr of their exhausts made a pleasant travelling companion on convoy escort duty.

By the 1960s, the speed of newer military vehicles had increased to the extent of allowing the lorries the motorcyclists should have been policing, to frequently outpace the sublime, although laggardly, TRWs. They were frequently hefted secretly into the back of the trucks they were supposed to be escorting. One in good fettle produced about 23bhp and the top speed, with an illegally prone rider, was 75mph (121km/h) so long as the breeze was following. Normally they would accelerate to about 65mph (105km/h) before eventually topping out, which made the 'leap-frogging' of mile-spaced convoys, sometimes moving at over 50mph (80km/h), close to impossible.

With the exception of especially adapted civilian models, such as the 6T Trophy 650s adapted for use by the Royal Signals motorcycle display team, Triumph produced no more military models. With the arrival of ultra-sophisticated telecommunications, the world's soldiery at last had little use for motorcycles as a means of either policing or message duties, and bikes were limited to non-general role of specialist operation vehicles, often in throwaway roles.

4

Brooklands, before, during and after

Record breaking, the four-valve Riccy, the science of its development, TT racing and failure, the Horsman two-valve

The awesomely banked 2.767-mile (4.452km) circuit through Surrey woodland was an arena of speed unlike any other. Brooklands dominated the British motoring fraternity so completely that with the near exception of Sunbeam and ERA, few British car manufacturers paid serious attention to grand prix racing until the 1950s, long after it had closed. Fortunately for British motorcycling the Isle of Man closed its roads for racing and its fine, natural contours developed into a testing shrine to motorcycle racing unequalled in all the world. As a consequence of this, and in contrast to their four-wheeled cousins, British motorcycle manufacturers through the challenge of their home road race circuit in the Irish Sea, quickly developed a superior breed of grand prix motorcycles.

Racing at Brooklands was, therefore, less popular amongst two-wheel competitors than four-wheel, and it contributed much less to the development of the British motorcycle than did the whirling hills and unnumbered bends of the IoM TT Mountain circuit. Despite that, from its opening in 1907, the huge concrete circuit near Weybridge played an important role in the development of a particular type of motorcycle – the speed record breaker rather than the road racer. In truth, its designer, Colonel H. C. L. Holden, had not considered motorcycles in its planning because the general consensus of the period was that

they were too fragile to maintain high speeds for long. Be that as it may, Triumph featured large from the first days at Brooklands.

The first motorcycle race was held on 24 February 1908, as a one-off private match between O. L. Bickford on a 5hp (660cc) V-twin Vindec and W. G. McMinnies on a 3½HP Triumph. As betting was encouraged at Brooklands, as a means of attracting the affluent uncommitted and thus boosting revenue, the single-lap race probably had its origins in a wager. McMinnies won by 100 yards (91m) at 53mph (85km/h).

Following their remarkable early successes in the IoM TT races, Triumph riders continued to enjoy great success. In 1909 W. F. Newsome finished third, with other Triumphs arriving in fifth, 11th, 14th, and 15th places. The following year Triumph rider W. Creyton was third overall, with more Triumphs finishing 4th, 6th, 7th, 8th, 11th, 13th and 15th. Then in 1911, the first year of the Senior, in which singles up to 500cc and twins up to 585cc, and Junior classes, in which singles up to 300cc and twins up to 340cc were allowed, Indian swept the Senior leader board with their superb V-twins, but a Triumph was the first single in that class to arrive. Frank Haswell, Triumph's brilliant works all-rounder, kept factory honours high in 1912 against formidable opposition from F. A. Applebee on one of the radical

new Scotts. Their outrageous cornering ability and stupendous, howling power from their water-cooled twin-cylinder engines were destined to achieve legendary status in their lifetime and thereafter. Triumph's most determined 'enemy', Harry Collier on one of his Matchlesses, was as relentless as ever. At 46.41mph (74.68km/h), Haswell secured second place behind Applebee's 48.69mph (78.35km/h) and ahead of Collier's 44.89mph (72.24km/h). More Triumphs came in fifth, sixth, seventh, ninth and 16th. Evidently, the remarkable Haswell, rather like the even more remarkable Alfred Scott, had decided that two gears were enough. Because the racer's hub gear change was no less quirky than the roadster's, his machine's transmission was simplified by the removal of bottom gear.

Haswell was equally successful at Brooklands. In the Six-hour race of 1913, on his 3½HP single-speed TT model, he finished first after covering 351 miles (564km) and 1,315 yards (1,197m) at an average speed of 59mph. He was 53 miles (85km) ahead of V. V. Cookson, who on a 1,000cc V-twin Matchless managed just 298 miles (479km) and 1,180 yards (1,079m).

It will be appreciated by now that Triumph's huge sales successes did not depend on successions of increasingly important TT wins; people bought them because they finished high on

End to End Record   June 12th & 13th 1911 on 3½ Triumph
886 miles in 29 Hours 12 min

Humphhrey
WICK,

Ivan. B. Hart Davies

In his own handwriting the heroic Ivan Hart-Davies notes his end-to-end record. Over roads that in modern times could be mistaken for farm tracks, and without suspension or brakes he averaged 30mph (48km/h) – a decent enduro schedule today! VMCC

the leaderboard. This was their great strength – stamina partnered by dependability. With this in mind, who knows what Triumph's future would have been without the First World War, because in the Senior TT of 1914 Triumphs came home fifth, ninth, 16th, 27th and 37th. For all their success, however, it was undeniable that against formidable new designs from rival manufacturers, the old 3½HP was slipping.

After the war, Triumph convulsed. Schulte left and the range began to alter drastically, as did company policy. The faithful old Type H Trusty was at last equipped with chain final drive, including a transmission shock absorber. Inflation, following an industrial slump in the wake of the war, doubled the price of the new chain-driven Type SD, as the chain-modified Type H was listed, to £115.

A recently retired Army officer, Major H. B. Halford, began racing a sv Triumph single in 1920. Halford had been recently recruited by Harry (later Sir) Ricardo. They had met in 1915 when both were engaged on the development of an efficient high-altitude engine with which British fighters would be able to tackle the Zeppelin airships, which at 20,000 feet (6,000m) were bombing London with impunity, beyond the reach of existing aircraft. Halford was in the process of concluding a new aeroengine design for which he was largely responsible. He was also a discerning motorcycle enthusiast.

This was years prior to the discovery of the advantages of lead oxides as a means of stabilising the combustion process, a subject on which Ricardo was an expert. He was, with his company's engineers, a leading world

authority on what now would be termed 'gas flow' technology, as well as metallurgy.

Halford was a skilful racing motorcyclist who had evidently chosen his bike carefully. Ricardo was impressed by the quality of its engineering but dismayed by its low compression and lack of turbulence within the combustion chamber. As a means of earning some extra cash at Brooklands his company's chemists had evolved an alcohol-based racing fuel which would allow higher compression ratios than the normal limit of 5:1. In the last race of the 1920 season, Halford raced his 3½HP on the new fuel and won his class easily.

Thus inspired, Ricardo's engineering company decided on a programme of engine development. In the normal course of events it may not have done so, but it lacked sponsorship, times were hard and the company needed a stronger public image. Past experience persuaded Ricardo engineers to exchange the old sv top end for an ohv conversion, employing the existing valve operating mechanism in the timing chest. The most startling new item, however, was a four-valve cylinder head cast in special high conductivity hard bronze. It is this which has turned the 'Ricardo' Triumph into an undeservedly respected motorcycle, because in fact four-valve heads had been employed by engine designers for many years previous, although mainly in big engines such as the Bentley cars, and also in Ricardo's own RHA aero engine. They were not generally favoured by motorcycle engineers who, through empirical development, had discovered the superior combustion chamber filling obtained from

two valves. Only recently has the power advantage of 'tumble', as the incoming fresh charge rolling into the chamber around a horizontal axis is described, been scientifically observed and measured ('swirl' is inducted mixture movement around a vertical axis). And tumble is more easily obtained with two valves than four. Ricardo was more interested in placing the spark plug centrally, from where the flame front of the burning charge would expand equally, thus more quickly, in all directions. The valves were placed at 30° in a pent-roof head rather than at the previous 45°, as a means of accelerating gas flow.

As a guarantee against the distortion that affected some hard-pushed, overheated racing Triumphs, Ricardo manufactured a cylinder barrel machined from a billet of 45 per cent

high carbon steel. Each head and barrel required lapping (time-consuming face-to-face fine hand grinding), because to improve heat exchange between barrel and head they were fitted together without a gasket. Rare in those days, a domed (according to Ricardo) aluminium piston, drilled for lightness and with a 'slipper', or split skirt, to minimise the effects of distortion, replaced the usual iron one, raising compression to a then astronomical 8:1. Because of the rising significance of the 500cc racing class, engine size was reduced from the SD's 550cc by the simple expediency of bore contraction from 85 to 81mm, leaving the stroke very long at the original 97mm. Finally, flywheel weight was lowered by skimming, largely as a means of reducing oil drag on a tiny reservoir held in the other-

The other great long-distance record breaker of the period, Albert Catt, who almost crippled himself proving that Triumph motorcycles did not break down or wear out. One wonders what philosophical musings brought about his clubman chum's tank legend. VMCC

wise total loss dry sump, but also to take advantage of the improved acceleration that would result from the lower mass of the lighter engine.

In Ricardo's dynamometer house, regular readings of 24 and 25bhp (18 and 19kW) at 5,000rpm were obtained on the modified engine. At the start of the racing season at Brooklands in 1921, Halford entered his new bike in an Open Class race and won hands down, despite competing against big twins. Continuing successes brought his employers, Ricardo, to the attention of two interested parties – competitors who believed, not without good reason, that the experimental Triumph's power originated from its fuel, and later on, from the Triumph factory.

The venture succeeded. Ricardo began to earn valuable royalties from the rise in racing fuel sales to Shell, to whom they were contracted. More significantly, though, Triumph had taken the bait and engaged Ricardo to further develop a new model for racing and volume production. That it occurred this way around is important – Ricardo alone designed and developed the engine, which only *after* its

early racing success, was engaged by Triumph. It was not vice-versa. As *The Motor Cycle* reported, making it plain that both press and public expected great things from the alliance of Triumph and Ricardo: 'The present engine, so far as the cylinder and valve gear and parts above the crankcase are concerned, has been entirely redesigned under the supervision of Mr H. R. Ricardo. The modifications comprise ideas which embody the most up-to-date internal engine practice.'

In TT format the basic engine specification of these still formidable singles included a cast-iron, wasted, two-ring piston and twin-caged roller big end, and roller cam followers with rocker arms between cams and valve stems to reduce side thrust, Amal TT carburettor, ⅜ x ¼in chain, clutch with inbuilt shock absorber and the option of a foot-change gear lever (modified hand-change system) for TT model owners wanting it. Its oil pump was foot operated. The designer, or more correctly the development engineer, behind these models was a Mr Stanley.

Now, while Shemans, Triumph's best hope on his works 'Riccy', man-

aged 43.30min (52mph/83.7km/h) in practice compared to Norton's H. Hassel at 42.13min, F. G. Edmonds on his semi-works TT sv single actually achieved the fastest TT lap at 40.08min (56.40mph/90.76km/h). This was faster than the winning trio of Howard Davies on one of the exceptionally powerful ohv AJS 350s, and Freddie Dixon and Bert le Vack, both on Indians. However, Edmonds was forced to retire on the last lap when three consecutive engine seizures followed his bike's oil tank split. Technically obsolete Triumph's big single may have been, but in view of the performances achieved in 1921, one is forced to conclude that its maximum power output must have equated roughly to that of the high-tech, four-valve, Riccy, which on petrol was averaging 20bhp as measured on a dynamometer. It was the end of Triumph's serious road racing involvement for a long time.

Although the Riccy, as it has become affectionately known, suffered mixed fortunes once it had reached production, none of these could be laid at Ricardo's door. Its speed in Ricardo's race specification was

It should have been a world-beating, record-breaking, race-winning super-sportster, but the 3½hp Type R, or 'Riccy' was never quite that after all. However, it has become an ultra-civilised sporting tourer beloved by modern vintage enthusiasts. VMCC

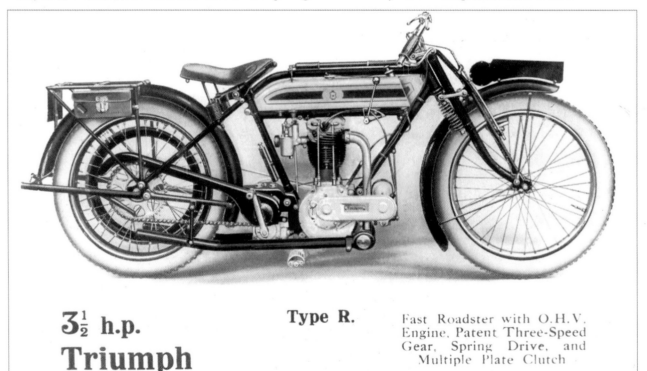

3½ h.p.

Triumph

Type R.

Fast Roadster with O.H.V. Engine. Patent Three-Speed Gear, Spring Drive, and Multiple Plate Clutch

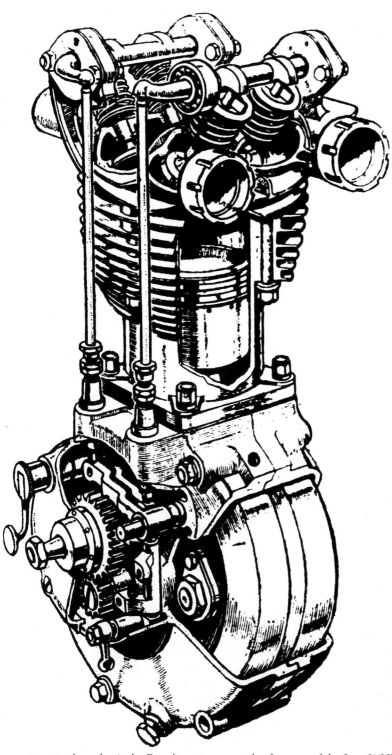

One may perceive how the 4-ohv Riccy's engine was a development of the 2-sv 3½HP. VMCC

valve trouble and while Shemans lay a creditable sixth for four laps, trouble with his gears forced him down to a final 16th place. Severe handling problems should have awakened Triumph to the deficiencies of its hopelessly obsolete fore-and-aft front fork and whippy old frame, as pointed out by its racing team, who to a man demanded the latest Druid front forks. They got them.

One should never judge a manufacturer by the tribulations of its racing team's first year's campaigning. By 1922 Triumph had replaced its old front fork with a new one of its own built to Druid patents, although ironically Norton, which was beginning to seriously challenge Triumph, was itself rejecting what it felt was the outmoded Druid fork in favour of the superior Webb. Following further development the Type R engine had been further improved. Its bore and stroke had been almost squared at 85 x 88mm, which not only improved combustion chamber shape but allowed an increased valve area by 25 per cent. The entire valve train had been strengthened, the exhaust ports had been splayed from parallel to improve cooling and lubrication had been improved; its total loss system had given way to a high pressure, double action, oscillating pump in a recirculatory system. Perhaps because of the greatly superior cooling provided by the new high volume, recirculating oiling method, an experimental engine equipped with a water-cooled cylinder head was abandoned. Alternatively, as cast iron had been adopted at the request of Triumph for cylinder barrel and head, possibly the water cooling was an attempt to cool an engine no longer suited to low-cost cast-iron construction.

By this time the Riccy had been adapted to run on petrol, whereas it had been conceived as a 'dope' burner (ethyl, benzole, acetone, water, two per cent castor oil as an upper cylinder lubricant, plus a pinch of smelly bone meal to satisfy the race-besotted public's olfactory conviction of fearfully secret chemical wizardry by Ricardo's sly boffins). Despite the 1922 engine improvements, dynamometer readings of 20bhp between 4,400 and 4,600rpm were recorded,

astounding. In the 1921 Brooklands Six-hour (or 500-mile) race, for instance, once its slipping clutch had been corrected, George Shemans's works Type R (Riccy) equalled the lap speeds of Bert le Vack's 1,000cc Indian

V-twin! During testing at Brooklands, Shemans maintained speeds up to 79mph (127km/h) during a non-stop 100-lap ride.

Triumph's Riccies in the TT of 1921 performed poorly. Two retired with

which on petrol-fed TT racers was reasonable enough.

Great things were expected. The young Walter Brandish finished second at 56.52mph (90.9km/h) in the Senior TT on his Riccy to the great ace, Sunbeam's Alex Bennet at 58.31mph (93.8km/h). Shortly after that, in August, another Riccy in private hands won the German TT (Grand Prix) 500cc event as well as setting a lap record. While at Brooklands, Halford gained a fine clutch of records principally for Triumph publicity purposes: 50 miles (80.5km) at 77.27mph (124.3km/h), the flying mile at 83.91mph (135km/h), and the One-hour at 76.74mph (123.4km/h). To cap it, a team of Riccies won gold medals in the ISDT.

In the light of such successes, even greater things were expected for the 1923 IoM TT. They almost occurred when Brandish astonished everyone with his consistent fastest speeds during practice, until he crashed and broke a leg at what is now Brandish Corner.

The chance that it was this alone which prompted Triumph to unexpectedly drop all major racing interest is pretty remote. Power politics within the company were responsible for that. But with the Riccy apparently set to become a terrific racing machine, especially if given a decent frame, it was tragic end. For all that it is undeniable that the Riccy even during its development was an old-fashioned machine of the first generation reliant on second-generation technology for its power. Triumph engineers must have been aware of its lack of future development potential, at least within the confines of their production budgets.

Despite their works racing successes, Riccies in private hands did not do well. Triumph relocated the essential central plug to one side and head-cracking was not uncommon. Their brakes were appalling, even by the quixotic standards of the day, and a return to Triumph's own cheapskate forks in 1924 combined with a frame sufficiently limp to frighten any rider unwise enough to use full racing engine power into discrete surrender. Roadster Riccies developed only half

the power of the racers and, although pleasingly civilised to ride, their top speed was disappointingly low at little more than 60mph (96km/h). On introduction they were priced at £120 cash, £129 on Triumph's Easy Payment Plan. When they finally ceased production in 1927, the contingencies of the period's recession had crushed this to a stark £55 for the basic model and £62 15s (£62.75) for the Lucas magdyno-equipped prestige example. A twistgrip throttle control cost an extra £1.

A road test report in *Motor Cycling* of January 1924 was full of praise for the Riccy. 'We have never ridden a better balanced single . . . very quiet . . . not the fastest sports 500 but [capable of] effortlessly superior high averages.' It was flexible down to 10mph (16km/h) in top gear, gave no trouble in three weeks' usage, covered over 1,000 miles (1,600km) including competing in the Exeter Trial, and managed the 56 miles (90km) between Salisbury and Beamish in 1 hour 40 minutes without extending ('scratching' as we say now) the machine. One is forced to query the impression given of fine stability because in reality, as we now know, it was poor and Riccy handling remains equally suspect. As the VMCC's Founder, Charles 'Titch' Allen commented about front fork action in his famous *First Vintage Roadtest Journal* (Bruce Main-Smith): 'Over anything like bumps or ripples the suspension becomes confused, getting out of phase with the bumps . . . going down on rebound when it should be coming up on bump.'

Quite possibly the Riccy, with its real need for a turned steel barrel and a bronze head, was simply too expensive for Triumph to persist with, especially in those fearfully austere times. Thus ended the brief life of a motorcycle which only a few years earlier had promised all the potency necessary to return Triumph to its former state of grace. Curiously, the Riccy, whose potential was rarely matched by its performance, has become one of the great icons of the modern collector.

To replace the Type R 'Riccy', Triumph produced the Two Valve. As late as 1925, Victor Horsman, one of the great bunch of professional race

engineer-rider-record breakers all nurtured by Brooklands and unquenchable thirsts for speed, had been doing well on a Triumph. *The Motor Cycle* reported in April that on a 607cc sv Triumph single Horsman had been timed over the flying mile at a mean 100.67mph (162km/h), and on a 599cc sv outfit had managed 69.54mph (112km/h). This may well have been the harbinger of Triumph's new Type 500, which was first sold to the public in 1927 as the ohv TT sports single which created so much press enthusiasm. To disassociate it from the four-valve Riccy, the Horsman-designed new Triumph was nicknamed the Two Valve.

Unlike any previous Triumph, the Two-Valve was recognisably modern in appearance, specification and performance. It started easily, usually first kick, the clutch was without quirks, the gearbox operation was simple and its mechanism robust, the frame was heavy and stiff, the forks strong and well sprung, the engine ran with solid assurance and its lubricant circulated unnoticed. Most of all, however, it was equipped with the new wire-beaded tyres, the introduction of which contributed as much to high-speed motorcycling then as tubeless radial tyres did in the 1980s. The congratulations of so many journalists to the fine shock absorbing qualities of the new front forks then making headway must in practice have owed a great deal to the lower tyre pressures needed by the self-secured wire-beaded tyres: 17 and 19psi (1.17 and 1.31 bar) front and rear had become normal recommendations.

Motor Cycling in March 1927 found the model to have intriguing 'Jekyll and Hyde characteristics', which in top gear without any ignition retard allowed a 14 to 73mph (22 to 117km/h) sweet tractability yet which was also powerful enough for fast touring. Its speed and high top gear of 4.39:1 deceived the tester into believing he covered his first 100 miles (161km) 20 per cent more slowly than he had, until the optional speedometer was fitted and the truth revealed. Braking efficiency conformed to a more historic tradition however. The best test distance was a distance of 18 yards (16m) from 30mph (48km/h) with both brakes on full. Summarising the bike the tester observed it was: 'So different from former Triumph productions . . .' *The Motor Cycle* noted in its test report how much more nimble was the Two Valve than the Riccy.

Unfortunately for Triumph, Norton by this time had begun reaping huge successes with its own new ohv machine, the 490cc ohv Model 18. It had appeared in 1922 and hounded the Two Valve. At Brooklands in 1925, Victor Horsman was concentrating on record breaking with the as-yet publicly unreleased Two Valve. He and Norton's Bert Denly over the next couple of years were to enthral the public with their high-speed duelling, during which, on a Two Valve, Horsman won as many as 140 national and international speed records for Triumph. In the autumn of 1925 he secured the prestige of becoming the first rider of a 500cc machine to average over 90mph (144.8km/h) within the hour at a recorded 90.79mph (146.10km/h). Then in the spring of 1926, Horsman raised the circuit's 500cc hour record to 94.15mph (151.6km/h) with his Two Valve, only to have it whipped from him in June by Denly on one of the race-prepared Norton Model 18s at 95.02mph (152.9km/h). A week later, Horsman saw further records slide further out of each when Denly, recording 100.58mph (161.86km/h) on the same Norton, became the first man to exceed 100mph (161km/h) for an hour on a 500cc machine.

Triumph did not give up road racing, although its interest had waned. All of Horsman's record breaking development was put into a road racing two-valve model for 1927.

On one of these machines Tommy Simister made third place in the Senior TT of that year. That it was not a second place behind Alec Bennett was due more to 'pilot error' than machinery flaw. On the first lap Simister crashed lightly and restarted quickly. By the fourth lap his times were among the top four – Stanley Woods and Bennett (works Nortons), Jimmy Simpson (AJS) and Tommy Spann (Sunbeam). Simpson and Woods then retired, leaving Simister free to overtake Spann into second place, but then Simister crashed again. He restarted, but either undisclosed machine damage or personal injury caused him to swing wildly and slow at Ramsey, where he lost a minute's time and was unable to make it up on the flying Guthrie who had slipped ahead. Bennett, on one of the new ohc Nortons, won at 68.41mph (109.65km/h) approximately eight uncatchable minutes ahead of Guthrie at 66.02mph (106km/h), while courageous Simister limped in on his battered Two Valve at 65.75mph (105.80km/h).

The Brooklands-inspired TT race model was actually much more lightly developed than its rivals, which conformed to Triumph's policy of racing only what it sold for road use. The model designation is confusing because Triumph listed a TT which was a mildly pepped Two Valve as the sporting partner to the standard model. In this trim they would return an impressive 75mph (120km/h) at least, which was comparable to anything else in its class. Triumph tuning for racing was simple and orthodox, involving a high compression piston, fiercer cams and bigger valves and

carburettor. To this specification the racer had a top speed, depending on circumstances, between 90 and 100mph (145 and 161km/h). In order to secure engine reliability at sustained high speed the 'automatic' lubrication system was reinforced by an extra large capacity oil tank under the saddle plus an auxiliary foot-operated oil pump, presumably for emergency or extreme contingencies.

Triumph, along with its customers, began at last to appreciate the need for powerful front brakes, so it exchanged the standard 5in (127mm) drum for a special 8in (203mm) device which, by the accounts of the day, returned an impressive performance. Its Triumph-built, Druid-type forks were oddly enough fitted with softer twin springs than standard, along with a Bentley & Draper friction damper. A pannier, or rounded, saddle tank was for the first time standard specification.

A 350 version was offered and returned an excellent performance virtually equal to the 500 in speed, but its sales were low and ceased after just two years. To illustrate their potency, the highway performance of the Two Valvers at least equalled and probably exceeded that of the greatly respected Sunbeam equivalents, at the time the standard by which most were judged.

Until the advent of the Val Page singles of 1933, the Two Valve was Triumph's top-of-the-range foundation machine. It deserves greater recognition than is usually granted because it was so utterly faithful and was, without doubt, the bike that hauled staid Triumph out of the Edwardian era.

5

Turner and beyond

*Pioneer Schulte's enforced retirement, Triumph winds up, the
Sangster connection, the car farce, Ariel, Turner and Page, BSA
steps in, Lady Docker steps out, Daimler V8s*

Triumph made Edward Turner no less than Edward Turner made Triumph. But before Turner there were other prime movers.

An ambitious man, although also a generous philanthropist, market-focussed Bettman saw diversification as the means of achieving his goal. Engineer Schulte alone perceived that a necessary rise in product quality had to come from within: metal fabrication skills at the turn of the century were frequently more venturesome than exact, and therein lay the rift. As early as 1914 Bettman had become the Standard Motor Company's chairman and by 1922 he had initiated car production in Coventry under the Triumph badge. By this time, Bettman had became part of Coventry's Establishment, attaining its Mayorship in 1907, only relinquishing it out of propriety at the outbreak of the First World War as he was German.

Schulte must have seen the end coming, when in 1919, the Triumph board invited Claude Holbrook, the very man who as an Army captain in 1914 had placed the first urgent order for 100 despatch rider machines with Triumph, to become, as Colonel Holbrook, the company's general manager. That same year, 1919, Triumph's board of directors invited Schulte, whom they probably saw as obstructively old fashioned, to resign. Schulte did so with a £15,000 gratuity.

Holbrook engineered the purchase of Hillman's abandoned car plant in Coventry and established the Triumph Motor Co.'s production of the Ricardo-designed 1.4-litre four-cylinder sv-engined light saloon, all in 1922. As predicted by Schulte, the diversification proved calamitous within the decade, although not even Schulte could have predicted the Depression of the late 1920s and early 1930s which inevitably caused Triumph's decline.

Fortunately, motorcycle production had been continued at the old Priory Street factory while cars were made at Much Park Street. In a doomed attempt to save its unprofitable car business the Triumph Motor Co. decided to sell first its bicycle plant in 1932 and then, in 1936, its motorcycle plant. Production of these had continued under the old Triumph Cycle Co. name.

During the mid-1930s, Triumph got itself into a real old pickle, as did so many manufacturers at that time. It sought to rise above the Depression by appealing to the comparatively unaffected wealthy classes of buyer. In a muddled attempt at sporting glamour the company invested heavily in its new 2.3-litre Dolomite sportster. As this was a barely disguised Alfa Romeo 8C to be built under a loose-knit licence, it surely was fated to fail because these GP race-based, eight-cylinder, supercharged, craftsman-assembled Italian thoroughbreds were complicated and highly strung cars that needed the deft touch of a master

to build, maintain and drive. Then Alfa stepped in, denying all agreements and, via threats of litigation, put a stop to the whole venture. Innocent of the abyss yawning between Italian promises and Italian commerce, Triumph loudly cried foul but retreated. On top of that, after its highly publicised Monte Carlo Rally Dolomite entry had crashed spectacularly enough with a steam train to generate even more adverse publicity, Lloyds, the company's bankers, also stepped in, surrendered to panic and put the second part of Triumph Cycle Co. up for sale.

The man who bought Triumph motorcycle manufacturing was Jack Sangster. No more influential figure would ever feature in the British motorcycle industry. Sangster was raised in an atmosphere of industry. His father, Charles, was a rare combination of trained mechanical engineer and astute businessman who, by 1897, was head of a large engineering company, Components Ltd, which manufactured parts, and even vehicles, for the British motor industry. With this around him, an excellent education behind him and one of the most perceptive and decisive brains of any industrialist in his head, Jack Sangster was destined for greatness. Following technical college the young Sangster received an engineering apprenticeship in the more advanced German and French auto-industries. When the First World War began he was 18

Edward Turner as a dashing young bowler-hatted engineer, contemplating the first production 500cc ohc Ariel Square 4 in 1930. VMCC

years old and was quickly commissioned into the Army, which appeared to have stimulated his imagination.

Components Ltd also owned Ariel, one of the great pioneers of British motorcycling. Ariel had won a reputation as a manufacturer of unusually high quality motorcycles. They were rarely exciting or innovative and were sometimes criticised for their rather dourly orthodox design. As well as excellence of execution, Ariel performance came from what would now be termed hand-selected component assembly. In the business of high production values, Ariel was proud to be Triumph's equal.

Triumph's demise in the Depression was common knowledge among industrialists of course. Ariel too was suffering, perhaps unsurprisingly in close parallel with Triumph, inasmuch as its venture into cars during the mid-1920s had not been successful

either. Jack Sangster learned a powerful lesson, one preached by Schulte before him – specialisation. When, in the hands of Charles Sangster, Component's Ltd folded in 1932 it seemed all was over for Ariel. But in his son, Jack, lay the company's new strength and through his powerful connections, private wealth and astute business dealing, the marque thrived again although reduced in both premises and product range.

When Charles Sangster died in 1934, Jack blossomed. He saw Triumph's potential as motorcycle makers and bought the bike division. Everyone felt relieved that one of the great marques was not after all terminally exiting with so many others. *Motor Cycling* had reported solemnly in January, 1936: 'The Board of the Triumph Co. Ltd announce that as from 31 January 1936 the manufacture of motorcycles will discontinue.

This action is a further step in the reorganisation of the company to which reference was made at the annual meeting in December last. Machines sold prior to this date will continue to be serviced by the company and spare parts will be available. The entire activities of the company are being concentrated on the new range of Gloria cars at the new works recently purchased.'

In this period of what seemed to be remorseless decline, Jack Sangster had earned a fine reputation as one of the kings of British industry, having turned around Ariel's fortunes. Thanks to this he gained the confidence of Lloyds Bank and acquired Triumph for £50,000.

Aware of Triumph's precarious position as one-time leader of the British industry yet with a lacklustre range, he cannily reintroduced Siegfried Bettman as Triumph's chairman. Even

One of Britain's greatest-ever all-rounders, the hugely talented Alan Jefferies, astride what appears to be a 5/10, possibly at Donington in the late 1930s. VMCC

though he was little more than a titular figurehead, Bettman's reputation and presence were living evidence of Triumph's strength and stability to the world at large.

What Sangster did lower down the management chain was to have much greater repercussions. He recognised the need for invigoration and in 1936 introduced two new men, both from Ariel, both hugely talented. They were Edward Turner as works manager and Bert Hopwood as designer. Val Page was already in the company, having been installed as chief designer in 1932.

Page had already started a programme of brand-new models, the most famous of which was the 650cc 6/1 parallel twin, but the most influential was the long-forgotten 250cc L2/1 single. He had also commenced consolidating the Triumph range from 18 models to a proposed eight, based around his new modular-based 2/1, 3/1 and 5/1 singles.

Precisely why Sangster allowed Turner to dismiss Page is now a matter of conjecture. Unquestionably it was not a matter of inadequate talent, as amply demonstrated by Page's past and future record. There are three probable alternatives. The first is that Page was not dismissed but had resigned in protest at Sangster's ruthless reduction of pay rates at Triumph. The second was more personal: Turner was not a true engineer and was known to demonstrate what amounted to fear of talented design engineers with impatience and bluster, presumably feeling that his professional skills were under threat. Finally, it may be that Page, a committed engineer, lacked the general works management qualities Turner found so desirable.

Page at the time was probably Britain's most talented design engineer. In 1908 he cut his apprenticeship teeth with the Clement-Talbot car company in London and by 1910 was employed at JAP as a design and development engineer. Here in particular, Page played at length with what were then dark forces invoked during cam design, valve operation, porting and combustion chamber shape, now all part of the computer-formulated science of gas flowing. In this Page stood head and shoulders above his two-wheeled rivals. It was he more than any other who made JAP and its competition singles and V-twins so world renowned. In 1920, for instance, Page set a 350cc sv JAP single spinning at the improbable speed of 10,000rpm, which even now is hard to imagine.

In all probability, Sangster was dismayed by the loss of Page to rival BSA

Few, if any, British engineers have shown the extraordinary design flair of Valentine Page. Here he stands beside one of his final motorcycles, the radical Ariel Leader. Seated is Ken Whistance, also of Ariel. VMCC

Giants of Meriden's Experimental Department (Comp' Shop), left to right: Jack Shemans, Arthur Jakeman, Doug Hele and Les Williams watching, evidently with some apprehension, a T120 racing engine on the 'brake'. Brian Nicholls

because in the following year, 1937, Page was back in Ariel's employ. In the meantime, Turner displayed what was to become his signature by redesigning and restyling Triumph's Page singles into the three Tiger singles, but sadly as mere transient heralds to his own new twin.

Edward Turner is a bit of a mystery. A great man, perhaps the greatest in the history of the British motorcycle industry, certainly the most influential, he was not necessarily a flawless human being. He was born in 1901 and, after displaying an aptitude for basic machine shop practice in his father's business, he joined the Merchant Navy at the outbreak of the First World War but remained about six years beyond. Always fascinated by cars and motorcycles, on leaving the sea he started a motorcycle business in Peckham, South London and by 1925 had become proprietor of a Velocette agency. Apparently he was a very persuasive salesman who found wheeling and dealing in large numbers of second-hand machines more rewarding than the rarer, however individually profitable, sales of brand new models.

During this time, Turner built his own machine, an unorthodox 350 single. He flogged it unsuccessfully around British factories until he met Jack Sangster. Ariel's managing director was impressed, less by the bike than by the man, whose grasp of management, finance, production and marketing were sufficient to win Turner a job as a development engineer at Ariel under Val Page, with a young Bert Hopwood working as his draughtsman.

Turner first achieved public recognition when his 500cc ohc square four was released in 1932. Although a very sweet engine, it was somewhat fragile and under-powered in its production form. In redesigned 600cc style it was more robust and as a 1,000cc ohv model was better still. But not until Page transformed the whole machine in 1950 did it begin to truly impress.

All went well with Turner until 1942 when, following what is usually regarded as growing hostility between himself and Sangster, they finally appeared to disagree so strongly over a string of company operating procedures, Sangster sacked Turner. With all the major factories working flat out on war materiel, BSA welcomed Turner. He remained with BSA for little more than a year before returning to Triumph with his extraordinary confidence in his own remarkable abilities, not one whit bruised.

Precisely why he disappeared and returned remains conjectural. But he found great difficulty working as a simple team member in BSA's huge management structure, and Sangster recognised his value to Triumph despite his egoism.

Turner, however, had one talent unequalled in the entire British auto-industry: he was an obsessive costings analyst. Alone amongst his contemporaries, and perhaps even among those who lived before and after him, Edward Turner knew down to the last ha'penny what every one of his motorcycles cost to build. This was so rare as to be almost unique. Most motorcycles, like other similarly complex high volume products, are priced at the maximum their market will accept and their cost accounting is as much retrospective as whimsical. With Triumph fighting for survival following Coventry's destruction by bombing in November 1940 and a company transfer to Meriden, Sangster saw that only Turner had the will to lead small Triumph against the growing might of the BSA and AMC consortia. Turner came home to Meriden.

When he took over Triumph management in 1942 Turner was faced by innumerable problems, the most pressing of which was a truculent workforce. As long ago as 1916 Triumph production workers, attempting to protect their higher-than-average wages and their localised security, challenged the government. The Ministry of Munitions (formed to administer materiel supply) had introduced a system of key worker employment control. If a production operation was found to be within the capability of semi or unskilled workers, the skilled worker could be transferred elsewhere as a means of maintaining production quality throughout British industry, or even transcripted into the military as a technician. To avoid localised imbalances, rates of pay were nationally standardised. Most of the unskilled and semi-skilled workforce replacing Triumph's craftsmen were women, and they were paid much less.

This was to have repercussions in Triumph's advertising of the 1920s when, apparently back to its 'men only' policy it proclaimed that none of its motorcycles were assembled by women. This was not in fact the wholly misogynistic claim that currently popular PC lore would have. With rare exception then, men alone possessed the kind of craft-based technical skills needed to produce consistently high-grade motorcycles, and they wanted their old jobs back.

Triumph's workforce in 1916 reacted angrily to what it saw as the destruction of its rightful standards of employment. It struck and this spread to involve 10,000 allied workers in Coventry before moving into Birmingham, with all the dire consequences of military supply rupture at source.

At this point the Ministry of Munitions moved quickly and harshly. Unequivocally it threatened instant, and active, military conscription for all participants in militant action. Triumph workers backed down, the national danger passed, but the threat was never forgotten by Triumph's workforce. Their aggression certainly worked because they were eventually paid higher rates than almost any other production workers in the British auto industry except for Jaguar's. To do them justice however, their pride in their product was second to none and the high quality of the product reflected this.

As Sangster had minimised Ariel expenditure in 1936 by reducing pay scales, so Turner did with Triumph in the same year. From that point on he remained aloof and uncommunicative from a workforce that was frightened of him and of which he was no less frightened himself. By and large all communications occurred through his secretary, the greatly respected, highly intelligent and supremely diplomatic Nan Plant. During her 21 years with Turner she was quietly courted by more desperate men than any princess ever dreamed, although all her suitors had motorcycles on their minds.

For a man of Sangster's all-too-evident commercial sagacity, Turner's post-1944 employment contract with Sangster remains a mystery. From his earliest days with Triumph, Turner been a regular visitor to the USA. There he made close friends with Bill Johnson, who ran a business importing Triumphs and Ariels, among other

British makes, and retailing them in the Los Angeles area. Doubtless Turner showed enthusiasm for Johnson when he discovered that he was running his own Triumph distribution operation, in which he ordered model batches ahead of sales, franchising them to selected dealers in southern California.

Johnson had also organised his own immensely successful Triumph racing team. Turner was mightily impressed.

On the strength of this relationship, Turner obtained a first-hand intimate knowledge of the American motorcycle scene that placed him at least a decade ahead of his greatest rival, BSA. When the Second World War ended, thanks to Turner's unequalled US experience in partnership with Johnson, Triumph shot from Britain's export starting blocks before the starting pistol had even been lifted. Turner quickly began spending

Jack Sangster, one of the most influential men in the history of the British motorcycle industry, receiving a commemorative gift at his retirement party at The George hotel, Solihull. John Nelson

half of every year in California, and it riled the various middle management experts under him in Meriden. While he was away the company ran smoothly; when he returned he created havoc, generally by arrogantly dismissing whatever decisions and new projects had been necessarily introduced during his absence and replacing them with his own tempestuously conceived alternatives.

He particularly riled Bert Hopwood, as Hopwood's seminal autobiographical book, *Whatever Happened to the British Motorcycle Industry?* reveals all too clearly. Hopwood was a hard-nosed, no-nonsense, Midland industrialist who rose rough-handed through the Birmingham hot metal industry via Birmingham Technical College and an engineering apprenticeship at Ariel. Turner's jealousy of what he saw as rivals, his lack of engineering nous, his petulance, his bombastic manners, his denial of aught but his own objectives and projects, so

frustrated Hopwood, Turner's head of engineering, it embittered Hopwood, who was a team man through and through, for life. What did not become generally known until his career was in its latter stages, was that Turner suffered from diabetes, and the characteristics of this illness can include extremes of mood, unpredictable changes of character and irrational behaviour. Coupled to that was the death of his wife, Edith, to whom he was utterly devoted, in a car crash in 1939. Then consider the effect on him of a second and somewhat tempestuous marriage late in life to a very young and excitable woman, and Turner's often inexplicable behaviour takes on a different hue. If anyone can be held responsible for nursing Turner through this dreadful period it was his super-secretary, the ever-faithful Nan Plant. Her constant vigilance on such matters as prescribed medication to schedule (during working hours) did more than provide the dismissive

Turner with essential equilibrium, it probably kept him alive.

In 1951, Sangster sold Triumph to BSA. At this time the giant BSA engineering group was making more money than sense and Sangster had promised BSA first option on the purchase of Triumph as part of Ariel's contract of sale to BSA in 1944. For all his apparent industrial perspicuity, this move actually revealed Sangster to be much less interested in the manufacture of motorcycles than he was in the safeguarding of his personal wealth. It was to set a trend.

Ariel was sold to BSA for £376,257, because Sangster claimed he needed the money to capitalise the potentially greater Triumph company's expansion in the post-war period. There was some truth in this of course and, indeed, the new factory at Meriden was expanded and new production equipment installed. But not quite enough though. During the 1950s when the USA especially was howling for many more bikes than Triumph appeared capable of producing, Turner initially decided to create a demand for Triumphs by limiting production to an absolute maximum of 10,000 units annually, thus restricting sales and thus ensuring vacant agency displays. Retailing experience in the 1920s had taught him to dislike full showrooms. It was a short-lived policy.

Not until he died in 1977 did it become apparent that Sangster's goal was death duty avoidance. Following its wartime government contracts, Ariel was indeed profitable, so he sold it, fearful of bequeathing little but death duty debt to his heirs. As Turner's unprecedented American export drive lifted Triumph into heady profitability, so Sangster apparently quailed again at the thought of the high death duties involved, so he sold it too. He sold it for £2.5 million ($10 million in 1951). He sold it cheap, very cheap, because Triumph was by far the most profitable bike maker in Britain, and the purchase price included Triumph's £1 million banked assets. BSA, alas, seemed not to appreciate the quality of the bargain it had struck.

Sangster, however, remained on the BSA board, as contracted during his sale of Triumph to BSA. For a few

Behind every great man . . . Nan Plant, Turner's great secretary, whose organisational talents disciplined Turner as no-one else ever managed. She was his anchor, and throughout the entire British industry, respect for her was absolute. John Nelson

years all went swimmingly. Triumph remained fiercely autonomous within the BSA group, more aggressive towards its giant owner than ever before. What had been 1946 sales of 9,529 motorcycles (5,254 UK, 4,275 export) by 1957 had risen to 13,047, a 27 per cent increase. For most of this period the BSA group's chairman was Sir Bernard Docker. For all practical purposes, as well as those of the national press to which rank glamour parallels scandal in the greed for headlines, Docker's personal 'chairman' was his wife, Nora. Her contemptible attitude towards the men and machines who made her wealth for her was exceeded only by her spendthrift devotion to glittering ostentation, of which her gold-plated Daimler car – as a prerequisite of her husband's noble position as a lion of British hot-metal industry – was the most notorious. And Daimler, part of the BSA group, was bleeding to death.

Not until 1956 was the Docker's behaviour called to account, by which time it was too late. Decadent behaviour had sowed the seeds of decay, although their germination passed unnoticed for some years to come by the greater majority of people. BSA group's profits were still good at £1,604,941 and a share dividend of eight per cent was made. In 1955, profits had been £2,865,676 with a 'divi' of 10 per cent, and in 1957, they were to be up again to £2,202,600 and 10 per cent. The fact that to offset the losses incurred by the car division – namely Daimler – BSA found it necessary to sell off its bicycle division to Raleigh and its Birtley heavy plant division to Caterpillar for approximately £2 million perturbed no-one. Except Jack Sangster, who had been retained by BSA on its board for his motorcycle industry expertise. Almost alone, but with the support of BSA's managing director, James Leek, at a specially convened shareholders' meeting Sangster courageously moved that Docker be removed as chairman of the BSA group, '. . . due to group losses through Daimler, his (Docker's) profligacy, scandalous conduct and over his extension of his position at board meetings.' By a vote of six to three in favour, Docker was removed

Bert Hopwood (left), discussing the then new Triumph Tigress scooter with New Zealand importer Bill White, and Bill Robertson. The twin-cylinder ohv 250cc Tigress was in all respects an excellent 'big' scooter, but by 1958 when it appeared, the scooter boom had run its course. John Nelson

to be succeeded by Sangster. The words come easily now but, as surely as the sun rises in the morning and goes down in the evening, that meeting must have been singularly memorable in BSA's history.

Although part of a giant industrial group, the motorcycle division of BSA was by far its biggest. In 1960, when the group's profits amounted to £1,663,748 and it paid an astonishing, even incredible, 17.5 per cent dividend to its shareholders, motorcycle operations accounted for 41 per cent of group turnover. Thus, Sangster's opinions held strong sway.

Where, though, did Triumph fit into all this? Triumph's profits for 1957 amounted to £719,575 which, while the most successful in the history of the British motorcycle industry, was quite typical for Triumph in that period. Sangster was full of praise for Meriden because despite the fact that Triumph produced only 20 per cent of the volume of motorcycles produced by BSA, and therefore lacked BSA's massive purchasing power, it was much more profitable. For this remarkable prosperity Turner could rightfully claim full credit. His position within BSA was therefore unassailable.

As Triumph's managing director, Turner was also a BSA executive, so his maintenance of his showbiz lifestyle alternating 50/50 between California and Warwickshire, is therefore revealed as less of a mystery, as is the accomplishment of his refusal to work at BSA in Birmingham. In modern parlance, the man had clout. So much so that the rest of the British motorcycle industry acknowledged him as its oracle, chancellor and engineer all in one, which eventually would have dire consequences. At some time in the 1950s Turner registered his own design company, from which issued much of consequence. Only an executive of the most extraordinary nature, and from a position of equally extraordinary influence, could hope to set up what amounted to his own personal subcontracting business within the heart of a company by whom he was already employed.

In an attempt to reverse moribund Daimler's ironic slide into a grave (as befitted Britain's premier hearse manufacturer) BSA engaged Turner to design some new engines for two new cars under shape from Hooper, Daimler's principle coachbuilders. Perhaps unsurprisingly in 1956 at the project's outset, when good quality large cars from such as progressive Ford were opening the high-priced old quality car clientele's wallets, Hooper was not much less threadbare than Daimler itself. The new engines would both be V8s. Turner, seduced by golden California, saw to that. A 2.5-litre version developed 140bhp and would power the company's brave venture into what was then a fiercely competitive sports car market. This was the 125mph SP250, popularly but incorrectly known by its code name, Dart. A larger version would be the 220bhp, 4.5-litre unit for Daimler's projected luxury limousine, the Majestic Major. Intriguingly, the wryly styled glassfibre-bodied sportster earned public acclaim, largely because the London Metropolitan police force bought some to catch the city-scratching rockers, who favoured Bonnevilles for their suburban grand prix. But its handling and roadholding left something to be desired. Against this, the stately Majestic was the SP250's equal in speed and, as the dashboard-biting author had revealed to him by a madman during one indelibly imprinted drive through Suffolk, it out-cornered the sports car through curves.

Such was Daimler's impecunity, however, that not until Jaguar bought the company from BSA in 1960, did the Majestic belatedly enter production. For £3.4 million, Jaguar got what it wanted – Daimler's neighbouring factory and the new engines, the excellence of which it recognised, desired and feared.

One should not be surprised to discover that the new engines were very closely related to Turner's pride and joy, the 6T. Or at least its cylinder and combustion chamber dimensions were, the latter being hemispherical of course, with 90° valve angles. Despite company suggestions for overhead camshafts, Turner relied on his familiar pushrods because they cost less and reliably returned all the revs any commercially built engine would ever need. He was right of course. The 2.5 engine was slotted easily into Jaguar's own Mk II saloon, where it outperformed Jaguar's own 2.4 ohc six by miles. Infuriatingly, these two magnificent engines were finally discontinued in the 1970s through British Leyland's mind-numbing policies when BL perceived a threat to its own inferior Rover V8. Val Page's 1933 250cc model L2/1 had indeed, come a long, long way.

Sangster retired in 1961, after which time BSA sunk inexorably into decline, and with it, kicking and screaming all the way, profitable Triumph. Following Docker's disappearance from BSA in 1956, Turner was promoted to managing director of all BSA's motorcycle divisions, from which time necessity moved him to BSA in Birmingham. One year later his position was expanded to incorporate BSA's automotive division, which was principally Daimler of course.

When Jack Sangster, who had sold Ariel and Triumph for a combined near-£3 million, died in 1977 he left an estate valued at £651,538. When Edward Turner died in 1973, he did so as a rich man although one who throughout his life had only ever been employed, he left £316,239.

6

Out with the old

*War's aftermath, a fight for survival, the 'Baby', TWN, living with
the Model H, the rise of chain drive, a three-speed gearbox, a
brand-new engine*

As early as May 1914, *Motor Cycling* made it plain during its summary of the forthcoming IoM TT that Triumph was passing into racing history and could no longer be considered as a winner, the favourites being Rudge and Sunbeam. In fact O. G. Godfrey on an Indian won at 49.5mph (79.6km/h), although the best Triumph was G. Boyton's fifth place at 46.3mph (74.6km/h). That year also Indian won the Scottish Six Day's Trial.

To be fair to Triumph, it tried. Early in the 1920s experiments were made with a proprietary quarter elliptic sprung swinging rear fork modification to a 3½HP model, but the results were not made public. In his 1926 *Book of The Triumph* (one of Pitman's *The Motorcyclist's Library series*) the well-known technical journalist and author E. T. Brown stated confidently: 'A spring frame is not employed, however, as it is questionable whether any frame of such design is really effective, but as the saddle is fitted with excellent coil springs the comfort of the rider is ensured.' One may query the truth of the implication over a solid frame's comfort, but there is no doubt that Brown's statement reflects the popular opinion of the time.

In all probability, Triumph's reluctance to change was rooted in a commercial philosophy charged by its founder's Teutonic methodism. Schulte especially would alter nothing until it had proved itself consistently

over a protracted test period. For this reason, Triumph had won itself a reputation equalled by few, if any, other factories. It cherished its Trusty image as its principle attraction. Once the war had ended, however, Triumph began an intensive development period.

Certainly Triumph's apparent tardiness was unconnected to a lack of capital. The company's profits for 1913 after factory maintenance, depreciation, directors' salaries and tax, was a remarkable £74,393 9s 3d, plus a balance brought over from 1912 of £15,024 16s 7d amounting to a combined total of £89,418 5s 10d.

In 1918, the figures were much the same. Profits of £60,048 19s 3d, which together with a rollover from the previous year, amounted to a total of

£76,647 5s 2d. Only the previous year Triumph shareholders had enjoyed a massive dividend of 30 per cent, and when Bettman announced a proposed expansion through share issue, stock leapt from 97s (£4.85) to 122s (£6.10). Triumph was in extraordinarily fine health.

Triumph's operations may have been conservative, but they were sound. In November 1913 it announced one of its most popular and enduring models, the currently overlooked 223cc, 145lb (65.8kg) two-stroke 'Junior', which the public immediately nicknamed the 'Baby' Triumph. Only in the final two years of its life, from 1923 to 1925, did it change much as a 249cc machine with the addition of a clutch, kickstarter and gear-lever, but for the rest

A first attempt at multiple gearing, the 1914 three-speed model. VMCC

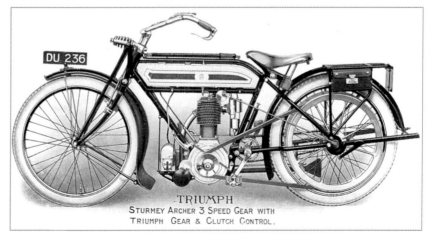

TRIUMPH
STURMEY ARCHER 3 SPEED GEAR WITH
TRIUMPH GEAR & CLUTCH CONTROL.

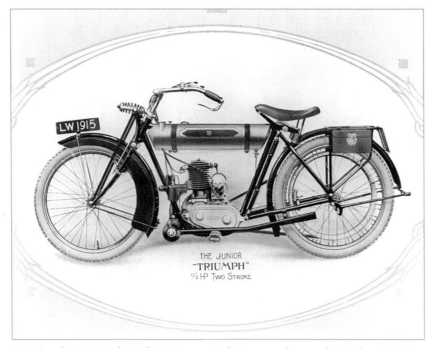

Introduced in 1913, the 2¼hp Junior, or 'Baby' two-stroke was designed to appeal to women. In fact, it proved to be so rugged and reliable it became a favourite with colonial travellers. VMCC

it remained as a basic little utility designed specifically to encourage women riders, rather like the current range of 50cc super-scooters do. It originally had two gears – low (8.4:1) and high (5:1) – smoothly operated by a simple handlebar trigger. These were increased to three (12.5, 8.5 and 5.5:1) for the final model. The engine was designed to be so unusually tractable that it would pick its way along at sub-walking speeds in low gear and down to 3mph (5km/h) in top, and it resisted stalling even when provoked. Cruising speed was anything up to its top speed of 30-35mph (48–56km/h). To Triumph's great satisfaction this tough little scallywag also won the hearts of huge numbers of colonials working in the far reaches of the old British Empire, where it competed in popularity with the rugged reliability of the big Model H.

The author has a vivid memory of a district nurse who rode her rounds through the Surrey countryside through and beyond the Second World War on one of these, although a repair following a minor accident with a horse-drawn milk float had necessitated the adoption of a non-standard front fork. It finally disappeared in 1953 on the nurse's retirement. Neither its distinctive trail of blue smoke nor its hollow, almost musical, gently popping exhaust will ever be forgotten.

Unlike any other Triumph, the Babies were ordered by overseas dealers in bunches so frequently that Triumph coded the order numbers in Latin for the sake of accuracy over the often untrustworthy telegraphic system. *BABY* =1, *DUO* = 2, *TRES* = 3, *SEI* = 6, *NOVE* = 9, *DOCE* = 12, *KINCE* = 15, *VENTI* = 20. Triumph's telegraphic address was simply 'Trusty Coventry'.

In March 1914, *The Motor Cycle* published a service record of its year with a staff Baby. It had returned 103mpg (2.74 litre/100km) in its 2,300 miles (3,701km) of mainly London use. Petrol costs had amounted to £4, oil 10s, accessories spares and repairs (new tyre and belt, plus a chain, piston, rings and gasket following some very uncharacteristic engine trouble), £12 9s 1d. Licensing had cost £1 15s, and it was sold for its original purchase price due mainly to the scarcity value of all vehicles then.

So successful was the little popper that by 1920 it was being built under licence by the American Excelsior company (the third member of USA's 'Big Three'), although with its engine bored to its maximum of 296cc; and by a German offshoot of Triumph – in where but Nuremberg of course. The German arm had started motorcycle manufacturing as early as 1903, two years prior to the all-Triumph 3HP model. The Knirps, as TWN (Triumph-Werke-Nuremberg) named it, was the model that restarted manufacturing in the plant after the First World War. Significantly, TWN supplanted Triumph's fore-and-aft fork with a more orthodox Druid-type fork of its own. It preferred an engine capacity of 248cc for German licensing convenience. Up to the war, TWN, or Orial-TWN to employ the full name, produced machines that were essentially identical to British Triumphs (one wonders how many British despatch riders may have puzzled over field-grey TWN near-Trusties in the hands of the Kaiser's couriers). After the war, TWN gradually bought itself out of Coventry's control until by 1929, it was independent. From thereon it relied on Swiss MAG engines until after the Second World War when it produced its own range of superbly engineered lightweight two-strokes. Amongst them was a magnificent 250 single employing a double piston induction system, closely resembling Puch's inspiringly original 1929 engine of similar type, in which one larger piston in tandem with another on a 'Y' type split connecting rod force-fed fresh compressed mixture into the smaller combustion chamber via a disc valve. In 1957, TWN was purchased by Grundig and turned over to office machine manufacturing.

The old sv range of long-stroke singles continued after the First World War of course. The 550cc singles may have started to get a bit long in the tooth, but they could still show a surprising turn of speed, as a *Motor Cycle* road test of 1918 proved, when its test Model H TT sportster managed 76mph (122km/h). But as so many other manufacturers were following the lead of Royal Enfield, P&M, Scott, HD, Indian etc by adopting all-chain drive, Triumph was forced to follow suit.

Despite the sales recession, Triumph in 1922 managed a net profit of £36,482 5s 4d and shareholder dividend of 10 per cent, whereas the previous year's profits had been a mere £9,834 6s 6d.

The Model H was sliding into history, so what could an owner of one of these expect from his machine? In August 1921, *Motor Cycling* published a detailed Model H log and top-end overhaul recommendation, as carried out on their own staff machine. Every 2,000 miles (3,200km) they had checked and reground the valve faces and valve seats, changed the valve springs and decoked the combustion chamber and ports. Every 5,000 miles (8,000km) the cylinder bore had been measured for wear and the piston rings renewed as a matter of course. Every 10,000 miles (16,000km) the crankcase had been flushed out with paraffin. The foot-operated clutch cable had shown signs of wear at 250 miles (410km) and had worn out by 1,000 miles (1,600km). As a means of ensuring reliability, (Triumph's own handbook states that the majority of engine failures were caused by lubrication breakdown) one full return stroke of the hand oil pump had to be delivered faithfully every 4–8 miles (6–13km) depending on speed and gradient. Most noteworthy of all, however, was the statement that normal cruising speed was 20–25mph (32–40km/h). A motorcyclist's touring handbook of the same year warns that 100 miles (161km) a day is about the maximum distance most riders should attempt.

Then one reads a Triumph advertisement for a Model C of 1914. The C was simply the H, but with a three-speed hub gear. One of its owners, a Mr J. Jones of Pontllanfraith, near Cardiff, had written to Triumph on 12 September 1913: 'Perhaps it would interest you to know that I have covered between 25,000 and 26,000 miles [40–42,000km] every year, during the last five years, and as for mechanical trouble, I don't know what it is. I never even carry a spare plug.' He continued to explain that as a commercial traveller he had already done 17,000 miles [27,000km] without a single hitch on Triumphs, even with the Model C's gears. If one equates *Motor Cycling*'s maintenance standards with Mr Jones's remarkable

mileage, one reaches some even more remarkable conclusions. Namely, that during his 142,000 miles [229,000km] of trouble-free Triumph ownership, Mr Jones must have replaced 60 piston rings in his Triumphs and 142 valve springs, as well as flushing away enough paraffin to run an old-fashioned farm tractor for a year. Either advertisers' honesty has improved a great deal since then, or the legendary durability of those old Trumpets has improved with the passage of time. Plainly, the truth of both lies somewhere in the middle, but the magazine's maintenance schedule, which was largely inspection for the sake of reportage of course, gives an idea of the period's necessity for constant mechanical attention. While Mr Jones's letter paints a picture of the kind of reliability that was available to the punctilious even then – at 25mph (40km/h) of course.

In November 1918, Triumph's first all-chain-drive model, the SD, was announced in the motor cycle press, presumably for 1919, although its retail distribution was not to occur for another 12 months, in early 1920. Although Triumph was far from alone in the adoption of chain drive, the change from belt drive incurred greater applications of technology, both known and unknown, than would arise again until the advent of environmentally enforced electronic engine management systems in the 1990s. Before the Great War the overwhelming majority of the existing manufacturers, of which there were 150 approximately, opted for belt drive over chain at a ratio of 2.7:1;

after the war chain models exceeded belts by 1.75:1. Understandably, Triumph was proud of its new transmission system, although factory intimations that it was a world first were pretty cheeky.

One gets the impression from the guarded comments of the period, when press and trade were usually perceived by a much more innocent and trusting public than now as twin heads of the same animal, that Triumph had become impatient with Sturmey Archer. It had previously with carburettor manufacturers, when it developed and manufactured its own superior instrument, the famous twin-barrel carburettor which remained in use from 1908 to 1927. Rather than wait patiently for the transmission specialist's anticipated new gearbox Triumph went ahead and designed its own. Even now transmission design is the overlooked vital partner of the power train, but in the second decade of motorcycle production it could be recognised only by those bold enough to stare long and hard into the future.

In all probability, Triumph's first three-speed gearbox was Schulte's last contribution to the company's products he had so valuably designed, developed, improved and maintained. In the same year as the SD was launched, Triumph's brilliant first engineer reluctantly resigned. To calculate the myriad chain drive mysteries wrought by transmission shock absorbers, primary, gearbox internal and final drive ratios, gear selector mechanism, engine power/torque/rpm delivery, clutch operation/strength/

Chain drive for the first time after the First World War, the model SD. VMCC

durability, the effects on the frame plus the consequences on riding methods must have stretched Schulte's team to its engineering limits. In reality that very first company gearbox was so successful in every respect that it continued in production, modified to suit, until the advent of the Val Page singles in 1934.

From the SD onwards gear changing required deliberation because modern type twistgrips were something of a novel rarity and most machines, including Triumphs, were speed controlled through a right-hand Bowden lever (akin to a post-Second World War air/choke lever). The right hand had also to shift the tank-mounted lever through its gate incorporating stepped gear-stops. The wet clutch's plates were alternating steel and copper. Few modern motorcyclists can imagine the dextrousness required to correctly change gear on those pioneering cog-swappers. Those who have experienced it usually find their confidence in their familiar motorcycling skills severely shaken. It was no easier for the riders of the period, whose familiarity with their belt driven machines' conciliatory natures in most cases had innocently coarsened, or at least had not honed, the finer points of benevolent gear changing in concord with the unforgiving chain.

Triumph's singular front fork; it pivoted around the bottom yoke. VMCC

Despite its chain drive, these first SD's nevertheless retained a great deal that was rudimentary, such as the stirrup (bicycle type) front brake, the dummy rim block rear brake, acetylene lighting, a hand-pumped total loss lubrication system and that shaky old fore-and-aft front fork. What was noticeable however, was the extra finning of that venerable old side valve engine, which remained visibly related to Triumph's very first 3HP model. Sidecarists in particular took a liking to the SD's astounding torque development which, top speed apart, rivalled V-twins of much greater capacity. And sidecarists, as well as solo riders, delighted in using their gearboxes to force the 550cc big singles up hill and dale in a sort of careless rapture of easy speed impossible with the old semi-fixed gear ratios of belt drive. This was especially hard on hot running old sv engines without the heat dispersing qualities of recirculating engine oil.

During its life, the SD was modernised with a Lucas mag-dyno and accompanying 6V lighting system, drum brakes, and a greatly improved front fork manufactured under licence from Druid. An ordinary SD in the hands of an ordinary rider would wiffle uncomplainingly along at 55mph (88km/h) all day. A normal top speed would be around 65mph (105km/h) but these engines responded well to tuning, so a keen type in tweed Norfolk jacket, riding breeches, gaiters and reversed cap lying prone over his finely fettled model could, with exceptional patience and a clear highway expect to experience, if not see with his own eyes because speedometers then were rare and expensive items, a maximum speed approaching 70mph (121km/h). Captured by a sidecar an SD would cruise at 35–45mph (56–72km/h) and produce a top speed 5–10mph (8–16km/h) greater than that.

Immediately following the cessation of the First World War, and as a consequence of its apparently insatiable appetite for machinery and equipment of all types, a huge surplus of industrial capability suddenly lay idle. A great deal of this was turned to civilian vehicle manufacturing, yet much of the western world had been hurt by the

war and lay exhausted, as yet unable to buy so much of what was on offer. Overproduction in Britain and protected markets abroad weakened economies all round, while slow but persistently rising unemployment and increasing tariff barriers lead irrevocably to a weakening of the pound Sterling. Yet no-one seemed to notice at first, because while the numbers of motorcycles on use in Britain rose from 123,678 in 1914 to 152,960 in 1916 and an extraordinary 571,522 in 1925, there was an excess of manufacturers. Although in 1920 21,285 motorcycles were exported, it was insufficient to support the great mass of producers, of which there were approximately 160 in Britain, but in truth many were simple assemblers of proprietary parts. In a vain attempt to tempt everyone, each of these producers on average was offering between five and six models. Triumph was no exception. By 1926 the brief boom was over and for a few years sales levelled out until, by 1929 and the catastrophic Great Depression, they began to fall fast.

Besides, mass produced cars were for the first time proving not much more expensive than motorcycles to buy and probably cheaper to run. Ford in Britain, for instance, heavily publicised its famous £100 8hp four-seat saloon, while in that same period a Riccy and sidecar would cost £120.

Having seen sense by its acceptance of chain drive on the SD model, one year later in 1923, Triumph made a second stride towards dislocating its eventual, and plainly reluctant, connection with the Model H and derivatives. Its first brand-new four-stroke engine since 1905 made an appearance. This was the 346cc (72 x 85 mm) Type LS, a sv single sporting all mod-cons, including a three-speed gearbox, mag-dyno and electric lighting, a Druid-type front fork, a high pressure mechanical oil pump and automatic oil return from a dry sump, a rugged all-metal wet clutch and, perhaps best of all, small, but comparatively effective drum brakes on both wheels. Press, trade and public alike sang its praises at the November Olympia show, London, even though its battery (or accumulator as it was often called then) appeared to be mounted as an afterthought over the petrol tank. In fact,

APPROXIMATE RUNNING COSTS

Model	1935 Price	Tax	Average Insurance Premium – Comprehensive	Petrol Consumption	Cost of New Cover and Tube	On 5,000 miles p.a. basis; per mile	On 10,000 miles p.a. basis; per mile
	£ s.d.	£	£ s. d.	m.p.g.	£ s. d.	d.	d.
3–46 h.p. Type L.S.	56 15 –	3	3 – 15	100	2 3 9	.66	.48
4–94 h.p. Type P	42 17 6	3	6 – –	80	2 3 9	.81	.59
4–94 H.P. 'Popular' Combination. Type P.X.	58 12 6	4	6 – –	60	2 3 9	.90	.75
4–99 h.p. O.H.V. Fast Roadster. Type R.	69 10 –	3	6 – –	80	2 13 4	.83	.61
4–99 h.p. O.H.V. 'Sports' Combination	91 5 –	4	6 – –	60	2 13 6	1.03	.78
4.99 h.p. O.H.V. 'Super' Combination	98 5 –	4	6 – –	60	2 13 6	1.03	.78
5–50 h.p. Type S.D.	66 10 –	3	4 – –	75	2 13 6	.85	.63
5–50 h.p. 'Sports' Combination	88 5 –	4	6 – –	55	2 13 6	1.05	.82
5–50 h.p. 'De Luxe' Combination	92 – –	4	6 – –	50	2 13 6	1.09	.85
5–50 h.p. Commercial Combination	87 30 –	4	7 15 – approx.	45	2 13 6	1.22	.94

Modern enthusiasts may like to compare their own running costs with these of 1925. Author

the frame had been constructed small as a means of minimising overall weight and dimensions. But despite the little piece of battery nonsense, in all other respects it was superbly made and, to quote *The Motor Cycle* road test summary: '(It) had the performance of the average 500'. At 50mph (80km/h) the magazine's test model returned 100mpg (2.42 litre/100km) and, wonderfully, its oil change period had been extended to 500 miles (804km), thanks principally to an efficient filtration system.

The engine was unusual: its overhung crankshaft was forged and ran on plain bearings, although a single outrigger ball-race supported the outrigger flywheel and, even more radically, the unitary engine and gearbox shared the same lubricant and the layshaft was pressure fed. Gear ratios were 12.5, 8.5 and top 5.5:1 and the whole thing weighed 240 lb (109 kg). Priced at a competitive £69 when it was finally released a year later, albeit with a primitive dummy rim rear brake that let the whole side down, it should have taken the showrooms by storm, but the period was a strange one as entire nations, let alone individuals, lost confidence in themselves and the future. So the superb new 350 teetered about until 1927 when it was axed as a sales flop.

Inflation had gripped Britain as a consequence of an industry, and thence commerce, made hollow by lack of stimulus. Fortunately Triumph management kept its head long enough to swallow some pride. By rejecting all its hard-won heritage of high quality, Triumph, world renowned for its magnificent material standards, decided to cater for a new class of motorcyclist – the bare-bones utility rider needing nowt but low costs. It designed and built the Model P.

By this time, Schulte and Hathaway, the two great partners behind the policy that had made Triumph great – trustworthiness – had gone. Perhaps mercifully in consideration of the Model P.

7

And in with the new

*Hard times, the profitability in humble pie, the Model P, 150cc ohv
singles, the Silent Scouts*

The Siamese twins of spiralling inflation and unemployment were decimating the British motorcycle industry in 1924 and most manufacturers were offering low-priced specials in an attempt to boost sales. Most of these by 1926, like BSA's famous 3½ (493cc sv single) at £44 and Douglas's 350cc EW model at £41 10s, were actually budget-built examples of existing models. Triumph, however, took the brave decision to meet the anticipated sales decline lying directly ahead with a brand-new model. To achieve this, part of the

workforce would be required to metamorphosise from engineering orientated idealism to one of penny pinching pragmatism. Amazingly, this astonishing about-face worked and the company survived and even prospered while others, like Sunbeam, Rudge, Calthorpe, Levis, Chater-Lea, NUT, Scott and a host of others entered a period of terminal decline.

Following a century of peace, apart from isolated actions like the Boer and Crimea wars which had had no direct material effect on the populace at large, the British nation's arrogant

conviction of its natural superiority was shattered by the Great War of 1914–18. Apart from a flash of industrial expansion in 1919, the centrally organised industries of wartime once returned to private administration were unable to cope with the harshly competitive new world order, in which abandoned traditional overseas markets had been forced to find alternatives. By 1918 the national debt had risen to an unprecedented £7,000 million. Fuelled by speculation, tariff barriers, shrinking industry, increasingly militant unionism and a general loss of national confidence, the pound Sterling collapsed. By the late 1920s, however, order began to rise out of chaos, as new industries such as vehicle and chemical manufacturing arose. As equilibrium returned British prosperity seemed also to improve. Two million were unemployed but it was hoped that this would improve once the national workforce had accepted the need for large scale redistribution and diversification.

When Triumph's utility special, the Model P, was announced in October 1924, its rock-bottom price of £42 17s 6d was highly praised as the lowest by far of any 500 of the period. In some respects the machine was crude because of a specification that even then was outmoded: it retained hand-pump lubrication and had an appalling, contracting band front brake, plainly borrowed from industrial hoists. The best that even the

By 1915, changes were coming. The old 4HP model was equipped with a three-speed countershaft box. It was getting too fast for its brakes. VMCC

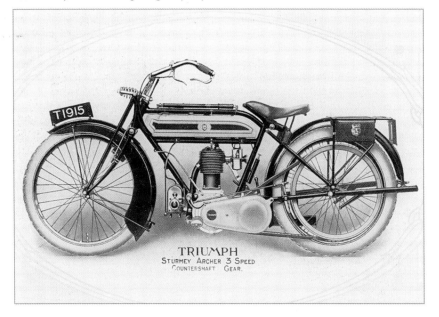

traditionally uncritical *The Motor Cycle* road test could report in December was a cryptic: 'We did not note that the application of this brake exerted any important effect on the forward motion of the machine.' Equally wry comment was made regarding the same brake's usefulness for parking on hills. On the improved Mk II brake in 1926 the same magazine observed, after a half column devoted to a lavishly ironic description of the improved brake's new mechanism and its clever 'servo' action, '. . . but the brake functions almost equally well backwards.' Reading between the lines then of necessity had been developed to a fine pitch by magazine readers. The clutch's crossover lift mechanism gave trouble as well as snagging rider's ankles, the engine ran big-ends, fixed valve guide holes wore out, crankcase oil leaks were not uncommon, clutch slip from leaked gearbox oil occurred, and starting could prove tricky. Fundamentally, however, the Model P was soundly made and handsomely finished and its performance surprised and pleased everyone.

Top speed was modest at 50mph (80km/h), but it would cruise indefatigably at 40mph (64km/h) and without changing down from top gear would easily climb most steep main road hills. Typically for Triumph, the P's engine ran exceptionally quietly and with bags of torque, a consequence of its designed intention to appeal to sidecarists, as proved by special cast-in frame lugs. A model with a Lucas mag-dyno and full lighting sold for £50 12s 6d. Weight was a mere 240lb (109kg). But, best of all, the P offered all-chain drive and a three-speed gearbox, with ratios of 14.12, 8.2 and 5.06:1. As *The Motor Cycle* columnist 'Friar John' commented in April 1925, after a week or so with a Model P sidecar outfit: '. . . accompanied by a 10-stone (63.5kg) sidecar passenger, the sturdy engine towed this load with ease . . . and enabled the machine to be pushed along at "thirty something" without impressions of flogging the engine . . . Top speed with loaded sidecar was in the neighbourhood of 40mph (64km/h).' Price of the strictly utility outfit (Triumph sidecar) was a mere £58 12s 6d.

Sidecars sold like hot cakes. This is Triumph's standard commercial box attached to the Trusty's successor the 3½hp (550cc) Type H of 1921. With three-speed Sturmey Archer countershaft and belt drive it was immensely powerful yet smooth and would carry a load at an easy 40mph (65km/h). VMCC

Of greater significance than the bike itself was the method introduced to produce it. By the time of the P, Triumph's original works manager, Charles Hathaway, had given way to Joe Phillips. More-or-less forgotten by history, Phillips deserves better because it was his complete redesign of Triumph's production system that was probably responsible for the company's survival. When Bettman decided the company needed a four-square budget bike, Phillips, more than anyone, helped to design a motorcycle most suited to a stream-lined volume production operation. To this end he cleared a section of the old Coventry factory and devoted it to a radical semi-assembly line operation using a minimum of skilled workers, then a major departure from the old craft-based and widely distributed assembly group method. Considering Triumph employees well-known militancy, this was no mean feat.

Nor was the P solely a budget bike. Triumph's long experience with the old British colonies had persuaded the company that what it also needed was an inexpensive, rugged big bike with low maintenance demands, the £83 SD being too pricey and the Baby too small. Hence the P was designed to fulfil three expectations – low cost pro-

Increasingly popular among family enthusiasts was the SD, actually a Type H with chain drive. Less smooth perhaps but power was transmitted positively, regardless of weather or incline. It also boasted Triumph's superior three-speed gearbox. VMCC

TRIUMPH FAMILY SIDECAR

By 1925, outfits had changed. This is the specialist sidecar model CSD, with a massively torquey 548cc sv single engine hauling a standard Triumph lightweight chair. It is equipped with full electrical equipment and good drum brakes. VMCC

duction, home utility and colonial stamina. This it eventually managed admirably.

Ample evidence of the newly installed mass-production operation may be seen in the sales figures. Despite the inbuilt flaws, Triumph was unable to improve the P until 20,000 had rolled off the line. To reduce component prices to a minimum, Triumph had 'squeezed' its subcontractors to a rock-bottom price, which meant, of course, both parties were contractually bound to huge volumes of unalterable components. This is standard practice now and modern Triumph at Hinckley has suffered similar problems, for example with unsatisfactory rear suspension units. To Triumph's credit, while its guarantee turnover was probably held down by the unsympathetic attitudes of the day, it did offer buyers a cheap and quick exchange system, by which, for instance, a ruined big-end bearing would be replaced at minimum cost by an improved version.

Within the first year, Triumph had sold its entire 20,000 first batch of Ps, warts and all, which probably covered capital investment with a small profit. From thereon greatly improved Mk II Ps left the factory. They were, in fact, more conventional, with orthodox clutch pushrod activation replacing the untrustworthy old scissor action lift, an oil retention device prevented gear oil from penetrating the clutch, replaceable cast iron valve guides were installed in

the barrel, an improved caged roller big-end was fitted, and what appeared to be a drum brake installed in the front wheel. This, the 'spring-ring' type, nevertheless remained stubbornly unorthodox and feeble. Instead of two brake shoes activated by a cam, a steel strip held by springs and lined by brake material was forced into drum contact against drum rotation.

Oddly enough, considering the parlous state of the nation, by 1927 it was more-or-less all over for the cheap P.

After selling at up to 1,000 models per week through 1925, sales declined fast after a maximum of 10,000 more were sold. Why? Probably because, like so many motorcycle and car manufacturers, Triumph had learned that in reality, the buying public at large needs more than cheap utilitarianism to maintain its interest and brand loyalty. In April 1926, even *The Motor Cycle*, duty bound at last, reported that the Model P as '. . . prematurely marketed [with] poor brakes and clutch . . .'

However beggarly the P may have been in the classic motorcycling perspective, as a commercial enterprise it had been masterful, although its production as a cheap utility machine had for the first time in its history placed Triumph squarely in the rub-a-dub market alongside rising commercial heavyweights like BSA. Perhaps stimulated by all the new models offered by manufacturers, but more likely by what appeared to be a strengthening of the home market's confidence following a return to peacetime industrial and social structures, Triumph in 1927 began to expand its range with new models. If there was a year which so well represented the overlap of the old and the new it was this.

A range of eight distinct models was offered. It began with the sub-

Last of the flat-tankers and first original ohv Triumph, the 500 (497cc) Two Valve TT 70mph (113km/h) sports single of 1927, right at the halfway stage of old and new, with both mechanical and hand oil pumps. VMCC

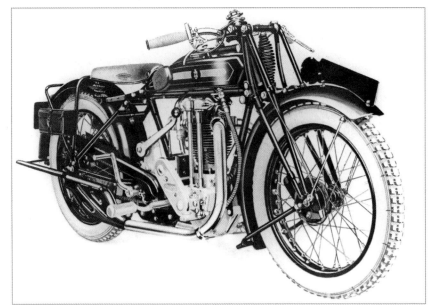

200lb (91kg) licensing 277cc (road tax) model W and continued through the 346cc LS, the 494cc P, the 494cc N de luxe, the 494cc QA, the 498cc ohv TT (Two Valve), the 550cc SD, and the 499cc ohv R. Of these the SD was the sole recognisable survivor of the original 3HP type, developed over 22 years to a quite extraordinary degree and by this time equipped with a Pilgrim mechanical oil pump (although supplemented by the retention of a hand pump also) and, if ordered, Lucas mag-dyno electrics. Ageing fast, it still enjoyed a devoted following, especially amongst family sidecarists for whom its utter dependability, its stupendous torque, its uncannily quiet engine, its smooth running and its incomparable finish were not merely functionally admirable. Better than any other model the SD exemplified Triumph's fine pedigree, in which a mature owner could take immense pride.

The N (de-luxe) and QA (Sports) models were improved variations on the P of course and, with the undeservedly short-lived LS, were not to survive much longer. Nor was the R (Riccy), with its technical feet uncomfortably in both pioneer and progressive camps. The W was newly released along with the TT model, which everyone had been excitedly anticipating for over a year thanks to Victor Horsman's highly publicised record breaking exploits at Brooklands.

By 1928, the range had grown to eight models: 277cc sv Model W £36; WS (sports) £37 17s 6d; 348cc ohv CO £52 17s 6d; 494cc sv NL £44 10s 6d; 498cc sv CN £46 17s 6d; 549cc sv CSD £47 17s 6d; 498cc ohv ST (Two Valve) £59 17s 5d.

The Two Valve's racing progress and performance is described in Chapter 4. It deserves greater acclaim than history has afforded it because it was Triumph's first 'modern' motorcycle, inasmuch as it provided all the convenience and reliability necessary for an owner to expect with good reason to start a journey easily, continue it pleasantly and finish it on schedule with no more distraction

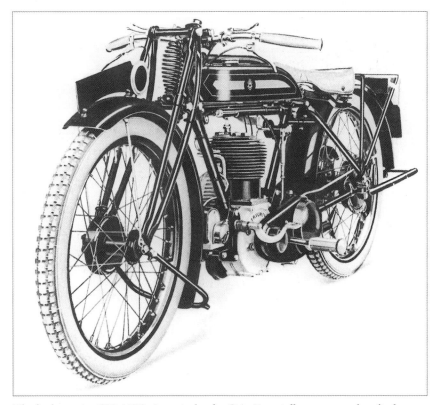

The budget price 500 (495cc) sv single, the QA. Especially constructed to fit the government's under-250lb cheap tax class. VMCC

The 277cc go-to-work cheap model W of 1929. Basic but sound. VMCC

A design revolution – the saddle tank of the 1928 Model N. VMCC

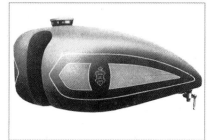

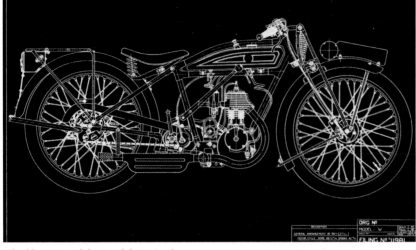

The blueprint of the Model W. Author

Triumph brochure: The way we saw ourselves in the Twenties. Cyril Ayton

ered to his huge delight and the chagrin of an accompanying pal on his prestigious 493cc ohv Sunbeam sportster, that the Trumpet had the heels of the Beam.

Or perhaps the demise of the Two Valve singles was not so untimely after all. Fine sportsters though the Horsman singles undoubtedly were, BSA's new Slopers, which were destined to become one of the truly great classic roadster designs of the inter-war years, in daily use were superior. In the first place, the Two Valve engine demanded sensitive manual ignition control at low speeds and/or during hill-climbing if combustion chamber temperatures were not to rise

than the owner of a current Hinckley-made Triumph would experience. For all the glamour of a Riccy, a Two Valve had the sort of dependability and performance that would far outstrip the wayward four valver. This completely orthodox ohv single with its understated manner, was as rugged as they came then, with a top speed of at least 70mph (113km/h) and the stamina to cruise indefinitely at 60mph (96km/h).

In March 1929, *The Motor Cycle* published a test report of a 350cc (72 x 85mm) two-valve TT model in which the journalist concerned was allowed to display an immodest degree of excitement. '. . . impressive starting on cold mornings . . . immensely powerful brakes . . . superb roadholding . . . 80mpg (3.5 litre/100km) and 1,500mpg (0.19 litre/100km) oil . . . superb finish . . . silky smooth engine . . .' And, typically for these remarkable models, high praise for an average speed capability exceeding a modest top speed of 65mph (105km/h). It cost £52 17s 6d, had 7in (178mm) brakes front and rear, weighed 336lb (152.5kg) and, like its bigger brother, was equipped as standard with a twist-grip throttle control. Yet it seemed Triumph was cursed never to produce the big-selling 350 it needed to please what was the fastest growing and most popular class in Britain. Within two years it had gone, highly praised by the few who knew it, unnoticed by the majority, unmourned by all. The author has a friend who, when he owned one of the even rarer sports models, discov-

unduly while in the second place, Triumph's clever gear stops either side of middle gear required the rider to develop a knack of slight lateral gear lever movement during the shift. BSA's Slopers were in every respect utterly forgiving and possibly smoother, they also generously accommodated the rougher elements of motorcycling and they cost about the same – Two Valve 350, £52 17s 6d; 350 Sloper, £54 15s.

Sadly, the Depression arrived with a vengeance in 1929 following the collapse of the USA's financial establishment, industry and dollar. The rest of the western word was sucked into the fiscal maelstrom. Had this not occurred then maybe the Two Valve would have become the foundation of Triumph's future. It was not to be, even though Triumph had sold a total production volume of 30,000 motorcycles in 1929.

In September 1930, Triumph announced its new range ready for the 1931 season. Apart from a 175cc utility two-stroke at a mere £23 17s 6d (Triumph cost accountants were in an obsessive six-penny phase), there was a new range of slopers on which a great deal depended. *Motor Cycling* expressed it best when it reported these two new 350s as 'Exemplifying solidity'. The sv model was priced at £37 17s 6d, and the ohv model at £44 17s 6d. They may have been new, inasmuch as their wet sump engines were canted fashionably forward, and they were undeniably built to Triumph's traditionally high standards, but they were also undeniably dull. It was as though Schulte's

Teutonic spirit of dependability over and above all else persisted to haunt Triumph and blunt what elsewhere was actually a period of high excitement.

In 1929, Velocette was just about to emplace its milestone positive-stop, foot-change gearbox into its KTT 'cammy' 350 racers. On one of these prodigiously quick machines F. G. Hicks covered 100 miles (161km) of

Brooklands speed bowl at over 100mph (161km/h) – a first for a 350 – as well as convincingly winning the IoM Junior TT at an average speed of near enough 70mph (113km/h) – in fact, 69.71mph. George Hack, chief engineer and race chief of Rudge, was introducing 4-valve heads with great mid-range power advantage to racing motorcycles. Norton's Joe Craig was exploiting the full potential of his old

TRIUMPH 2.49 h.p. O.H.V.   MODEL WO

TRIUMPH 4.93 h.p. O.H.V.   MODEL NT

Top: *A neat and sporty little 250, the 1931 WO.* VMCC

Middle: *An equally cobby 500 of the same type, the 500 NT.* VMCC

Bottom: *A major, although quiet progression. Employing the basic NT, Triumph stripped their ohv big single in 1932, equipped it with a foot-change four-speed gearbox, a high level exhaust, a 20-inch front wheel and knobbly tyres, and called it the 500 Competition Model. The Tigers followed five years later.* VMCC

TRIUMPH "500" COMPETITION O.H.V. MODEL CD. (WITH FOUR-SPEED GEAR)

The ST of 1929 was the basic Two Valve. VMCC

class and both engine sizes were available in either standard or Mk 5 sports trim. In March 1933, Triumph put one of its standard 150s on a 2,007-mile (3,230km) non-stop tour of England. On its 7.85:1 top gear it proved to have a top speed of 50mph (80km/h) and averaged 117mpg (2.4 litre/100km) petrol consumption and 2,100mpg (0.13 litre/100km) of oil on a ride without any unscheduled stops. As the whole point of the exercise had been one of economy Triumph was pleased to publicise running costs of under one farthing (approximately 0.1 of a modern penny) per mile. Great emphasis was placed on the low cost of Triumph's own fully comprehensive insurance cover plan, the annual premium of which for the 150 XO and mature rider, was £3.

Even lower down the utility scale were a couple of small-change commuters. When, in 1932, the government rationalised its vehicle licensing laws to some we now recognise as

boss Walter Moore's CSI ohc racing engine by developing the glorious International. In 1931, Tim Hunt riding a 490cc ohc Inter' broke through the IoM Mountain circuit's target barrier of 80mph (129km/h) during a lap of 80.82mph (130km/h).

Twistgrip throttle controls, attempted by many but finally commercially pioneered by Doherty, were becoming standard, as by 1930 were positive stop foot changes, thanks to the practically unpatentable Velo' original blueprint; the robustly superior Webb or Webb-type front fork with its single variably coiled compression spring had been widely adopted. The twin 'black arts' of cam design and combustion chamber dynamics were becoming sufficiently well practised for the third partner – exhaust pipe design, as witnessed by experiments with megaphone systems which harnessed shock waves – to be maturing nicely enough for engine power to be rocketing. Brakes were also finally being recognised as a vital counterbalancing equal partner to engine power in the quest for speed.

All this race-lead progress, yet Triumph through its new slopers seemed determined to resurrect the stolid Type H machine. Then for 1932 came new XO series 147cc, and 174cc ohv singles and the well-known Silent Scout models. The little ones were commuter models, priced at £28 10s for the 150.

Perhaps because of their small size and inclined engines, the XOs are

these days frequently given as early relatives of the 1950s 150cc Terrier and 200cc Tiger Cub, yet except for a sharing of common small four-stroke technicalities they are entirely unrelated. In fact, they were supreme examples of the rising super-utility

In 1930, a new ohv single was announced, the CTT de-luxe with electric lighting, and the more basic CO. VMCC

Triumph 4.98 h.p. C.N.

Side-valve singles were the staple work-horses of all manufacturers. These included the 1929 550 CSD, a sidecar tug, and the 500 CN which was mainly a solo. Both were built around Two Valve basics. VMCC

Triumph 5.49 h.p. C.S.D.

structed competition from an excess of similarly ambitious producers was too great and they disappeared within two years.

Following the first of the new style 350 slopers in 1931, Triumph launched its new big single range, best known for the Silent Scout model. They were probably the last Triumphs that attempted to appeal largely on their prestigious construction and finish quality, rather than on performance. There were three of them – the 548cc model A sv which came equipped with sidecar lugs, the 493cc (84 x 89mm) B twin-port ohv tourer and the similar BS sport model. Ever mindful of Sunbeam's exquisite finish or Ascot-Pullin's exclusive qualities, the material quality of these new Triumph slopers remains as supreme examples of two-wheeled craftsmanship. Their diamond enamelling, their polished plating, impeccable fasteners, finely contoured and perfectly matched aluminium castings, their instrument and control styling were classic examples of ergonomic aestheticism, their overall appearance was elegance personified, and they ran as smoothly and silently (for the period) as a good car.

Beneath the pressed steel panelwork that was offered as a de luxe extra on some models, the engines of both sv and ohv models were identical except for valve gear and cylinder head. Lubrication was actually dry sump, although a quart-plus (1.2l)

based on engine capacity rather than weight, it made Villiers, the engine manufacturer, rich. Half the motorcycle producers in Britain, starved of sales to a decimated national workforce, looked to Villiers for a power pack to meet the new 150cc bottom limit with its annual 15s licensing fee. As though out of a hat, Villiers met the challenge and supplied Triumph, along with a dozen others, with two engines complete with electrics, carburettor, gearbox and clutch. What Villiers charged Triumph for these poppers remains unknown but, as the 98cc model retailed at an astonishing £16 16s and the 150cc model £21, it must be assumed that it amounted to no more than pocket change. Although they were soundly con-

Slopers were all the rage in the 1930s. This is the 550ND of 1933. VMCC

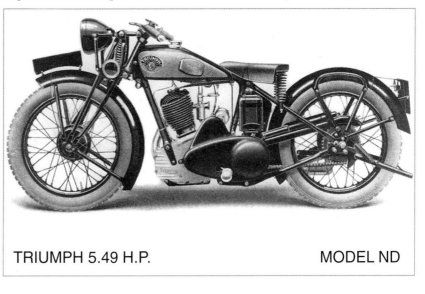

TRIUMPH 5.49 H.P.   MODEL ND

The pretty little 147cc ohv XO of 1933. It was not technically related to the post-Second World War Terrier, but there's little doubt it inspired Turner's baby. A Mk 5 sports version was also available. VMCC

tank cast ahead of the crankcase suggests otherwise. By this time Triumph had adopted a petrol tank-mounted hand-change lever gate and the shift through the four gears was simple, clean and positive and the ratios well chosen, with the 14.7 first gear spaced a generous step down from the top three of 9.6, 6.4 and top, 4.7:1. Unlike the new 250's steel fly-wheels, those of the Silent Scouts were cast iron and bolted to their crankpins, which revolved on ball and roller bearings.

Triumph had never forgotten the near-silent whuffle of its Type H engines and with the Silent Scout endeavoured to return to the quiet reciprocation of the old iron-piston engines. Because iron expands very little compared with aluminium, and because clearances remain equable between piston and bore, the old all-iron engines ran without the familiar cacophony of early aluminium-piston units. The company had been one of the pioneers of aluminium pistons, thanks to Ricardo's introduction on the four-valve R. Despite its early use of slipper pistons, in which the skirt is split to provide expansion room without distortion and microscopically sprung to take up cold play, Triumphs, like most reliant on the same technology, rattled. After a great deal of piston development, the company very nearly achieved the old time whisper with the Silent Scouts. Much of this was owed to the incorporation of car-type 'harmonic cams' as Triumph dubbed them. In fact, luxury car engineers had for some years known that by incorporating quietening ramps into the cams and matching

carefully radiused followers to suit, another major source of rattle could be eliminated.

The Motor Cycle in April 1932 road tested the B tourer and found it to be 'Quiet but slow [with a] 70mph (113km/h) maximum yet utterly quiet, tireless and untiring to the rider.' It was all Triumph had hoped for – a beautifully made, handsomely understated, serenely civilised tourer. Unfortunately for their maker, the Silent Scouts, for all their honourable ways, remained unpopular, no more than 2,000 in total being sold during their brief, three-year lifespan, of which 50 per cent were B tourers, 30 per cent model As and the remainder the BS sports. When one considers that a cheaper OK Supreme ohv 500 single of the period, with its high-cam JAP engine would manage a genuine 80mph (129km/h), however more roughly, it is perhaps unsurprising. Besides, lightly modified OK Supreme sportsters won lots of road races as club level . . . That apart, *The Motor Cycle* reported that their 343lb (155.7kg) B tourer averaged 86mpg (3.2 litre/100km) unless cruised fast over 50mph (80km/h) when it returned 70mpg (4 litre/100km). Triumph had still not quite perfected combustion chamber design because the tester found a need to harmonise the left-hand ignition advance twist-grip with the right-hand throttle twistgrip to avoid pinking and to extract the best performance. The machine's road holding was exemplary and its 7in (178mm) brakes were merely fair. As an indication of the future, speedometer, electric horn and ammeter were provided as standard equipment. The price was set at £55 10s.

Then Val Page appeared.

8

Sowing the seeds of greatness

*Turner's bête noire Valentine Page, foundation 250, the first 650
twin, the Mk 5 racer, BSA fights back*

No-one, probably not even the man concerned, knew it at the time, but Valentine Page's employment by Triumph in 1932 was to so profoundly influence world motorcycling that it remains in production with us today, almost 70 years later, subtly reflected in Kawasaki's 1999 W650 – a salute to the 650 Triumph twins. Triumph was in serious difficulties. A consequence of diversification ventures led to a loss of motorcycle application, and a range of uninspiring, somewhat middle-aged motorcycles stumbled futilely into a generally disinterested market.

It was small, and of no apparent significance, but the 249cc model L2/1 of 1934 contained the seed-germs of Triumph's post-war greatness. At £40 10s its price was high, although lordly Sunbeam's equivalent 350 cost £60. Probably because the name Triumph had lost its lustre after well over a decade of dithering, neither press nor public paid serious heed when the entirely orthodox and apparently modest little ohv machine appeared. Fortunately the section of Triumph dealers who either directly entered or sponsored racing did, so suitably modified, the L2/1 began notching up places on the winner's rostrum at club and national level and as late as the 1950s the engines were still very much in demand.

The engine proved to be as tough as they come, thanks to a forged steel crankshaft and flywheels that proved capable of absorbing the most extreme power tuning methods. Although the high cam engine (in which the camshafts are situated high in a raised timing chest, thus shortening pushrods) was becoming popular, this conventional low cam engine's capacity for sustaining high revs in safety was extraordinary. A 6,000+rpm peak accompanying rare stamina made it the racer's inexpensive darling, so few have survived.

A standard model had a top speed of around 65mph (105km/h) depending on extraneous conditions and it must be one of the first road-going motorcycles that earned itself a reputation for sustained full throttle riding, as they used to say, 'With the taps wide open'. Its dry sump lubrication system worked efficiently and the valve gear exhibited a fine tolerance of wild throttle application and clumsy gear changing, a rare commodity then. A pair of good 6in (152mm) brakes stopped it and a stiff single-loop frame with a duplex engine cradle kept the wheels nicely in line. Perhaps best of all was a fine four-speed gearbox with ratios of 15.5, 10.55, 7.32 and top, 6.10:1. In short, it was about the best of its type available.

The 350cc 3/1 of 1936 was an uninspiring utility whose life was surely extended by the materiel necessities of the war. VMCC

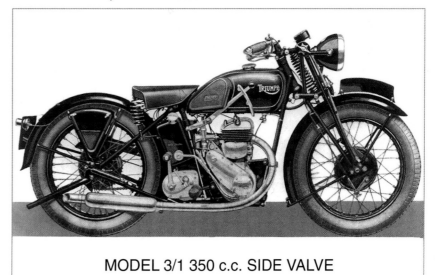

MODEL 3/1 350 c.c. SIDE VALVE

Of all the motorcycles produced by Triumph the modest looking little 249cc ohv L2/1 is probably the most influential, thanks to its superb engine layout. VMCC

British motorcycle industry. With sidecar attached the 6/1's top speed was around 65mph (105km/h) equating to 4,050rpm, it would return a little over 40mpg (7.1 litre/100km) and according to reports of the time, it ran smoothly and quietly, with very mild vibration above 45mph (72.4km/h) third gear and some rattles from the only semi-covered valves and rockers.

Precisely why the press was so pleasantly surprised by the 6/1 is no longer possible to identify. However, it must be remembered that while the previous two new prestige singles from Triumph (Two Valve and Silent Scout) had been well received and had given a fine account of themselves, even for their time they were pretty conservative and both demanded sensitive manual spark

Late in 1933, presaging the 1934 season, Triumph exploded into the news. The relief felt by everyone over clear indications that the decline of what had been Britain's premier manufacturer was over, was almost tangible as they expressed unbounded admiration over the brand new 6/1 ohv 649cc parallel twin. Without exception press, trade and public raved. It may not have been a racer, but it represented the magnificent image of the Triumph they had carried for so long in their mind's eye. Above and beyond all else in an age when singles seemed to fill 95 per cent of the market and V-twins the rest, the 6/1 was intriguingly different.

In retrospect we can now understand why the new 650 ran so well, although few people did at the time. What is plain to see now is the undiluted enthusiasm for the engine's refusal to pink or knock however provoked, the ease with which it started: 'Not once did it need a second kick, even after three nights parked outdoors in sub-zero temperatures', its remarkable tractability: '20mph (32km/h) in top gear', and 'Its fine, perfect combustion.' There, the press was truly on the right track, for Page at this time was in the forefront of combustion chamber and gas flow engineering and from his extensive research in all probability knew more about it than anyone else in the

MODEL 2/1 250 c.c. O.H.V

Val Page developed the L21 into the superior 2/1 of 1936 . . . VMCC

. . . and the 350 3/2 of 1936 . . . VMCC

MODEL 3/2 350 c.c. O.H.V

placement and throttle exploitation if their combustion process was to remain efficient. The 6/1 was by all accounts impervious to rider provocation. If ever proof were needed that the heart of an engine was its combustion chamber, this was it.

Despite a clutch which, in a tradition of Triumph beginning with the first free hub models and persisting until the end of the Meriden-made twins, stuck overnight, the 6/1's transmission was a delight. Its gear change was superb and the positive lubrication system of the Silent Scout was carried over to the 6/1's rear chain. Gear ratios were 12.6, 9.2, 6.2 and top, 5:1.

Although a 1933-designed motorcycle, in many respects it displayed the characteristics of later models, such as increased capacity for petrol (3.5 gallons/16 litres) and oil (4 pints/2.2 litres), an unusually robust duplex cradle frame and a pair of fairly advanced brakes. These were much bigger than most at 8in (203mm) diameter and ribbed into the bargain. More than that, they were not the usual cast iron, but nickel-iron, in which 4 per cent nickel is added to produce an alloy of extraordinary toughness more usually found in highly stressed engine parts. The reason for this was simple: the 6/1 had brakes mechanically coupled at the foot pedal, although the front one could be operated by the handlebar lever alone. In consequence they were extraordinarily powerful, although without the high weight penalty of cast iron drums of equivalent strength. There was also a ratchet-type catch on the foot pedal intended to be used as a parking brake. Why so much attention to braking? Because Triumph's first 650 was designed specifically as a sidecar tug, hence its massive girder forks, whose one-inch (25mm) diameter tubes tapered elegantly towards their ends. Thus negating the popular sporting sidecarist's dodge of attaching a third laterally bowed tube on one fork leg to resist the lateral flexing caused by charioteering's side loads. Thoughtlessly, factory management assumed that sidecarists, who by nature or inclination were even more conservative than their solo brothers, would prefer a good old-fashioned hand gear change to foot change,

. . . and the 500 5/2 of 1936 . . . VMCC

which was then in the ascendant of course.

After only three years in production and poor sales, the 6/1 was withdrawn from production, a fact since variously attributed to its unorthodoxy, its excessive 405lb (183.7kg) weight, its high, 28in (711mm) saddle height, its low, 80mph (128km/h) solo top speed, its hand gear change, its high, £70 price and all manner of wise-acre flummery. By comparison with other machines of similar class none of these stand up to objective analysis. For instance, the 5/5 weighed a mere 25lb (11.3kg) less and it was a 500 single, while the 6/1's numerous super-sports imitators a few years ahead would adopt a further porcine penalty of another 25lb without incur-

ring sales retribution. In its final year of production it was offered with foot gear change, although in truth it was a pretty clumsy adaptation of the original. No, in reality, the creation of the 6/1 was a consequence of poor market research at a time when small, cheap cars were replacing outfits, and its cessation was a result of vital company and product consolidation. Plus a little Turneresque politicking, maybe.

During its brief life the 6/1 proved beyond all doubt that it was laying down an extraordinary pedigree for itself, thanks mainly to Harry Perry, Triumph's dynamic sales manager and talented motorcycle enthusiast. In the Llandrindod Wells-centred ISDT (now ISDE) Perry, driving a 6/1 hitched to one of Triumph's own

. . . and the full race 500 5/10 of 1936, but which remained undeveloped following Turner's policy of company consolidation and twin-cylinder engines. VMCC

MODEL 5/10 500 c.c. O.H.V

It should, and could, have been one of Triumph's greatest models ever, but Page's 650cc parallel twin was brushed aside by Turner's Speed Twin. VMCC

Gloria sidecars, earned a silver medal with a loss of five marks only. This occurred when, following a tyre-shredding morning spent hill-climbing mountain tracks around the Welsh course, the 6/1's front tyre gave out on the way to Donington Park race circuit for the final speed tests, leaving Perry to repair it and thus arrive late. Immediately following this the outfit was decoked and inspected under ACU observation, by which time it had clocked over 2,000 miles (3,200km). The same crew then drove to Brooklands and covered 500 miles (800km) under mostly dangerously foggy conditions. Fortunately the fog eventually lifted and they began circulating at a regular 67–68mph (108–109km/h), which just got them inside the coveted 500

miles in 500 minutes target at 498 minutes, averaging 60.2mph (96.8km/h). Good going for an unmodified touring outfit. Back at Coventry under ACU observation once more it was stripped and found to be suffering from absolutely no measurable wear. Unsurprisingly, presentation of the ACU's Maude's Trophy followed these achievements.

The following year, 1934, Triumph attempted to win *The Motor Cycle* trophy for the first multi-cylinder 500 to exceed 100 miles in one hour. For this purpose they relied on the 6/1, reduced in bore and stroke to 63 x 80mm and force fed by a Zoller (rotary vane) supercharger, gear driven off the primary drive double helical gear. Although designed for a 1,100cc engine, Triumph engineers restricted

it by gearing it to 0.6 engine speed and a pressure of 7 or 10psi (0.8 or 1.13 bar) as set. With the exception of the blower's mounting castings, all the engine components were standard. Compression ratio was 7:1 and a 1⅛in (28.5mm) Amal racing carburettor was fitted ahead of the blower. The engine was dynamometer tested to 46.7bhp (34.8kW) at 4,600rpm, the supercharger absorbing a measured 5bhp (3.7kW) less another 2bhp (1.5kW) through associated pumping losses. The standard 6/1 engine developed 25bhp (18.6kW) at 4,500rpm. More power could have been forthcoming but Triumph wanted their record breaker to be as standard as possible, which had it not been for its supercharging would have been wholly creditable, so material limitations imposed a 4,600rpm limit. In the event, the engine revved beyond that, the machine being geared at 3.78:1 in top to provide 100mph (161km/h) at 4,700rpm.

The stresses involved were considerable, mainly those of heat, so to combat this a five-pint (2.8-litre) oil tank feeding a high volume oil pump was fitted. Proof of stress may be found in the exchange of the gearbox's standard plain bearings for caged roller bearings. And to combat the high fuel consumption a 6-gallon (26.3-litre) fuel tank was fabricated.

Sadly, New Imperial just pipped Triumph by claiming the trophy before the 6/1's Brooklands' development had been completed. During testing it had burned out spark plugs, thrown tyre treads and hiccoughed a bit. Even so, its rider, Tommy Spann, proved its potential by achieving a standing start lap of 92.57mph (148.9km/h), a flying lap of 104mph (167.3km/h) and a top speed of 109mph (175km/h).

The blown 500cc 6/1 disappeared from public view until its 650 highway brothers fell from commercial grace, then late in 1934, McEvoy bought it with the avowed intention of developing the model as a sports roadster. Now the odd thing here is that McEvoy ceased production in 1927 after the death of its leading rider-engineer Cecil Birkin in the IoM TT practice week, who was brother of the famous 'Bentley Boys' car team racer,

Tim Birkin. McEvoy promised to be a high flying company, if only because its chief designer was the extraordinary George Patchet, previously of Brough Superior and who, following employment by FN (Belgium) and Jawa (Czechoslovakia), turned his talents to submachine gun design. Michael McEvoy, the company's founder, was a former Rolls-Royce engineer and one of Britain's top supercharging experts who also handled the distribution of German Zoller superchargers.

McEvoy planned to greatly improve the power delivery quality of the blown 6/1 with a sophisticated induction system which, he claimed after testing, actually did eliminate the uneven cylinder filling and stalling which, evidently, had plagued the original. He was convinced that the engine's stresses, which were ruining the plugs and causing stalling, originated not from its combustion but from induction inertia. He designed a system which would have altered supercharger pressure to suit from 4psi to 15psi (0.27–1.03 bar), and compression ratio was to be reduced to 4:1.

Then, as with so many exciting projects, no more was heard of it, but it was far from the end of the 6/1, or at least a good many of its features.

Study one of the early BSA A10s some time, and compare it to the 6/1. The most obvious similarity lies in the semi-unitary construction of the engine and gearbox, which are flat-wall bolted together in tandem. Equally similar are the two engines' valve trains. Both rely on a single camshaft running transversely across the crankcase behind the cylinder barrel activating the rockers by four long pushrods via wide radii cylindrical tappets. No plainer example of a close relationship between the two could exist however, than the bore and stroke of the 6/1 and the A10, which are identical at 70 x 84mm = 649cc. And, for what it is worth, the wheelbase is identical at 54.75in (1391mm) while BSA's early duplex cradle frame bears a striking resemblance to that of the 6/1.

The one great dissimilarity between the two lies in the consummate virtue of the 6/1's bottom end and primary transmission construction, compared with the A10's accountancy-enforced compromise. The 6/1's crankshaft was machined from a single forging, with crankpin dimensions of rare size – 1.75 in. (44.5mm) diameter x 1.25in. (31.8mm) long. It was supported on twin ball-races, while the big ends ran plain white metal bearings. Against logic, its flywheel was taper-fitted outside the crankcase, although within the primary transmission housing. In the opinion of most experts now this was forced on the idealistic Page by Triumph's inability to manufacture crank and wheel in one piece. This, no less than the crankcase-located oil tank (not wet sump), gave the false impression of mass apparently disliked by so many prospective buyers. Famously, the engine spun backwards, or clockwise viewed from its drive side, because of its split or counter-helical gear primary drive. Had the gears meshed as a pure helical then their powerful lateral forces would have necessitated even more robust crankcases, and straight-cut gears would have whined. The engines never, ever, broke.

Page must have worked long hours because, coinciding with the release of the 6/1, was the announcement of the new 250, 350 and 500 singles in 1934, popularly, although not accurately, known as the Mk 5 range in honour of the sportsters they were to become.

1934 MODEL RANGE

XV/1 (150cc Villiers two-stroke) three-speed £25 10s. X05/5 (150cc Triumph ohv) three-speed £29 15s. X05/5 150 Sports four-speed £33 10s. X07/1 (175cc ohv) three-speed £30 15s. X07/5 Sports four-speed £34 10s. 2/1 (250cc ohv) three-speed £42 10s. 2/5 Sports four-speed £50 10s. 3/1 (350cc sv) three-speed £43 10s. 3/2 (350cc ohv) £52 10s. 3/5 Sports four-speed £55 10s. B (500cc ohv) four-speed £55 15s. BS Sports four-speed £58 15s. 5/1 (550cc sv) four-speed £51 10s. 5/2 (500cc ohv) four-speed £54 10s. 5/3 de luxe (550 sv) £59 5s. 5/4 de luxe (500 ohv) £62 10s. 5/5 Special Sports (500cc ohv) four-speed £71 10s. 6/1 (650cc ohv twin) £75 15s.

Before Edward Turner became general manager of Triumph in 1936, Val Page in 1934 had already set Triumph along the commercial route of modular design. Despite the excellence of the L2/1 250 single, Page discontinued it, principally because for his purposes, he needed a brand-new range more suited to optimum commonality. Even so, Page knew sound design and retained its fundamental merits for his new Mk 5 range.

The new singles – 249, 343 and 493cc – were offered in standard and sports specification. Thus the 250 was listed as the 2/1 standard and 2/5 Sports; the 350 as the 3/2 standard and 3/5 Sports; and the 500 as the 5/2 standard, 5/4 de luxe and 5/5 Special Sports. Within a year, all sports models were designated 'Mk 5', including the peppy little ohv 150. This was further complicated by Triumph and the press referring to the different model specification types as 'Mk 1', 'Mk 2' or 'Mk 3'. All three were entirely orthodox singles in the British tradition. As a matter of interest, it is these models which first featured the twin plunger oil pump that was to lubricate most subsequent Triumphs until the production of the twins finally ceased in 1988. A study of an Ariel oil pump will reveal a near identi-twin. It may be imagined that this was 'borrowed' from Ariel after Jack Sangster's (Ariel's owner since 1932) take-over of Triumph, but Sangster did not take control until 1936. Page, on the other hand, had been Ariel's head of engineering and design and was the brains behind that company's classic Red Hunter singles.

As they are so similar, we will concentrate on the largest of the trio, the 500. With a bore and stroke of 84 x 89mm the engine was unfashionably 'square' for its time. Despite its new image, it reflected most of the qualities so beloved of Triumph enthusiasts: the quality of its workmanship and overall finish was exemplary, its power delivery smooth and torquey from the lowest revs, and in regular use it was fuss-free and undemanding yet with terrific high speed stamina. All of which allowed big mileages to be covered at unusually high average speeds without tiring the rider.

More unusually for a Triumph, per-

The style of the 5T and its numerous derivatives may be perceived in the 500 sports/competition 5/5 of 1935. VMCC

haps because the 500 model relied on a rolling chassis very similar to the massive 6/1, even retaining the parking brake, it held the road superbly and with its 8in (203mm) brakes carried over from the 6/1, it braked magnificently. To cap it all, Triumph had equipped its new machines with one of the latest Webb-type girder forks, complete with fully adjustable Hartford-type friction dampers on the top link, and they absorbed bad roads as supremely as they swung unerringly around good bends.

If the 500 had a fault, it was its mildly weighty nature, which as it employed a massive duplex cradle frame like the 6/1, is perhaps understandable. At 380lb (172.5kg) this was heavier than most big singles, but many people found it a small price to pay for its other fine qualities. Standard models had a top speed of 70–75mph (113–121km/h) while the 5/5 Sport Special would manage up to 85mph (137km/h). Road testers of the time all admitted to being especially impressed with the 5/5's terrific high cruising speed stamina. That 70mph could be maintained indefinitely when by far the majority of vehicles on the road had a top speed at least 10mph (16km/h) slower than that. In July 1935, *Motor Cycling* tested a 5/5 and reported gear speeds of first (13.3) second (8.7) 52mph (84km/h) at 6,070rpm, third (6.0) 71mph (114km/h) at 5,650rpm and top (4.8:1) 83mph (133km/h) at 5,320rpm, and minimum non-snatch speed in top gear on full ignition

retard was 15mph (24km/h). Petrol consumption average through the test period was 84mpg (3.35 litre/100km). In its test report's finishing paragraph *Motor Cycling* summarised: 'The model 5/5 Triumph is a handsome and superbly finished mount with an excellent all-round performance and a wealth of really practical refinement which stamps it as a machine of unusual merit.'

Triumph appeared at long last to have the very machine it needed as a replacement for the legendary Trusty. Its closest rival was perhaps BSA's highly respected big single, the 496cc Empire Star. Fundamentally they were of the same kidney – air-cooled, ohv, dry sump, perpendicular singles with four-speed, foot-change gearboxes slung on heavy brazed lug frames. The Triumph was a modicum heavier, a degree faster, perhaps a shade more agile, but both cost about the same, at £66 for Coventry's sportster and £65 10s for Small Heath's. And BSA, too, had racing in its corporate mind for its Empire Star. To prove its point under ACU observation BSA put one of its Empire Stars through a week's endurance testing. At Brooklands it covered 500 miles (805km) at a remarkable 73.3mph (118km/h), then spent the rest of the time storming all the notorious English hills of the period. Apart from scheduled maintenance stops, the Beesa flew unhindered, averaging up to 55mpg (5.1 litre/100km).

BSA, no more interested in international road racing than Triumph,

was for all that impressed by its Empire Star's performance and decided on a policy of developing a clubman racer from its sportster. So also was Triumph. By 1935 it had finished the development of a new 100mph-plus super-tuned road racer, the model 5/5 Mk 10, or as it came to be known, the 5/10. Standard 5/2 tourers developed around 22bhp (16.4kW), sports 5/5s about 25bhp (20.1kW) but the 5/10 depending on engine specification turned out a minimum of 30bhp (22.4kW).

Its specification was impressive. In order to increase leverage on the crank-pin the 5/10 was fitted with a longer connecting-rod, which necessitated a longer barrel. Twin exhaust ports were retained but exhaust pipe diameter was reduced to increase exhaust gas velocity. Compression was raised from the 5/5's 7:1 (std was 6:1) to 7.5:1 for petrol and 11:1 for 'dope' – usually methanol based. The camshafts were special high lift items with tappets set slightly off-centre to resist 'scrub' as they revolved, and the gas tracts within the cylinder head were polished and flowed.

Good though they were, the standard cast iron flywheels were replaced by some machined from solid steel billets, because to improve bottom end reliability at racing speeds, the tolerances of the press fitted flywheels around the crankshaft pins were decreased, thus demanding a much higher tensile strength from the flywheels. The ordinary main bearings were retained – two ball races on the drive side and one on the timing side – but the big-end bearing was changed from a conventionally fabricated twin-row ball race cage to a superior type with a cage machined from a billet of aircraft quality Duralumin.

Dry sump lubrication was maintained but with an increased flow from a higher capacity pump and a greatly improved flow incorporating positive oil feed to the rockers and the rear of the cylinder. Cast-iron valve guides were replaced by bronze.

As a Lucas racing magneto replaced the roadsters' mag-dyno, the long induction tract necessary to carry the touring Amal carburettor over the mag-dyno was replaced by a racing

Amal instrument on a short induction stub. A close ratio gear cluster of 7.9, 6.3, 5.4 and top, 4.5:1 was employed as standard, with a foot-change selector mechanism.

Perhaps the most unusual aspect of the machine, and which indicates Triumph's serious intent, was the exchange of the usual aluminium or pressed steel engine covers for Elektron. This is a magnesium-based ultra-lightweight alloy containing approximately 4.5 per cent copper, 12 per cent aluminium plus small amounts of zinc and manganese. It is very expensive.

Before the project got into its stride, however, Triumph found itself in serious financial trouble. The company changed hands and with that in 1936 Val Page found his position as head of engineering design taken by Edward Turner, who was also general manager. Turner changed company policy and with it Page's new singles. Page was immediately snapped up by BSA and given the responsibility of developing its David Munro-originated Empire Star sports single into full-blooded competition models. With the assistance of Munro and Herbert Perkins he managed this with such formidable success that the great Wal Handley in 1937 won a BMCRC (British Motor Cycle Racing Club) Gold Star award at Brooklands. These were awarded to ton plus-lapping heroes. Handley averaged 102.27mph (164.6km/h) for the race and achieved a fastest lap of 107.57mph (173.11km/h). BSA riders on five of the same models that same year also lost no marks in the ISDT.

So the super-sportster Beesa single took the name Gold Star for its own

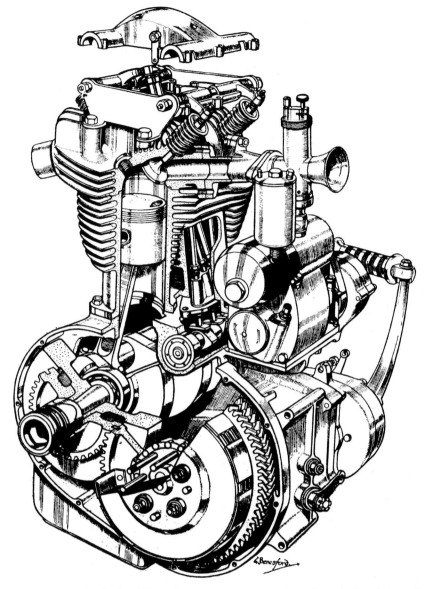

A great engine. Study this 6/1, exchange its gear primary drive for a duplex chain and you have the main features of a BSA unit A10, including bore and stroke. VMCC

and went on to greater and greater competition glories, on and off road.

And the potentially greater Trumpet super-sportster sank forever.

9

Tiger! Tiger! burning bright

Triumph by name and deed again, record breaking, Turner's curves, the Speed Twin, the world reels, Freddie Dixon and the Riley connection

Only slight mention has been made of the two smaller Mk 5 singles, the 2/1 250 and the 3/2 350 sports models. They shared the same cycle parts, which were in all but reduced dimensions, the same as the 5/5's, and much the same comment applies to their engines.

In the late summer of 1934, Triumph took a selection of its machines to Brooklands, where they were timed for an hour. The results were fascinating and tend to corroborate general opinion regarding the probable superiority of the 350. A standard 2/1 250 ridden by S. Slader averaged 49.17mph (79.12km/h); a standard 3/1 350 averaged 70.72mph (113.8km/h), a speed which concurred more-or-less identically with an accompanying 5/5 500 sportster; a solo 6/1 650 twin managed 69.72mph (112.19km/h). Jock West, later to become famous as the only British member of the 1938/39 BMW 'blown' Rennsport road racing team and then to become post-war sales manager of AJS/Matchless, demonstrated the superb potential of the experimental 5/10 by circulating at a steady 86.46mph (139.13km/h). Disappointingly he was black flagged because it was felt that the 'Racing risk was too high' whatever that portentously Turneresque statement may, or may not, have signified.

In September 1936, the range for 1937 was announced. Turner, the new hard-headed shrewd economist had,

following Page's lead, reduced it to just eight machines in a supremely successful consolidation exercise that would eventually return Triumph to a position of pre-eminence once more, even if for different reason from old. Pride of the range were the new Tigers – 70 (250), 80 (350) and 90 (500). Although so undeniably based on the existing Mk 5 range, they had been cleverly remodelled in what was to become a Turner trademark. Of course they performed well, but above all other considerations, they were as clean-cut handsome as a naval hero.

Under Turner's guidance, the old singles' entire bottom end had been left untouched, but all else was new. A new, compact gearbox with greatly improved selector mechanism no longer even distantly related to hand-change systems had been fitted, and this, frequently modified, was to remain with Triumph until the end of the Meriden twins. The entire valve mechanism in the cylinder head was encapsulated within a neat rocker box, while spring-loaded pushrod tubes set into rubber gaskets sealed them too. To accommodate this new cylinder heads had been made with twin ports giving way to single exhausts. The smaller two shared 7in (178 mm) cast iron drum brakes while the Tiger 90 was equipped with 8in (203 mm) iron-lined drums in ribbed cast aluminium. A larger capacity oil pump, certainly on the two bigger models, improved lubrica-

tion. This may well have been borrowed from the 6/1.

For the first time, Triumph displayed the silver-blue enamelled tanks that were to become such an identifiable signature. Richly chrome plated, they were almost sensually curvaceous, as was the headlamp too, and what had been an angular oil tank was now prettily rounded, although thankfully for the sake of heat radiation, it had been left black enamelled. Oh how the Tigers sparkled. All this overlayed a compact frame and promised perfect pitch. Prices were T70 £52, T80 £57 and T90 £65. They looked so right they had to go right. And they did.

The Motor Cycle put a T90 through its paces in January 1937 and loved it. In a standing start quarter-mile sprint the machine achieved 60mph (96km/h). It had a sitting-up top speed against a stiff breeze of 82mph (132km/h) and in still air managed just over 85mph (137km/h). The tester changed into top gear at 70mph (113km/h) and noted that acceleration began to decline only above 75mph (121km/h). Its minimum non-snatch speed in top gear was 14mph (22km/h) and at 40mph (64km/h) petrol consumption was a measured 40mpg (7l/100km). Compare this to contemporary four-valve Rudge's much more highly respected 500 single, for Rudge raced internationally. By the end of a standing quarter mile its speed was 58mph (93km/h), it

Rarer than hen's teeth these days, a 5/10 in a current vintage race paddock, viewed by an appreciative Charles 'Titch' Allen, founder of the VMCC. VMCC

had a top speed of 73mph (117km/h) and its minimum non-snatch speed was 16mph (26km/h). In its favour, it recorded 91mpg (3.10 litre/100km) but at 377lb (171kg) it weighed 5lb (2.2kg) more than the T90. Prices were identical.

The ACU selected at random from Triumph dealers' showrooms, a T70 from Brandish of Coventry, a T80 from Glanfield Lawrence of London and a T90 from Colmore Depot of Birmingham. They would be ridden around Donington Park for brief running-in, a standard first service, then would be raced for three hours around the circuit. Following that they would go to Brooklands for a timed fastest lap. Riders were Ted Thacker on the T70, Allan Jefferies on the T80 and Freddie Clarke, Triumphs own development engineer-rider, T90.

In sub-zero temperatures with sheet ice across parts of the circuit, the trio of riders began easing the brand-new bikes towards high speed. Fortunately the temperature rose just enough to melt the ice for the three-hour high-speed session. By the end Thacker on the 250 had covered 79 laps at an average speed of 56.72mph (91.27km/h), Jefferies T80 89 laps at 57.4mph (92.4km/h), and Clarke T90 84 laps at 54.4mph (87.54km/h). Frustratingly the 500 seemed cursed with gremlins: a piece of grit under the oil pump's non-return ball-valve lost oil pressure and defied repair, a rear tyre punctured and the HT lead worked loose in the magneto pickup, hence the poor speed.

Under the ACU observer's eagle-eye nothing other than scheduled maintenance was carried out before the fastest lap timing at Brooklands. There, the big single displayed its long legs, making a best time under Clarke's right fist of 82.31mph (132.45km/h). Next was Jefferies on the middleweight at 74.68mph (120km/h). Thacker wound up with a 66.39mph (106.83km/h) lap on the lightweight.

By this time, trials and road racing, which even into the late 1920s sometimes overlapped, had become clearly defined as the art of machine control and the quest for speed followed diverging routes. Yet they were still compatible, curiously so by current standards, and undeniably extant. Witness Triumph's determination to sell its bright sportsters as record breaking racers-with-lights-on simultaneous with the range's increasing success off road. By the end of 1936 public demand had forced the factory to offer Tigers in full trials trim. Turner must have loathed the added complication. Trials specification included an engine retuned for maximum torque, increased ground clear-

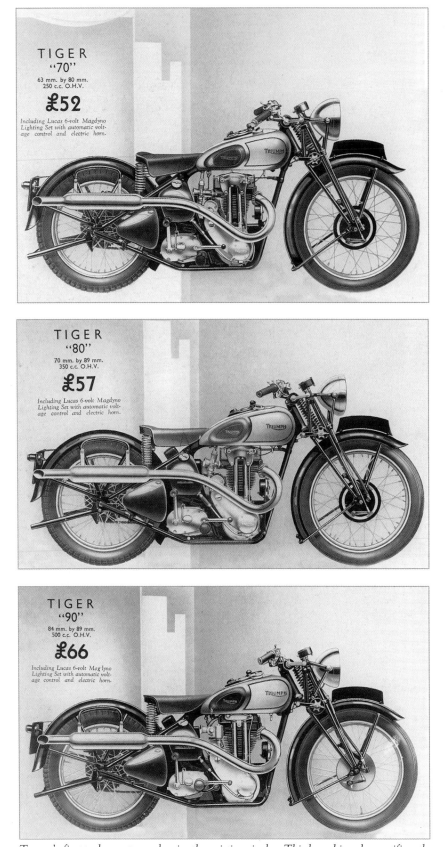

TIGER "70"
63 mm. by 80 mm.
250 c.c. O.H.V.
£52
Including Lucas 6-volt Magdyno
Lighting Set with automatic volt-
age control and electric horn.

TIGER "80"
70 mm. by 89 mm.
350 c.c. O.H.V.
£57
Including Lucas 6-volt Magdyno
Lighting Set with automatic volt-
age control and electric horn.

TIGER "90"
84 mm. by 89 mm.
500 c.c. O.H.V.
£66
Including Lucas 6-volt Magdyno
Lighting Set with automatic volt-
age control and electric horn.

Turner's first task was to modernise the existing singles. This he achieved magnificently with the range of Tigers 70 (250), 80 (350) and 90 (500). They were also available with low-level exhaust pipes. VMCC

ance obtained by 'dropping' the rear wheel spindle by simple sub-frame cut-and-shut methods, crankcase shields, uprated fork springs and wide ratio gears plus a range of optional sprockets. Prices were T70T £57, T80T £52 and T90T £69.

All this, though, was as nothing compared with what was impending.

When the Speed Twin came out in the summer of 1936 those who rode it were awe-struck. The only other motorcycle to have ever made such a profound impression was Honda's CB750 in 1969. Others, like the post-war Vincents, were wholly fabulous developments of what had gone before. Or possibly the early Scotts, but they were too radical to impress the conservative majority; besides, what did one expect of a race-born freak? The Speed Twin, however, was instantly familiar as your most uncommon-or-garden roadster, with a bewitching performance that outpaced everything of similar size and most of twice it. The Speed Twin, simply, and very nicely, sped with an easy zing. This was its chief delight.

That the Speed Twin when it appeared was a mere twin upset no-one. Throughout press and trade, common gossip had made Triumph's anticipated new 'multi' into a four which, considering Turner's entry ticket into motorcycle design had been the Ariel's ohc 500cc square four, is unsurprising. With no recorded exception, the Speed Twin heated everyone to a fever pitch of lyricism. 'Torrens' (Arthur Bourne) of *The Motor Cycle*, a grey-flannelled soberside most astutely aware of his pre-eminence, wrote in October after his first ride: 'If the general run of production models is around the standard of the machine submitted for test this new vertical twin will cause a furore.' He claimed that Turner telephoned *him* (!) the day following the test model's return with a request 'To chat the model over', but the only two improvements that came to his experienced mind were a need for improved oil pressure gauge illumination and a rear chain oiler control.

One has to accept the fact that, in common with most manufacturers, Triumph then ensured the press received for testing only models which had been meticulously prepared by its most skilful mechanics, often otherwise employed in the company experimental department. While they were not usually built to order (although it was known to occur), press bikes were individually fettled to an exceptionally high standard and were as near to 'blueprinted' as anything taken from a production line could be. One can hardly blame their makers for that. Thus, the familiar 90mph (145km/h) top speeds of pre-war Speed Twins recorded by road testers of the day should be regarded as mildly better than average, but for no other reason than careful engine preparation. *The Motor Cycle* recorded a mean top speed of 93.75mph (150.8km/h) and a best one-way maximum of 107mph (172.2km/h) on its test Speed Twin in October 1937: 'Truly an amazing figure for a fully equipped five-hundred.' It was indeed. Modern 500s, such as Honda's CB500 twin, produced to the same medium priced all-rounder performance standards, do not by much at all improve on it, save by stamina.

It will be remembered that when Val Page joined Triumph in 1932 his first machine was the 250cc ohc L2/1 announced in 1934. A fine little sportster, it was popular as an inexpensive yet reliable method of road racing at club and centre (regional) level thanks to an engine that responded well to power tuning. It had two significant features that were to prove Triumph cornerstones – an unusually efficient hemispherical combustion chamber and the memorable engine dimensions of 63 x 80mm. When Page designed the new range of Mk 5 singles for Triumph in 1933 for 1934, he used this as the basis for his 250, 350 and 500cc engines, although for all that they were brand-new engines. Page was by this time a world leader in combustion so with sound commercial sense carried over the efficient top end.

When Turner arrived to take responsibility of Triumph in 1936 he, in a more comprehensive operation than Page, also used what he had to hand as a means of improving the product by exploiting the best parts of Page's Mk 5s into the production of the Tiger range of singles. Then, in 1937, the Speed Twin arrived. It bor-

For a brief time before their production ceased, Tigers were available as competition (off-road) machines. This is a T80. VMCC

rowed the apparently flawless bore and stroke of the T70 née L2/1 as well as inheriting much of the 250's combustion characteristics, and in some compelling, almost indefinable way, the sum of those twinned little single cylinders' parts in unison far exceeded their individual performance.

As a matter of interest, the quoted power output of the T70 was 16bhp (14kW) at 5,800rpm and that of the 5T 27bhp (21.1kW) at 6,300rpm. The T80's was 20bhp (15kW) and the T90's 28–29bhp (21.3kW). These vary by 1 or 2bhp depending on the source, which range from factory brochures to press statements, but the above, and others in the 1930s range, are taken from publisher C. Arthur Pearson Ltd's highly respected book

Exploded view of the 3HW engine: The technical layout of a typical Triumph single, the 3HW of 1936. Author

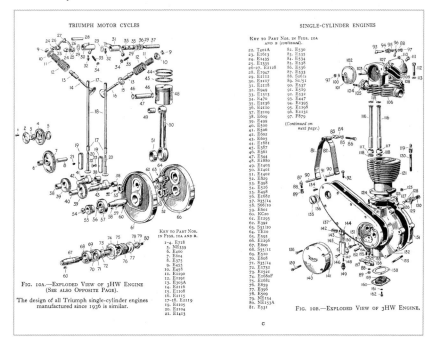

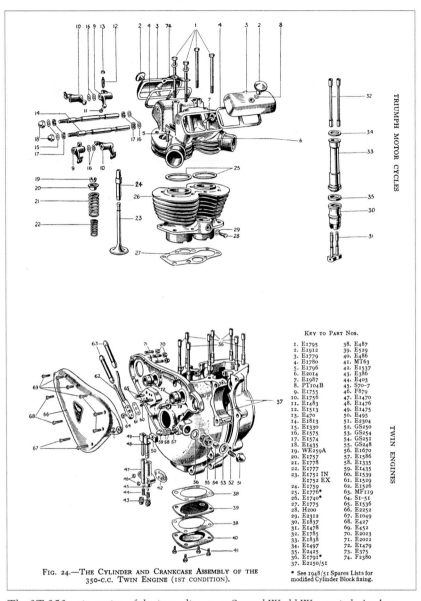

FIG. 24.—THE CYLINDER AND CRANKCASE ASSEMBLY OF THE 350-C.C. TWIN ENGINE (1ST CONDITION).

KEY TO PART Nos.

1. E1795	38. E487		
2. E1912	39. E529		
3. E1779	40. E486		
4. E1780	41. MT63		
5. E1796	42. E1537		
6. E2014	43. E386		
7. E1987	44. E403		
8. PT104B	45. S70-7		
9. E1755	46. F879		
10. E1756	47. E1470		
11. E1483	48. E1476		
12. E1513	49. E1475		
13. E470	50. E495		
14. E1813	51. E2304		
15. E1330	52. GS250		
16. E1575	53. GS254		
17. E1574	54. GS251		
18. E1435	55. GS248		
19. WE259A	56. E1670		
20. E1757	57. E1586		
21. E1778	58. E1335		
22. E1777	59. E1435		
23. E1751 IN E1752 EX	60. E1539 61. E1529		
24. E1759	62. E1526		
25. E1776*	63. MF119		
26. E1740*	64. S1-51		
27. E1775	65. E1536		
28. H200	66. E2252		
29. E2312	67. E1049		
30. E1837	68. E427		
31. E1478	69. E452		
32. E1785	70. E2023		
33. E1838	71. E2022		
34. E1497	72. E1479		
35. E2425	73. E375		
36. E1791*	74. F2380		
37. E2250/51			

* See 1948/51 Spares Lists for modified Cylinder Block fixing.

The 3T 350 twin engine of the immediate post-Second World War period. Author

Triumph Motor Cycles, published in 1938. The author was A. St J. Masters, who at the time was Triumph's service manager, the unrivalled sovereign over all Triumph technical matters. Triumph had its own Heenan & Froud DPX1 dynamometer, a genuine 'water-brake', which measured power from the crankshaft, as opposed to the popular, although much less demanding and accurate, rolling roads employed currently. In general, Triumph obtained its power figures from perfectly serviced engines turning the dynamometer from a jig. They were silenced to normal standards, were not especially carburetted or usually equipped with a dynamo.

Variations in power claims may well have been a matter of publicity minded employees selecting the best figures from a wide variety of bench tests. If one accepts the rule of thumb that a roadster of the period required a minimum of 30bhp (22.4kW) at the crankshaft to manage a bare 100mph (161km/h) in extremis, and 35bhp (26kW) to provide it regularly for a storm-suited owner, then the factory's claims are pretty accurate.

At the time of writing, enthusiasm is increasing for placing the responsibility for the technical origins of the Speed Twin engine within the Riley 9 car engine. Yet the Speed Twin's direct ancestry is clearly that of the T70, and

before that Page's L2/1 and possibly even before that the model W of 1930 out of Coventry's drawing office. After the passage of over six decades since the inception of the Triumph twin that was to revolutionise motorcycling, it is impossible to identify any more specifically generic identity with any certainty. All the personally responsible participants have, alas, died. And no engineer of normal human traits is likely to leave written records of technical innovations gleaned from his peers. However . . .

The Riley Register is the title of the Riley car club. Its historian is the diligent Dr David Styles, whose expertise and intense curiosity about all things Riley is probably unsurpassed. He is also the author of *As Old as the Industry*, the definitive Riley history, as well as holding down the editorship of the (British) Vintage Motor Cycle Club's magazine, *The Vintage Motor Cycle*. As Riley historian he enjoys unmatched access to the Register's comprehensive files, which include the diaries of Percy Riley, founder of The Riley Engine Company in 1903. He was its energetic dynamo until its absorption into the plebeian Morris car company in 1938. Percy Riley ranks amongst the world's great car designers, an equal of Vincenzo Lancia, whose ageless designs set the Italian industry into a motoring renaissance, and Hans Ledwinka, whose epoch-making Tatra's (Czech) inspired Ferdinand Porsche. The greatest of the Rileys was the four-cylinder Riley 9, which from 1926 to 1938, spawned not only its own progeny within the company but a host of imitators within and without Britain. Amongst non-Riley enthusiasts, the engine is perhaps most famous for powering the prodigiously successful ERA racing cars of the 1930s and '40s.

After a long series of discussions with the author of this book in the autumn of 1998, Styles was prompted to thoroughly investigate the Riley-Triumph connection. What he discovered prompted him to write about his findings, which he put into an article, *Riley's Triumph*, which at the time of writing had been adopted for publication by both British and American vintage motorcycle club magazines.

It is from these conversations that a great deal of the following information is culled. Our most grateful thanks to Dr Styles for his generosity.

It is a fact of Riley 9s that throughout their life these cars, in a variety of styles from pure racer to touring saloon, won every competition in which they participated, and the engines powered a wide variety of other makes and specials to victory with no less success, including grand prix events. One of the 9's most devoted drivers was Freddie Dixon, whose prowess on racing Douglas, Norton and other motorcycles through the 1920s, was equalled by his skill between four Riley 9 wheels during the 1930s. Because of Val Page's success as motorcycle engine designer and development engineer in his pre-Triumph days, he and Dixon knew each other well. Aware that Page had in mind a parallel twin (the 6/1) in 1932 and equally aware of the terrific performance of the progressive Riley 9 engine, Dixon arranged a meeting between Page and Percy Riley, although no written record was made of the meeting itself.

The outstandingly influential feature of the Riley 9 was its engine. Of even greater import was the philosophy of its designer, who was dismissive of patenting and believed that it was of eventual benefit to the British auto-industry at large if its good ideas were shared around. This is less insanely philanthropic than is immediately implied and was once surprisingly common amongst truly innovative engineers, certainly until the 1970s. Many of them sincerely believed that as their talent for advanced design had placed their company in the forefront of industry, so it would continue. The crumbs of their technology employed by smaller, lesser manufacturers, would be unlikely to lead to truly competitive commerce due to the accelerating pace of the more dynamically talented market leaders. The lesser, often idiosyncratic, producers served only to stimulate public desire for their own superior products.

When Turner took over Triumph management in 1936, he halted production of almost the entire, and unprofitable, Triumph range, and con-

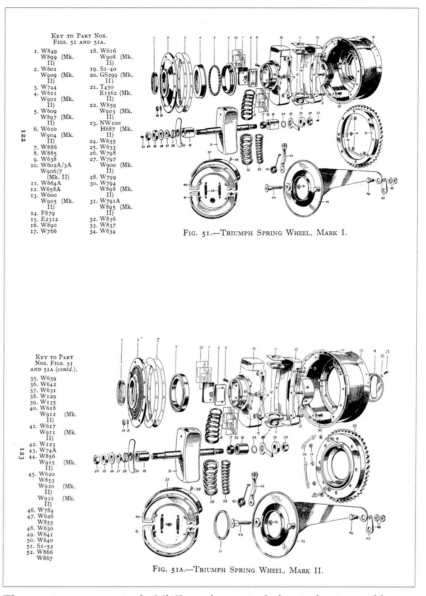

KEY TO PART NOS.
FIGS. 51 AND 51A.

1. W849
   W899 (Mk. II)
2. W601
   W909 (Mk. II)
3. W744
4. W611
   W901 (Mk. II)
5. W609
   W897 (Mk. II)
6. W610
   W904 (Mk. II)
7. W886
8. W885
9. W638
10. W602A/3A
    W906/7 (Mk. II)
11. W664A
12. W658A
13. W600
    W905 (Mk. II)
14. F879
15. E2312
16. W890
17. W766
18. W616
    W908 (Mk. II)
19. S1–40
20. GS299 (Mk. II)
21. T450
    E1562 (Mk. II)
22. W859
    W903 (Mk. II)
23. NW100
    H687 (Mk. II)
24. W635
25. W633
26. W798
27. W797
    W900 (Mk. II)
28. W799
30. W794
    W898 (Mk. II)
31. W791A
    W895 (Mk. II)
32. W836
33. W837
34. W634

FIG. 51.—TRIUMPH SPRING WHEEL, MARK I.

KEY TO PART NOS. FIGS. 51 AND 51A (contd.).

35. W639
36. W642
37. W631
38. W129
39. W135
40. W618
    W912 (Mk. II)
41. W617
    W911 (Mk. II)
42. W123
43. W74A
44. W856
    W915 (Mk. II)
45. W620
    W853
    W920 (Mk. II)
    W921 (Mk. II)
46. W784
47. W626
    W855
48. W630
49. W641
50. W640
51. S1–52
52. W866
    W867

FIG. 51A.—TRIUMPH SPRING WHEEL, MARK II.

The main improvements in the Mk II may be seen in the heavier bearings and bearing housing, better seals and more robust sprocket carrier. Author

centrated on improving the best of what remained. These were the Mk 5 singles which he remodelled into the appealing Tiger singles. And he designed the 5T Speed Twin. As explained, its engine was little more than two T70 top halves coupled to a common crankshaft, and they were Page's out of the L2/1.

Of outstanding merit in the 1926 Riley 9 was its hemispherical combustion chamber, which was very advanced for the time but by no means unknown. Each chamber aspirated through two valves at 90° to each other, or 45° from vertical. Percy Riley, like Page who when he was with

JAP gave the company most of its early power advantages, had studied engine breathing and combustion and was convinced that here – gas flow and flame front velocity – lay the secret of power. To this end the Riley 9 was meticulously developed. Maximum timing accuracy was ensured by helical timing gears turning twin high camshafts lifting pushrods. The layout was considered to be more reliable and less expensive than the ohc systems then showing promise, mainly at Velocette.

Sometimes quite erroneously criticised now, the introduction of the hemispherical combustion chamber in

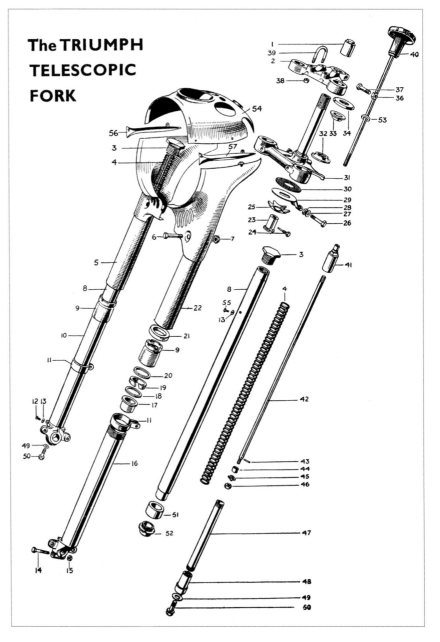

Compare this rider's eye view of a 1951 Speed Twin with the same of a 1938 Tiger 90. Turner knew how to 'clean-up' appearances like no other. Author

the 1920s was as much of an evolutionary step as electronic management systems were in the 1990s. The first and most popular all-ohv engines incorporated 'bath-tub' combustion chambers, in which the parallel valves descended vertically into the combustion chamber. When engine speed is low (sub-4,000rpm) this has many advantages, apart from simple assembly and low production cost. The bath-tub combustion chamber was often placed to one side of the engine as the best method of cooling the usually fractious spark plug. During the piston's ascent to compression, the turbulence in the cylinder caused by the effect of the bath-tub not only cooled the spark plug, it mixed the fresh charge nicely. Thus detonation and its accompanying evils, one of the devils of 'hot' side valve engines, was largely eliminated. But like sv units, the old bath-tub ohv engines were limited by their inability to breath freely, a consequence of their unsatisfactory valve angle and their semi-recessed valves, as well as slow and uneven flame front travel because of their offset spark plugs.

If we accept that a sphere would make the perfect combustion chamber shape, we can hardly disagree that a

modified sphere is the best compromise. A sphere minimises heat loss and thus maximises volumetric efficiency, and it lacks dangerous hot-spot projections as well as asphyxiating pockets. Two unavoidable practicalities deny us spherical combustion chambers, however. First, it is not possible to place the spark plug at the centre of the combustion chamber, where ideally it should be for perfect flame front travel; secondly, the concave in a piston needed to complete the sphere would result in a hopelessly low com-

pression ratio in a square dimensioned engine. Admittedly the familiar domed crown of a conventional hemi' piston and the offset spark plug intrude rudely into what otherwise would be a perfect little world, but there is no alternative. Besides, with two valves at 45° gas flow and transfer are so terrifically improved that the loss of the pure sphere's excellence is more than outweighed by the increase in high-speed efficiency and, thus, the power and the reliability of the compromise. Unfortunately in practice, the high

Triumph's tele was slim, because unlike most, its spring was contained within the stanchion. Author

TECHNICAL DATA

MODEL	3T	5T	T100	TR5	6T
Engine Type ... ... Bore and Stroke ... ... m/m	O.H.V. TWIN 55 x 73.4	O.H.V. TWIN 63 x 80	O.H.V. TWIN 63 x 80	O.H.V. TWIN 63 x 80	O.H.V. TWIN 71 x 82
Cylinder Capacity ... ... c/cm. (cu./ins.)	349 (21)	498 (30.5)	498 (30.5)	498 (30.5)	650 (4.0)
Compression Ratio ... ... Standard	6.3 : 1	7 : 1	7 : 1	6 : 1	7 : 1
B.H.P. and R.P.M. (Low Octane Petrol)	19 at 6500	27 at 6300	32 at 6500	25 at 6000	34 at 6300
Petrol Tank Capacity ... ... Gallons (Litres)	3½ (16)	4 (18)	4 (18)	2½ (11.4)	4 (18)
Oil Tank Capacity ... ... Pints (Litres)	6 (3.4)	6 (3.4)	6 (3.4)	6 (3.4)	6 (3.4)
Carburetter Main Jet	120	140	*150	150	‡140
Carburetter Throttle Slide	5/4	6/3½	6/3½	6/3½	6/3½
Carburetter Needle	5	6	6	6	6
Carburetter Needle Position	2	2	3	3	2
Carburetter Needle Jet	107	107	107	107	107
Inlet Valve Opens B.T.C. ... ... Degrees	22	26½	26½	26½	26½
Inlet Valve Closes A.B.C. ... ... Degrees	66	69½	69½	69½	69½
Exhaust Valve Opens B.B.C. ... Degrees	63	61½	61½	61½	61½
Exhaust Valve Closes A.T.C. ... Degrees	25	35½	35½	35½	35½
Ignition Timing Fully Advanced ... Inches (mm)	†¹¹⁄₃₂ (9)	⅜ (9.5)	⅜ (9.5)	⅜ (9.5)	⅜ (9.5)
Contact Breaker Gap ... ... Inches (mm)	.012 (.3)	.012 (.3)	.012 (.3)	.012 (.3)	.012 (.3)
Sparking Plug Gap ... ... Inches (mm)	.015 to .018 (.4 to .5)	.015 to .018 (.4 to .5)	.015 to .018 (.4 to .5)	.015 to .018 (.4 to .5)	.015 to .018 (.4 to .5)

	3T	5T		T100		TR5	6T	
Tappet Clearance—Cold ... ... Inches (mm)	.001 (.025)	.001 (.025)		.002 in. (.05) .004 ex (.10)		.002 in (.05) .004 ex (.10)	.001 (.025)	
Engine Sprocket—Solo ... ... Teeth	19	22		22		21	24	
Engine Sprocket—Sidecar ... ... Teeth	—	19		19		—	21	
		Solo	Sidecar	Solo	Sidecar		Solo	Sidecar
Gear Ratio ... ... Top	5.80	5.00	5.80	5.00	5.80	5.24	4.57	5.24
Gear Ratio ... ... Third	6.90	5.95	6.90	5.95	6.90	7.46	5.45	6.24
Gear Ratio ... ... Second	9.80	8.45	9.80	8.45	9.80	11.58	7.75	8.85
Gear Ratio ... ... Low	14.13	12.20	14.13	12.20	14.13	15.25	11.20	12.8
Primary Chain Pitch ... ... Inches	½ x .335 x .305	½ x .335 x .305		½ x .335 x .305		½ x .335 x .305	½ x .335 x .305	
Primary Chain Length—Solo ... ... Links	74	78		78		76	80	
Primary Chain Length—Sidecar ... ... Links	—	77		77		—	79	
Rear Chain Pitch ... ... Inches	⅝ x .400 x ⅜	⅝ x .400 x ⅜		⅝ x .400 x ⅜		⅝ x .400 x ⅜	⅝ x .400 x ⅜	
Rear Chain Length ... ... Links	90	93		93		90	93	
Front Tyre Size ... ... Inches	3.25 x 19	3.25 x 19		3.25 x 19		3.00 x 20	3.25 x 19	
Rear Tyre Size ... ... Inches	3.25 x 19	3.50 x 19		3.50 x 19		4.00 x 19	3.50 x 19	
Wheel Base Static ... ... Inches (cm)	53.25 (135)	55 (140)		55 (140)		53 (134)	55 (140)	
Overall Length ... ... Inches (cm)	82.5 (209)	84 (214)		84 (214)		80 (203)	84 (214)	
Overall Width ... ... Inches (cm)	28.5 (72)	28.5 (72)		28.5 (72)		29 (74)	28.5 (72)	
Saddle Height ... ... Inches (cm)	28.5 (72)	29.5 (75)		29.5 (75)		31 (79)	31 (79)	
Ground Clearance ... ... Inches (cm)	6 (15)	6 (15)		6 (15)		6½ (16)	6 (15)	
Weight—Dry ... ... Lbs. (Kilos)	325 (147)	365 (165.5)		365 (165.5)		295 (134)	370 (168)	

* For Maximum Performance, detach air filter rubber hose and fit a 160 main jet.
‡ " " " " " " " " " " " " " 190 " "
† For Low Octane Fuel reduce to ⁹⁄₃₂" (7 mm).

accuracy of the machining necessary to emplace the valves in their designated attitudes relied on the skill of Triumph's production craftsmen. The otherwise inexplicable performance variations between identical models, most especially in the final years under BSA management, could as often as not, be attributed to small variations in valve angle.

Technical data taken directly from the 1951 owner's instruction manual. Author

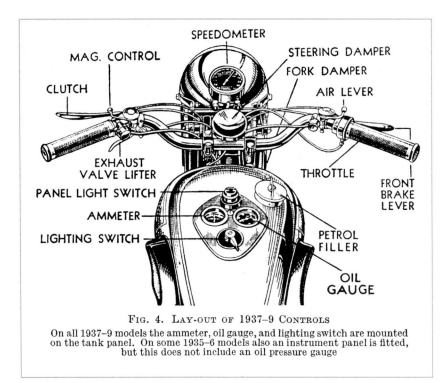

FIG. 4. LAY-OUT OF 1937-9 CONTROLS

On all 1937–9 models the ammeter, oil gauge, and lighting switch are mounted on the tank panel. On some 1935–6 models also an instrument panel is fitted, but this does not include an oil pressure gauge

The 1938 Tiger from the saddle. Author

Turner was already a Riley 9 buff. He had owned one – a Monaco Saloon – when he had worked at Ariel, and he loved it. During this period he joined the exclusive yet unofficial club of the West Midland region's car and motorcycle management. They mixed freely, both informally at pub lunches and formally at the Coventry Chamber of Commerce, of which he and Victor Riley (elder brother of Percy and in 1896 founder of the Riley Cycle Co. Ltd which was to grow into the Riley car company) were both active members. It is inconceivable that the exceptionally astute Turner did not discuss technical matters with Victor Riley.

At first sight, one may be forgiven for dismissing the Riley 9-Triumph 5T relationship. Remember though, unlike Riley, Turner's engine had been defined by appearance as much as performance. Page's massively profiled 6/1 for all its technical merits had not sold well, and Turner thought he recognised a significant reason – it was not pretty. So to keep the Speed Twin neat and compact, he was forced to drop the high cam Riley 9 layout. And to keep the cost down, for his engine with two camshafts was already bordering on the exotic, he

denied the new twin the helical cut timing gears it needed to run quietly and allowed it to whirr, in what was to become Triumph's chattering trademark, on straight cut gears. Similar too, was the Speed Twin's rocker gear and its associated positive lubrication via external pipes, while of greater import, the Triumph's valves were positioned identically to the Riley's.

The engine dimensions of the Riley 9 and Triumph 5T are not identical; a halved Riley 9 would result in 544cc while a Speed Twin is 498cc. It makes no difference to the close relationship and probably also has technical roots in the mid-Twenties when Turner was developing the Square Four for Ariel. A Squariel is little more than two transverse parallel twins linked by geared crankshafts. Turner took almost three years to turn his four-cylinder notion into a showroom motorcycle. The 5T Speed Twin incurred less than a year. With the Squariel, Turner was pioneering parallel twin dynamics and he learned the hard way they could be abominable, which he never forgot. Thus he was able to put the remarkable Speed Twin together in double quick time, which he never allowed anyone else to forget.

Whereas a Riley 9's cylinder dimension are typically long stroke at 60.3mm bore x 90mm stroke, the Speed Twin's are 63 x 80mm. Page had understood full well that his 249cc motorcycle engine did not require the high torque development of the car engine at low rpm which the high induction speeds of the long stroke Riley 9 provided. Besides the bore and stroke had proven ideal on the nippy little 250cc model W of 1930. The car engine developed a maximum of 27.7bhp (20.6kW) at 4,000rpm and a useful 14.75bhp (11kW) at 2,000rpm. Coincidentally, the Speed Twin also produced the same maximum power but at 6,300rpm. It was fortunate for Turner that Page abbreviated the stroke of the car power unit for his motorcycle engine.

While without records one can only surmise, using sensibly applied circumstantial evidence, the origins of the Triumph 5T Speed Twin appear to be thus. That in 1932 Val Page designed a 250 (in fact 249cc) single employing the well-known and highly respected combustion chamber of the Riley 9. And when Edward Turner doubled the engine up for his 500 twin (498cc) he dipped further into the Riley 9 honey pot by employing its camshaft layout and valve train. To give Turner his due, he never attempted to claim credit for the top end of the 5T. In all his published interviews the majority of his concern lies demonstrably with the engine's superior smoothness, torque development and acceleration over a single of the same size. Commercially he was justifiably proud of his multi's adaptation of ordinary single-cylinder production requirements and its low manufacturing cost. Its crankcase split vertically into two, just like a single, and it employed a duplicate of the single-cylinder T90's rolling chassis.

It is sometimes claimed that Triumph also won its oil pump from the same Riley source. This is doubtful because the design more closely resembles Ariel's than Riley's, which was remotely activated by concentric cam driven connecting rods. But in any case, Triumph had been moving towards this design through a series of similar designs in previous models and the type was not unusual. Besides, it is of small account.

When Turner changed from the Mk 5s to the Tiger singles in 1936, apart from encapsulating their valve gear and providing a specifically foot-change gearbox, he made one other significant alteration which was to profoundly affect all Triumphs for 30 years. He exchanged Page's torsionally stiff, if slightly heavy, twin-loop duplex cradle frames, for his own single-loop duplex cradle devices. Admittedly they alone brought the arguably over-weight 375lb (17.25kg) T90 into line with its big single peers at 362lb (16.4kg), but it was hardly to the otherwise excellent 500's advantage. Lighter yes, but no longer taut around the bends. While the T70 and T80 managed superbly, the heavier T90 misbehaved during fast cornering unless it was treated circumspectly.

Why did Turner engineer such a change? It was simpler to fabricate, absorbed less steel and it looked smart. That it was a poor frame is indicated by press reports arising the year following the 5T's launch. At the time, journalists had been utterly beguiled by the Speed Twin and in all probability assumed that any wayward behaviour must be an aberration. In fact, the early model's cornering abilities were miserable. It could hardly be blamed on the extra power and weight of the 500 twin because the 500 single produced 1bhp more and weighed 1lb more.

Only in 1939 was an admittance made by the press over the Speed Twin's 'flighty' rear end and 'dancing' front end. It followed the introduction of the notably faster super-sports T100 Tiger 100.

Before moving into the period which initiated Triumph's rapid rise to pre-eminence, thanks to the T100's extraordinary performance, let's pause at a might-have-been. Throughout the 1930s Triumph had never enjoyed much success with its 350s, and it had built a few. The 3TW military 350 twin of 1941 will be recalled, on which so much rested, yet was obliterated along with the factory in the bombing of Coventry. In partnership with its military twin, Triumph was busy developing a civilian sportster, the Tiger 85. If the ultra-enthusiastic reports from both *The Motor Cycle* and *Motor Cycling* over the Army bike are any indication, then the T85 would have wooed 'em harder and faster than did the 5T. However, against expectation the 3TW, which of necessity was intended to survive rougher handling than its civilian brother, was actually a measurably less substantial motorcycle than the T85. It had to be to meet War Office specifications regarding weight and performance.

Because of the outbreak of war in 1939, the T85 never appeared, although it had received advanced publicity. Probably no finer example of Turner's dedication to his beloved 'metal paring' exists than in the weight differential of the pair. Where the T85 met 263lb (119.4kg) fully equipped for the road, its khaki partner managed a starving 230lb (104.4kg) similarly togged. Turner's single minded resolution to minimise mass resulted in minimalisation as rarely seen on motorcycles. Whether Triumph's civilian customers would have been willing to compromise the usual rugged durability of the T85 for the sake of the squaddie's enforced fuel-sipping athleticism is debatable. But without a doubt, the extra 33lb (15kg) required for the T85 to meet even the simple requirements of the late 1930s is a perfect example of the unavoidable penalties to be paid for increasing civility.

In 1946, Triumph made another bid for the popular 350 class with a resurrected T85 in the form of the 349cc 3T. Evidently its blueprints escaped the Nazi bombs while the military model's did not. Although the £163 11s 3d 3T closely resembled the £180 6s 11d 5T in detail it differed enough to prove unequal to matching the 500's performance pro-rata, so never found much favour. While astonishingly smooth, tractable, quiet and docile, the claimed 19bhp (14.2kW) of the smaller twin must have issued from puny ponies because they were completely unable to match the muscley ones of the earlier T80 single's 20bhp (15kW). Most ran out of steam at 65mph (105km/h) and to find one that would exceed 70mph (113km/h) was a rare treat. But it was a remarkably economical machine, averaging up to 100mpg (2.8 litre/100km) and never less than 65mpg (4.34 litre/100km) however hard pressed. By 1950 it had been dropped. from the Triumph range.

10

Days of glory

Back on top form, American racing, Brooklands record breaking, supercharging, Bert Hopwood, Freddie Clarke, the T100, endurance, North America, Bill Johnson

If the Speed Twin provided the potential for success, the Tiger 100 was the proof of it, at least in the eye of the public, who saw in the super sportster the opportunity to own a motorcycle directly related to the record-breaking Triumph twins of the past year or so. The Coventry factory was about to reap the benefit of its 6/1 parallel twin's trailblazing record breaking because, however much it may have yearned for speed, the Great British Public was fully aware that Great British Road Racers on their Great British Singles beat all comers on their fancy foreign multis. Well, usually anyway. So even a British twin was viewed askance, as stockists of the 6/1 found.

By the time the Speed Twin arrived, the ice had been broken, and by the time the super-sporting Tiger 100 appeared, the world at large, let alone Britain, was convinced of the new twins' incomparability. American motorcyclists especially were captivated when in the 1937 American TT at Ontario, California, a race-prepared Canadian Speed Twin won the event's two premier races against mainly Harley-Davidsons of twice the size. One year later in Australia, Les Fredericks lifted the nation's 12-hour speed record from the previous 700 miles (1,126km) to 806 miles (1,297km) at an average of 67.62mph (109km/h) on another Speed Twin.

In Britain, the prestige of Brooklands ranked a fair second to the IoM TT. Freddie Clarke had set the pace for Triumph in 1936 with a potent methanol burning L/21 (250 single) then followed up in 1937 with an all-time 350cc class record of 105.97mph (170.5km/h) on a similarly prepared Tiger 80. One year later Ivan Wickstead followed suit with a blown Speed Twin, which like Clarke's T80 time, also stands at an eternal 118.02mph (189.9km/h), 1.7mph (2.73km/h) faster then the previous record holder Denis Minnet on an ohc Norton. At the outset of war in 1939, the bravely banked old circuit, which was proving inadequate to the demands of increasingly more powerful cars and bikes anyway, was seconded for military aviation, never to reopen.

Certainly the Wickstead machine was fundamentally a 5T, but he and its owner, Maurice Winslow, had robustly strengthened the machine. Turner's minimalist engineering principles first revealed themselves as Freddie Clarke, who following his Brooklands triumphs had been hired to head Triumph's development and competition department, brought the T100 into the world. Its 34bhp (25.3kW) was too much for the 27bhp (20.1kW) Speed Twin, which when its pace was forced, lifted its cylinder barrels, broke its crankshafts and snapped its con-rods. When the T100 entered production in 1938 it sported lightly strengthened crankshafts and con-rods, and a heavier barrel flange clamped down by eight rather than six studs, which it shared with the Speed

One of the world's most important and influential motorcycles, Edward Turner's 1937 Speed Twin. Life on and about two wheels has never been the same since. Cyril Ayton

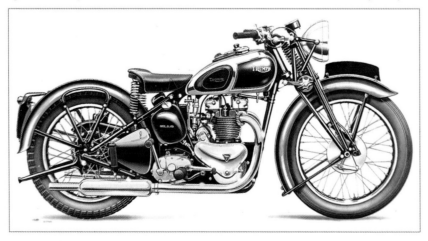

Twin. First-year 5Ts were also equipped with rolling chassis which performed not much better than the first engines did. Their almost unaltered T90 heritage was proving to be insufficiently substantial.

No ordinary machine, Winslow's Speed Twin's power was boosted twofold by supercharging and its speed, by half as much again as the original, could not cope. So over a four-month period of intensive re-engineering, Winslow and Wickstead reinforced the engine's crankcases and the crankshaft, strengthened the entire engine jointing system, and remodelled the frame to accept a belt-driven supercharger above the gearbox. Such prodigious accomplishments were unlikely to have much impressed Turner, who in the spring of 1939, made a public statement to the effect that Triumph no longer supported grand prix racing because it contributed nothing of value to road model development, whereas in the 1920s, 60 per cent of racer construction was from roadster parts. He (Triumph) would support only races for stock-type machines. Nor was he impressed by trials and scrambles because they did not demonstrate product reliability. Ho hum . . .

Fortunately for Triumph, and ultimately of course Turner himself, no-one took Triumph's general manager seriously. How could they when the potent T100 appeared undisguisedly equipped to deal sensibly with high speeds? Americans began dirt racing the T100 and the British began road racing it, although tragically the Second World War interrupted what gave every sign of turning a meteoric rise into unrivalled supremacy.

Hopwood, who in 1936 had left Ariel to join Triumph as Turner's design assistant, thoroughly approved of the improvements made to the 5T, but the real credit for the T100 must go to Clarke. Apart from the stronger major engine components previously mentioned and shared by both 5T and T100, much of the sportster's specification was different. The 5T's Amal 276 carburettor had a ¹⁵⁄₁₆in. (23.8mm) throat and 160 main jet, while the T100's was 1in (25.4mm) and a 140 main jet; compression was raised from 7:1 to 8:1 (sometimes quoted as 7.8:1)

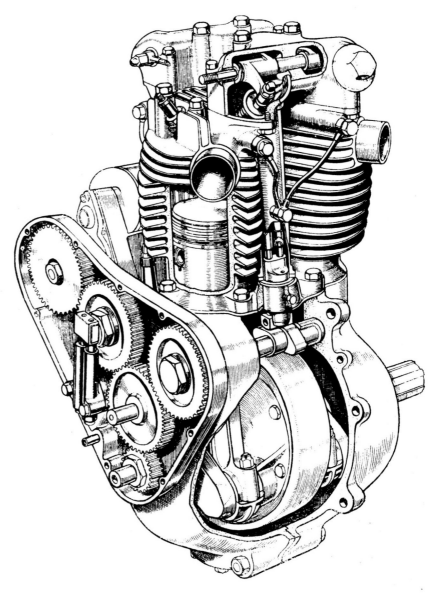

A cut-away of the 5T engine, which employed a mag-dyno because separate K2F (twin) mags were a device of the future in 1937. VMCC

with forged pistons for the T100; the T100's cylinder head gas tracts were carefully contoured and polished, and an optional bronze head for improved cooling was available for an extra £5. The T100's tappet blocks were phosphor bronze, the valve guides were bronze rather than iron, and the engine's internals were peened and polished to resist surface micro-cracking from flexure. Perhaps surprisingly to modern enthusiasts, the valves were seated directly on the bronze, unlike the later alloy heads which necessitated iron seat inserts. While

fine for the road, when subjected to earnest racing techniques of a regular 7,000rpm plus, the valves pocketed into the comparatively soft bronze, so almost all competition machines eventually had steel seats shrunk into place. Contrary to popular belief, both early models shared the same camshaft. Tellingly, the 6-pint (3.4-litre) oil tank of the 5T was enlarged to a full gallon (4.5 litres) on the T100 because, presumably, overheating was a problem on hard-ridden models. Some confusion exists over the actual, as opposed to the listed,

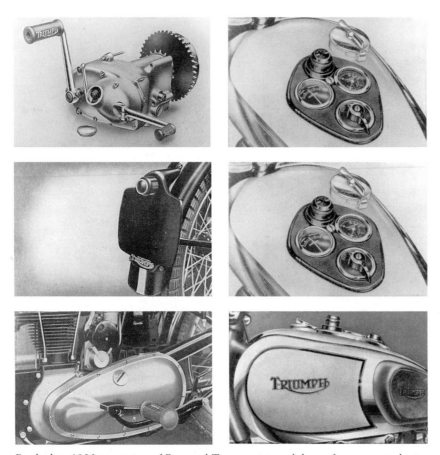

By the late 1930s, a variety of Page and Turner-originated design features were beginning to characterise the new Triumphs. VMCC

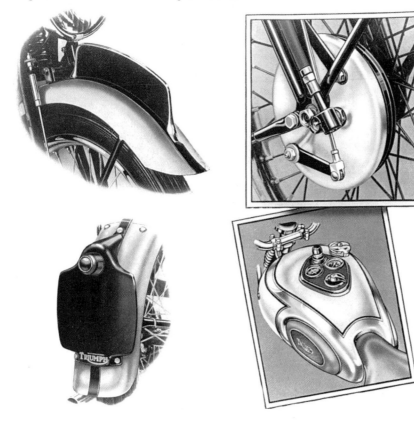

petrol tanks and brakes. Pre-war 5Ts and the very first T100s were listed with 3.25-gallon (14.7-litre) and later T100s with 4-gallon (18-litre) tanks. The front brakes on the 5T were plain dished 7in (178mm) iron and the T100's were ribbed cast iron for improved cooling and freedom from distortion. Any early 5Ts now equipped with big tanks and ribbed front brakes either had them fitted as an option by the original supplier or they have been since adopted.

Every T100 engine after initial running-in was then removed from its rolling chassis and was tested on Triumph's own Heenan & Froude DPX1 dynamometer, and tuned if necessary, to proof of 34bhp (sans silencers). When its customer took delivery, he would be issued with his machine's development shop certification of power delivery.

To prove a point, Triumph equipped the T100 with novel silencers. When their sleek outlet cone was detached, the tapered remaining silencer form became a megaphone exhaust, then as fashionable as carbon fibre or titanium cans are now. They were also functional because removal of the caps released an extra 2bhp (1.5kW).

This is actually quite an expensive list of parts that the economy-energised Turner would never have sanctioned unless vital. The Speed Twin cost £77 15s at its launch and the Tiger 100 £82 15s. Both weighed around 365lb (165.7kg) and all other dimensions were the same, including the wheelbase at 54in (1,371mm). And both enjoyed what in Britain became symbolic of a more leisurely age when riders had time to take their eyes off the road for a moment – a tank-top instrument panel comprising an ammeter, an oil pressure gauge and a night-time detachable inspection lamp. The theory was that as neither instrument was illuminated, a rider could simply twist out his inspection lamp and check that the 35W electrical and 60psi (4.14 bar) lubrication systems were up to scratch, as well as assisting with map-reading and emergency repairs. Numerous extras were offered, some of which were in practice essential. These were for both models: 3.50

To prove a point, being that you can't keep a good un down, John Armstrong thrashes his 1950 T'bird in a modern classic/vintage race, although what Freddie Clarke would have thought of the knee-out cornering style is not known, and that front brake, surely, is from a BSA A10? Cyril Ayton

front tyre (which definitely improved a flighty front end), a quickly detachable rear wheel, rear carrier, side stand, pillion footrests and seat, rear stop light, 120mph speedometer incorporating intermediate gear rpm scales, and a straight-through racing exhaust system.

Of the two machines, the 5T created the greatest impact because it was such a sensational surprise. *The Motor Cycle*, normally extreme only in understatement, let slip an almost audible scream of excitement: 'Truly an amazing figure for a fully equipped five-hundred,' after its testers had recorded a top speed of 107mph (174km/h) over a quarter mile (403m) with a light tail wind. Truly an amazing figure indeed for a 27bhp sports tourer of more than 60 years

past. On a standard 5:1 top gear at its maximum bhp revs of 6,300, top speed could only have been 97mph (156km/h). Even at the T100's 6,500rpm best it was 100mph (161km/h). One cannot but help wonder whether the wily Clarke had a finger in this little press pie because its mean top speed was 94mph (151km/h).

During development, the prototype 34bhp T100 was breaking crankshafts at 7,000rpm. Fourteen years later the great technical journalist and racer, Vic Willoughby, commented in *The Motor Cycle*, May 1953, that following a race at Snetterton in which he had been beaten only by a Manx Norton, a Moto Guzzi Gambalunga and a Roland Pike-prepared full-race tuned BSA A7, 'At 7,000rpm high frequency

vibration proved troublesome.' He was racing a factory-prepared but wholly road-equipped T100; 7,000rpm on a 5:1 top gear equates to 108mph (174km/h). One would have to blueprint a 1937 5T to the most excruciating exactitude these days to even get a sniff near a genuine 90mph. They were never as fast as this in the hands of Joe Rider, although as late as 1953 press testers were still recording top speeds of 90mph (145km/h) plus, but which by 1956 the 'superior' short-stroke 5TA had dropped to a more realistic 85mph (137km/h). Perhaps significantly, pre-production Speed Twins had been bench tested and found to be developing 29bhp (21.6kW) at 6,000rpm. The conclusions are that (a), the 5T engine was so innately

Technical Details

MODEL	Speed Twin	T.100	T80	T70	6S	5H	5S	3S	3H	2H and 2HC
Engine type	O.H.V. Twin	O.H.V. Twin	O.H.V.	O.H.V.	Side Valve	O.H.V.	Side Valve	Side Valve	O.H.V.	O.H.V
Bore and Stroke ... m.m.	63 x 80	63 x 80	70 x 89	63 x 80	84 x 108	84 x 89	84 x 89	70 x 89	70 x 89	63 x 80
Cylinder Capacity c.c.	498	498	343	249	597	493	493	343	343	249
Compression ratio ...	7 : 1	7.75 : 1	7.5 : 1	7.7 : 1	5.6 : 1	6 : 1	5.6 : 1	5.3 : 1	6.7 : 1	6.92 : 1
B.H.P. @ R.P.M.	28.5 @6,000	33–34@7000 (open megaphones)	20 @ 5,700	16 @ 5,800	18@4,800	23 @ 5,000	15 @ 4,800	12 @ 4,800	17 @ 5,200	13 @ 5,200
Engine revs : Top gear @ 10 m.p.h. Solo	647	647	711	750	618	618	674	788	711	788
Engine Sprocket No. of teeth Solo	22	22	20	18	23	23	20	18	20	18
Clutch diameter ...	6″	6″	6″	6″	6″	6″	6″	6″	6″	6″
,, Plates: Number	4 Driving 5 Driven	4 Driving 5 Driven	3 Driving 4 Driven	3 Driving 4 Driven	4 Driving 5 Driven	4 Driving 5 Driven	4 Driving 5 Driven	3 Driving 4 Driven	3 Driving 4 Driven	3 Driving 4 Driven
Friction Material	Cork	Cork	Cork	Cork	Cork	Cork	Cork	Cork	Cork	Cork
Clutch Sprocket No. of teeth	43	43	43	43	43	43	43	43	43	43
Gearbox Sprocket ,,	18	18	18	18	18	18	20	18	18	18
Gear ratios: Top Solo	5.0	5.0	5.5	6.1	4.78	4.78	4.95	6.1	5.5	6.1
,, ,, Third ,, ...	6.0	6.0	6.6	7.33	5.75	5.75	5.94	7.3	6.6	7.3
,, ,, Second ,, ...	8.65	8.65	9.5	10.50	8.26	8.26	8.56	10.5	9.5	10.5
,, ,, Low ,, ...	12.70	12.70	14.0	15.50	12.1	12.1	12.52	15.5	14.0	15.5
,, ,, Top Sidecar	5.8	5.8	—	—	5.23	5.23	—	—	—	—
,, ,, Third ,, ...	6.95	6.95	—	—	6.28	6.28	—	—	—	—
,, ,, Second ,, ...	10.03	10.03	—	—	9.05	9.05	—	—	—	—
,, ,, Low ,, ...	14.73	14.73	—	—	13.3	13.3	—	—	—	—
Rear Wheel Sprocket No of teeth	46	46	46	46	46	46	46	46	46	46
Rear Chain	⅝″ x .375″	⅝″ x .375″	⅝″ x .375″	⅝″ x .375″	⅝″ x .375″	⅝″ x .375″	⅝″ x .375″	⅝″ x .375″	⅝″ x .375″	⅝″ x .375″
,, ,, No. of pitches	93	93	90	90	93	93	90	90	90	90
Front Chain	½″ x .305″	½″ x .305″	½″ x .305″	½″ x .305″	½″ x .305″	½″ x .305″	½″ x .305″	½″ x .305″	½″ x .305″	½″ x .305″
,, ,, No. of pitches Solo	78	78	75	75	78	78	75	74	75	74
,, ,, ,, ,, Sidecar	77	77	—	—	77	77	—	—	—	—
Brake Drums, diameter and width ...	7″ x 1⅛″ F 7″ x 1⅛″ R	7″ x 1⅛″ F 7″ x 1⅛″ R	7″ x 1″ F 7″ x 1⅛″ R	7″ x 1″ F 7″ x 1⅛″ R	7″ x 1⅛″ F 7″ x 1⅛″ R	7″ x 1⅛″ F 7″ x 1⅛″ R	7″ x 1″ F 7″ x 1⅛″ R	7″ x 1″ F 7″ x 1⅛″ R	7″ x 1″ F 7″ x 1⅛″ R	7″ x 1″ F 7″ x 1⅛″ R
Tyres Dunlop: Ribbed to 'Tigers' and 'Speed Twin' front wheels	26″x3.00″ F 26″ x 3.5″ R	26″x 3.00″F 26″x 3.5″ R.	26″ x 3″ F 26″x 3.25″R	26″ x 3″F 26″x 3.25″R	26″x 3.25″F 26″x 3.25″R	26″x 3.25″F 26″x 3.25″R	26″x 3.25″ 26″x 3.25″	26″x 3.25″F 26″x 3.25″R	26″ x3.25″F 26″x 3.25″R	26″ x3″F 26″x 3.25″R
Saddle Height	27¾″	27¾″	27″	27″	27¾″	27¾″	27″	27″	27″	27″
Wheelbase	54″	54″	52½″	52½″	54″	54″	52½″	52½″	52½	52½″
Overall length	84″	84″	82″	82″	84″	84″	82″	82″	82″	82″
Overall width	28½″	28½″	28½″	28½″	28½″	28½″	28½″	28½″	28½″	28½″
Ground Clearance ...	5″	5″	5½″	5¼″	5″	5″	5½″	5½″	5½″	5¼″
Weight fully equipped lbs.	360	362	320	316	356	362	322	316	322	318

PRICE LIST OF EXTRAS

Rear stop light - -	**6 0**
Smith Chronometric Speedometer 80 m.p.h. Trip Type - - -	**2 10 0**
Smith Chronometric Speedometer 120 m.p.h. Trip Type - - -	**2 15 0**
As above 5 in. dial -	**5 5 0**
Pillion Footrests/pair -	**7 6**
Pillion Seat - - -	**12 6**
Rear Carrier - -	**7 6**
26 x 3.5 Dunlop Tyres over 26″ x 3.25″ extra	**11 0**
Crankcase Shield -	**10 0**
Prop Stand - - -	**10 0**
Quickly detachable rear wheel - - - -	**2 0 0**
Valanced Guards to 6S, 5T & 5H Models— per pair extra	**12 6**
'Straight through' exhaust	**7 6**
Extra for Pipe - -	**7 6**
Bronze Head to "T. 100" Model extra - - -	**5 0 0**

The technical specification of the 1939 range. Author

powerful that production models required subtle de-tuning, (b), the T100 was actually a 5T prototype rather than a further development and/or (c), the 5T-based twin actually responded to blueprinting with almost disproportionate eagerness, which was not far from the truth. Certainly it would account for the high efficiency of the press bikes.

More impressive, because it appears to be more representative, was *Motor Cycling's* 1938 report of its Tiger 100 test. A top speed of 98mph (157km/h) and a mean of 96mph (154km/h), and truly remarkably, the ability to lap Brooklands fully road equipped at just over 92mph (148km/h). During speed tests it was revved through the gears up to 7,000rpm when acceleration was 'breathtaking'. It covered the standing start quarter mile in 15.8 seconds, at the end of which it had achieved 80mph (129km/h) and its fuel consumption had averaged 60mpg (4.70 litre/100km). The Speed Twin exited the standing start quarter mile at 74mph (119km/h) and averaged 82mpg (3.4 litre/100km). Both machines provided minimum non-snatch top gear speeds of 10–12mph (16–19km/h).

Apart from the adoption of post-war tele-forks, differences existed between the 1930 and 1940 twins. The most significant of these was the pre-war use of a Lucas MN2 mag-dyno, platform mounted behind the engine. It was not a success on hard-ridden machines, which through a penchant for loosening their mag-dyno mounting bolts sometimes revealed the previously unknown inherent flaw of parallel twins – high frequency vibration. Although in fairness to these early models they seemed to run very smoothly apart from a brief period of vibration apparent at around 75mph (121km/h) (5,500rpm). Their rubber mounted handlebars, borrowed from the Tiger singles, may have helped, but neither footrests nor tank 'buzzed' much at all. In the late 1940s, by which time BSA, Ariel, Norton, Matchless/AJS and Royal Enfield's draughtsmen had become disciples of Edward Turner's new order of parallel twinning, Lucas awoke to the commercial advantage of manufacturing a magneto specifically for the plethora of new 360 twins and provided the K2F instrument separate from a dynamo. Fortunately, the adoption of the K2F magneto also lost the MN2's advance-under-tension manual ignition control penchant for slyly slipping into full retard during use, often baffling riders over their inexplicable loss of power and speed. The K2F thankfully employed the rather more logical retard-under-tension control.

Further indication of the 5T's tendency to overheating in extremis is revealed in Turner's claim that one of his reasons for employing aluminium con-rods was that they conducted heat away from the crankshaft better than steel. Their width improved their stiffness over steel although they were not in practice any lighter. The first year's models employed white metal big end bearings. This is a tin-based alloy also incorporating lead, copper and antimony (not unlike soft solder apart from the copper). From 1939 and the T100-on, all Triumph twin big ends were of the quickly replaceable, tougher and less expensive steel-shell variety. The shells were still white metal coated but no longer required the laboriously time-consuming 'scraping' to fit.

In Britain, a motorcycle of 1939 earned respect as a means of transport. Turner had yet to accept that America, since the advent of the cheap Model T Ford in the 1920s, saw it primarily as an exciting leisure machine. So in March of that year his company publicists organised a stunt that would yet again win Triumph the Maudes Trophy against severe competition. The ACU selected a 5T from a dealer's window in Bedfordshire and a T100 from another in Yorkshire. After a routine service they were each ridden by long-suffering yet unidentified factory test riders for 1,806 miles (2,993km) around Britain, including the northern and southern tips, and many miles of deeply snowbound roads, averaging 42mph (67km/h). After that, in the hands of racing men Ivan Wickstead and David Whitworth taking turns on the T100 and Alan Jefferies and Freddie Clarke on the 5T, they were thrashed mercilessly around Brooklands for six hours. The T100 managed a mean of

78.5mph (126km/h) and the 5T 75.02mph (121km/h), with no more trouble than a cracked oil pressure pipe to the Speed Twin's gauge. When stripped under ACU supervision apart from minor picking-up on one piston due to a lack of running-in, no measurable wear was apparent.

By this time the 5T's sinews had been stiffened by its adoption of T100 steering geometry and an improved front fork spring, which was stiffer and of greater coil diameter. Rebound tension springs were also fitted to improve damping (two coils of unequal rate tend to negate each other's 'bounce'). Reports over the previously unmentioned, 'flighty rear end' and, 'dancing front end' cure were highly publicised. As the author knows all-too-well from 35 years' experience with his own 1939 T100, the flexure of these slim frames during fast cornering can simultaneously loosen all those body parts a man needs must hold tight, and tighten all those parts he should relax.

Despite the war and its restrictions in British industry and on transportation, exports to the USA continued until early in 1941. Perhaps it was fortunate because during that period the increasing numbers of 5Ts and T100s

had time to make their presence felt powerfully over the Atlantic. By and large Americans realised the racing potential of the new Triumphs before the British. The reason was simple enough. In contrast to grand prix car racing, where Continental Europeans – Alfa Romeo, Mercedes, Maserati, Bugatti *et al* – fought in desperate rivalry largely without major British investment, British motorcycle factories fought their grand prix no less fiercely and Continental Europeans were made welcome, just so long as they did not get *too* uppity. The consequence was that with the rare exceptions of Sunbeam in early days and ERA in the latter 1930s, British competition cars were based around production cars, in similar fashion to American racing motorcycles. And just as European cars achieved astonishing heights of specialisation, British racing motorcycles did too. Who then, in Britain, would seriously consider campaigning a mass-produced ohv sports roadster twin like a 5T in grand prix orientated road racing, when almost two decades of ruthless survivalist technology had culminated in the IoM-proof ohc cam engine? Such machinery, as Turner had noted, may have distanced itself from your

No power 'curve' graph could ever climb with such graphic precision of course, but it gives a pretty accurate idea of Triumph's projected image at the time. Author

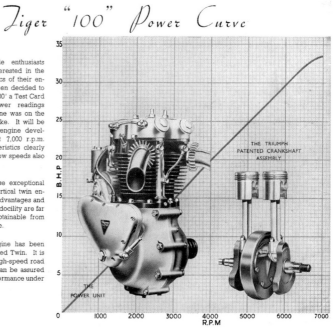

Tiger "100" Power Curve

BECAUSE motor cycle enthusiasts are particularly interested in the power characteristics of their engines, for 1939 it has been decided to issue with each Tiger '100' a Test Card showing the horse-power readings obtained when the engine was on the Heenan and Froude brake. It will be seen that an average engine develops nearly 34 b.h.p. at 7,000 r.p.m. and the curve characteristics clearly show that the output at low speeds also is very impressive.

Quite apart from these exceptional figures, the Triumph vertical twin engine offers many other advantages and the starting and general docility are far superior to anything obtainable from even the smoothest single.

The Tiger '100' engine has been developed from the Speed Twin. It is eminently suitable for high-speed road work and the amateur can be assured of a most creditable performance under racing conditions.

The author at Classic Bike Guide *magazine's annual April rally, Whitchurch, Shropshire. He has owned and ridden his bronze head 1939 T100 since 1965, hence its travel-stained appearance.* Author

common-or-garden roadster but their requirements of high power, low weight and great stamina demanded they were hand-crafted rare marvels, and unavoidably expensive ones.

Fortunately for Triumph's future, the AMA (American Motorcycle Association) had decided that if bike racing was to survive in the dark days of the Depression, it would of necessity need to be production based. This would ensure it remained inexpensive. It was a thoroughly laudable aim based on existing production model engine sizes of 750cc (45cu in) and 1,300cc (61cu in). What's more they had to be good ol' flatheads (side valve), unless you were willing to give away around 30 per cent displacement for the privilege of rocker boxes. Unfortunately, it stultified both Harley-Davidson and Indian design and development. American racing, while at least as spectacularly action packed as anything in Europe, ossified technically.

The first British bikes to vaguely interest America trickled over the border from Canada, then a nation retaining close cultural ties to Britain

– the Mother Country. Severely classic Ariels, rugged Rudges, strong and simple BSAs and sparkling Triumph Tiger 90s but, common-or-garden ohv one-lungers all, apart from a few ohc Velos and Nortons and a rare BMW or Vincent. While a few were campaigned with fair success in the USA, Americans stubbornly refused to perceive singles as anything other than utility machines. Even so, as late as 1946 Johnson Motors was sponsoring the acclaimed Bruce Pearson on a Tiger 90 in Southern Californian half-mile flat tracks.

Into this thunderingly exciting yet technically moribund scene in the later 1930s came a lithe, lean, entrancingly pretty yet stunningly potent new Triumph – the Speed Twin. It reeked of speed, and close on its heels an even zipper brother – the Tiger 100, with performance enough to exceed even the glamour of its silver and chromium-plated livery. The few that were imported in 1939 astonished the flat-top pilots, irreverently dismissing the disadvantage of their undersized 500cc engines in a thrill of zingy revs. Had American

racing not broken with European grand prix, Triumph would have no more enjoyed runaway fortune in the USA than it did in double-knocker-obsessed 'Blighty', of course.

Through the pre-war years, the 5T and T100 proved adept at all forms of American motorcycle sport. In exactly the same way that Alec Bennett, the supremely successful British grand prix racer of the 1920s and early '30s, commented on the valuable time saved per IoM TT lap when Velocette introduced the first positive-stop foot-change in 1926, so American Triumph racers exploited the time saved with a foot change on a Triumph.

Fun though it all was in those early days, not until the Second World War ended, did Triumph truly make its presence felt in the USA. It was to change the world.

In common with most of his countrymen, Turner's confidence in a successful cessation of war for Britain, encouraged him to search for overseas business. To this end in 1940, he initiated a business relationship with Bill Johnson of Los Angeles and satisfied himself on two counts – that the American market was ripe for exploitation and because of its size, America would require two centres of operation, one east and one west. In the long term, this would prove to be disadvantageous to Triumph because it divided what should have been a united operation.

By 1946, having already exported a few hundred twins to Johnson, thanks to Turner's acumen Triumph was measurably ahead of any other British rival, although Hap Halzina was about to become BSA's US distributor. Thanks to Johnson's clever West Coast strategy of promotion through high-profile race team sponsorship and his well-organised, franchised dealer network, Triumph had become a name to respect in California.

Back in Meriden, Triumph's new factory in 1946 was going flat-out in top on a variety of projects, its new tele-forked range of 3H, 3T, 5T and T100 going well. The 3H was a civilianised 3HW 350cc ohv single but while catalogued it was never produced due to a sustained need to devote all production facilities to the huge demand for twins. The 360lb

Vintage racing at its best. Note the rider's wind-flattened boots on this 1938 Speed Twin. Vintage class racing speeds are roughly comparable with GP class 125s. Author

(163.4kg) 350cc 3T twin was never a patch on its bigger brothers, to which it was only partly related, and its strangled, puny engine resisted even the ingenious Clarke's attempts to energise it beyond 70mph (113km/h) so within two years it, too, had gone.

Although the basic format of 5Ts had not changed since 1937, the 1946 models looked very different on account of their new tele-forks.

Was there ever such classicism? A 1949 T100. Author

Undeniably they set new standards in styling and are now generally recognised as one of the rare immortal classics of motorcycle design. So influential was Turner's post-war 5T styling, that despite Honda's best attempts to break away in the early 1960s with such as the 125 Benley and CB160, it was not until the end of the decade that the CB750 Four had it surrendered. To this day, the

Triumph's of the immediate post-war period command higher prices amongst collectors than the pre-war twins. Few motorcycles of any period can match the simple purity of their form.

No small credit must go to the tele-forks which, while elegantly slim, were also one of the best of that time, if only because they provided a genuine 6in (152mm) of deflection where others gave 4in (102mm) and sometimes a boney 2.5in (63mm). Off-road competitors quickly learned to exploit the advantage. Compared with the old Webb-type girder fork's 53lb (24kg) they weighed a mere 37lb (16.8kg), while less than half of that was unsprung weight to the girder's gross, and they were hydraulically damped on rebound. The improvement was magical, even if a few die-hards on both sides of the Atlantic wished otherwise. Rarely in motorcycling has form and function harmonised so well. Often criticised by devotees of other marques' tele-forks for their 'weakness', in reality they were slim purely on the merit of the routing of their spring inside the stanchion, rather than outside.

11

Racing again

*Racing, racing, racing, export or die, the Grand Prix, Turner's fury,
Ernie Lyons, Turner's joy, Hopwood and Clarke resign, the ISDT,
Henry Vale, T100C race kit, the Trophies, rear suspension,
America, America, America*

After the debacle of its 1934 IoM TT with three 5/10s, Triumph kept clear of racing. It had entered a team of three famous racers, Jock West, Ernie Thomas and Tommy Spann, in the Senior. In fact there was nothing much wrong with any of the bikes, but their conversion from hand gear-change to foot, employing the same gearbox, placed too much responsibility with the rider. Without the hand-change gate stop, riders could too easily override the foot selector's, and they did. One by one the bikes retired with mechanical problems probably as a result of accidental over-revving.

Despite official policy, people at Meriden in 1945 were relishing the freedom given them following the cessation of hostilities. Two men in particular were about to force Triumph into full-blooded competition once more. They were the irrepressible Freddie Clarke, head of development, and Henry Vale, head of the competition (off-road) shop. While Turner was in the USA early in 1946 organising Triumph's future, Clarke had been equally busy building a 'secret' racing machine, the prototype Grand Prix.

In much the same way that Turner's Delphic commercial wisdom during the late 1930s had given his company a near-decade start over its British rivals in the USA, so Triumph's wartime contract to provide the RAF with high-efficiency portable generator sets (used amongst other duties to

charge the 'trolley-accs', or trailer-mounted battery banks, required to cold-start heavy bombers) led to the development of the all-aluminium 5T competition engine. Inexpensive and commonplace now, aluminium was then anything but. To keep the 6kW/4,000rpm engine's temperature down, it was all-aluminium and fan-cooled.

Britain in 1946 was by any commercially applied standard, bankrupt to the tune of almost £5,000 million, literally spent by war. Prime Minister Clement Attlee of the Labour Party was by appearance and habit an astringent vegetarian who applied control of national expenditure by strangling imports through the Ministry of Supply. By such means he squeezed Britain's vital foreign currency earning manufacturers as tightly as he exhorted them to, 'Export or Die' in a fearfully applied parody of the Protestant work ethic. Everything consumable, including food, was tightly rationed. Life in Britain during the post-war years was grim and the nation was grey, if sinewy.

Fortunately, the generator engine was already in production so siphoning off a few for racing motorcycle adaptation was, for the nimble Clarke, like breathing or walking. The GP's crankcases were standard T100, so was the crankshaft but meticulously assembled and polished, as were its peened con-rods. Forged pistons of 8:1 or 8.3:1 were normal although

these could be varied to suit the customer. As, in Britain 'Pool' (nationalised and rationed) petrol then available, was limited to a maximum of 70 octane the, GP's standard compression ratio was right on the ragged edge of brave-maybe and could, and did, in the heat of racing induce pinking, with all entailed. Carburation was by twin 1in (25mm) Amal Type 6 competition instruments in parallel via a single, central remote float, and the exhaust was carefully dimensioned following development into a surprisingly wide twin megaphones. Uniquely amongst Triumphs the combustion chambers within the cylinder head were lined with iron skulls cast in at the foundry. Valves were the same size as the T100. Ignition was by BTH racing magneto and no provision for a dynamo was made. While irrelevant to the GP's purpose, these small instruments absorbed enough power to reduce top speed by at least 5mph (8km/h).

The heart of any competition engine is its camshaft. In total, 175 GPs were produced of which, surprisingly considering their demand for them, Americans received less than a quarter, so GP camshafts were never a generally available item. They were identified only as the 'Q' camshaft and are memorable because their cam form was the precursor of what has probably become the world's most famous profile – the legendary E3134. Americans claim it originated from

Rivals at the British MX GP, Hawkstone Park 1965. John Giles, T100A leads Sylvain Geboers, G80. Brian Nicholls

them and the British much the same. The truth seems to be that the E3134 cam form was developed by Freddie Clarke during his later GP period but was first available in the USA as part of Triumph's 1951 T100 Race Kit, which with all necessary race preparation, then metamorphosed into the desirable all-alloy close-finned 42bhp T100C. There is even an apocryphal story over its appearance. Turner, typically cavalier about the realities of technical development periods, wanted an instant special camshaft for 'his' T100 Speed Kit in double-quick time one Friday, or else! In despair, Triumph's Comp' Shop engineers copied the profile of a likely looking shoe heel . . .

As Stan Shenton, proprietor of Boyers of Bromley (London), Triumph agents since time immemorial and whose racing team's regular victories often equalled, beat and were even

assumed to be the factory's own in the 1960s and 1970s, states in his book *Triumph Tuning*: 'The E3134 is a Triumph designation for a cam form, not an actual camshaft, and no less than 14 different camshafts, each with their own part number, have been produced with this form.' Although published first in the 1970s *Triumph Tuning* is still regarded as the production racing 'Bible' by current Meriden tuners. Besides, if the incorrect tappet or follower is partnered to the E3134 it will not give of its best. The right one is the E3059R tappet. E3134 cams have been superseded by more recent computer-designed cam forms for racing, about which expert advice should be sought for classic racing.

As well as its engine, the GP offered an impressive specification. This superb racing motorcycle is all-too-frequently dismissed by the great unwashed as a tweaked T100, when

in fact it was built to order in the factory experimental department to a true grand prix racing standard. The frame was specially built and slightly shorter in the wheelbase, the clutch was heavily sprung and with hard racing inserts, brakes were sls 8in (203mm) cast iron ribbed, a Smiths competition rev counter replaced the speedometer, a steel 4-gallon (18-litre) petrol tank and 1-gallon (4.5-litre) oil tank held the fuel and lifeblood. It also weighed a mere 310lb (140.7kg) fully equipped, compared with the 365lb (165.7kg) T100.

Depending on gearing and preparation, the GP's top speed was anything between 110 and 120mph (177–193km/h). This was slightly higher than a period Manx Norton's best and the GP's superior power spread and acceleration gave it a further advantage on short and twisty circuits. Unfortunately, and unlike the

Britain's most successful production racing team was Boyers of London. Here, regular team riders Paul Butler and Dave Nixon flank manager Stan Shenton. Stan Shenton

Manx, it was blessed with neither great roadholding nor stamina. While its power spread was wide for a racing engine, it hit a 42bhp (31kW) peak between 6,500 and 7,500rpm, and at these speeds its engine life was strictly limited. Most engine failures concerned valves and springs, and pistons.

Optional gear clusters allowed that if all three 5T-based models were equipped with the same sprocket teeth (which they more-or-less were anyway), a T100's overall gearing was 12.7, 8.65, 6.00 and top, 5.00:1; a TR5 Trophy's was 15.34, 11.58, 7.25 and top, 5.00:1, and a GP's was 8.67, 7.20, 5.48 and top, 5.00:1. Unfor-

The foundation stone for Triumph's return to competition greatness in 1948 was the TR5 Trophy; 295lb, 25bhp, a broad spread of torque and rare agility, gave this 80–85mph twin an unrivalled enduro-winning nature. John Nelson

tunately for competitors, because the factory was working at maximum capacity up to 1950, the optional gear clusters were in practice infrequently available.

While Clarke was building the first Grand Prix he must have had Ernie Lyons in mind because in 1938 the Irish racer entered his Speed Twin in the IoM Grand Prix (a race held in September open to non-international FIM licence holders). He crashed leaving Ramsey but he must have impressed Clarke because in 1946 he was chosen to break in the new racing twin at the Ulster Grand Prix around the closed-road Clady Circuit. Because of poor carburation the twin ran weak and hot and burned through its supply of spark plugs long before the race ended.

A few weeks later, in September, Lyons won the Manx Grand Prix, which settled the model's name, had broken its frame's front down-tube and won Triumph more British acclaim than it had known since the days of the racing 3½s. It also maddened Turner when he returned from the USA to the point whereby his two best technical men – the fast-rising Bert Hopwood and the supremely talented development engineer-rider, Freddie Clarke – perceived no future for them in Meriden's suffocating climate and left to join Norton and AJS-Matchless respectively. Because of this the GP, which Turner belatedly agreed to list, was never seriously developed into the magnificent road racer it promised to become had Clarke been given even limited encouragement.

If any single model contributed to Triumph's eventual successes at Daytona, it was the GP. Fortunately by 1947 the AMA allowed compression ratios to rise to 8:1, although kick-starts remained *de rigueur* in its roadster-based racing formula. A T100 managed sixth in 1947, but in 1948 a GP ridden by Phil Cancilla made the same spot. Then, in 1949, Jock Horn riding on the JoMo team's 'works' GP utterly dominated the entire race for three-quarters of its duration, then a cylinder died and he retired to leave three previously trailing Manx Nortons to take over. In 1950, Triumph finally cracked it when, on his own GP, Rod Coates set a Daytona race record of 81.26mph (130.76km/h) in the Amateur 100-mile event after an elbow-to-elbow duel with Manx and HD riders. Fine racer though he was, Coates was destined to achieve legendary status as a race engineer in charge of TriCor's competition department through the 1960s. In the 200-mile race, while GP riders Ed Quartz and Ray Walloon set lap and speed records (90mph/145km/h), they failed to finish.

Road racing in the USA never achieved the popularity of the mile and half-mile, so while some GPs were adapted to flat tracking with great success, they were too few to impress the public. This, by-and-large, was the preserve of the more freely available modified 5Ts and T100s. By 1952, and after development mainly by a partnership between JoMo and Tim Witham, T100-based flat-track machinery was doing Harley Davidson serious national mischief despite HD's advantages of favourably home-brewed regulations.

A typical example of the GP's popularity and capabilities may be learned from the 1950 IoM Senior TT race, which was then, and will forever remain, the most punishing of international road races. Of the 75 starters, 40 were Manx Nortons, 11 were AJS 7Rs (two 350cc and nine overbored specials), and nine were Triumph GPs, followed by eight Velocette KTTs (two 350cc and six overbored), five Vincent Grey Flash/Comets and one each BSA ZB Goldie and Guzzi Gumbalunga. Geoff Duke (Manx) won at a mean speed of 92.27mph (148.48km/h). The first Triumph GP rider home was T. McEwan at 83.79mph (134.84km/h) in 13th place. Then followed David Whitworth at 82.14mph (132.18km/h) in 19th place. Four more GPs followed at 24th, 42nd, 45th and 47th out of 52 finishers. For what in fact was a cheaply race-tweaked pushrod sports roadster without serious road racing investment, a two-thirds survival record equal to the formidably blue-blood cammy racers is pretty remarkable

In fact, a GP won the IoM Grand Prix once more after 1946, when in 1948 D. G. Crossley came home first.

If Triumph owed a debt of gratitude to anyone, it was Henry Vale of Meriden's experimental department. In 1946, he recognised the off-road potential of the Speed Twin, and from it developed the Trophy. Here, he is riding one of his own. John Nelson

The following year GPs excelled in the IoM Senior TT when five of them finished behind 86.93mph (139.8km/h) winner Harold Daniell's Manx: 5 New Zealander S. H. Jenson at 83.17mph (133.8km/h); 6 C. A. Stevens, 12 C. W. Petch, 17 J. Bailey, 21 the evergreen A. E. Moule at 78.14mph (125.74km/h). In 1949 the noviciate Geoff Duke on a Norton Model 30 International won the IoM Clubmans TT at 82.97mph (133.52km/h). He was chased home by Britain's supreme all-rounder Alan Jefferies at 80.79mph (130km/h) on his GP, followed by another nine GPs in the same event, six of them at over 70mph (113km/h). Another rider, D. G. Lashmoor, won the 1,000cc Clubmans' TT at 76.30mph (122.78km/h), beating Vincent Rapides. As at this time no refuelling was allowed, it may not be a fair comparison because one unidentified Vincent rider, frustrated beyond endurance, threw caution to the winds and circulated at 85.55mph (137.67km/h) before running his tank dry on the third and final lap.

In 1952, Bernard Hargreaves brought home the Meriden bacon again in the IoM Manx GP, but on a

T100. Two years prior to that Triumph riders Ed Kretz Jr and Don Bishop had proved the T100's worth by coming first and second in what is generally regarded as America's first European-style road race. It was held at Santa Ana military airfield only after promoter Al Papp's valiant fight against competitor and public apathy. The 50-mile (80km) event was never repeated because the Korean War began on 16 July, the day of the race, and the base never reopened for racing.

Let's go back to 1947 and the first post-war ISDT. For reasons best known to itself, the FICM (now FIM) allowed the host nation, Czechoslovakia, to apparently 'fiddle' the regulations. Their proposed speed schedules so penalised the larger capacity classes in favour of the 'tiddlers', that all British manufacturer and club teams withdrew. Too late, the organisers, who had been relying on the value and support of the then prestigious British teams, changed the regulations. In a last-ditch attempt to wave the Union Flag, the ACU formed a scratch team from three privateers who had persisted. They were Len Sheaf on a 1938 ISDT 250cc SOS (Vale-Onslow's superbly engineered and Villiers' powered lightweight) modernised with a set of

Dowty's superb air-sprung tele-forks (as used by Panther) and a new Amal 276 carburettor; Alan Sanders on a barely modified 1938 Speed Twin, and Jock Hitchcock on an equally standard new Speed Twin. In the event, Sanders was forced to retire following unremitting tyre troubles on the first day, while on the fourth day the Mk 1 sprung hub of Hitchcock's bike was shaken to bits by the vibration caused by miles of log-laid forest tracks.

Unsuccessful? Immediately yes, but the seed had been sown at Meriden, where Henry Vale had taken notice. In time for the ISDT of 1948, and with Turner's full approval, Vale turned three pretty standard Speed Twins into formidable time-trial (enduro as we'd say now) machines. Mind you, their riders themselves were no less impressive – Allan Jefferies the great all-rounder, Jim Alves, who was unsurpassed off road, and Bert Gaymer, a supreme trials specialist. This time though, Triumph riders, far from lone British representatives, were up against the formidably combined might of the rest of the British industry's aces – the trials world's supremo Hugh Viney on a 500 Ajay, Charlie Rodgers and Vic Britain on 350 Enfields, and Jack Williams on a 500 Norton Inter'. They, with

Jefferies, formed the national ACU Trophy Team. The Silver Vase club team was represented by Bob Ray (500 Ariel), Jack Stocker (500 Enfield), and Alves. They all finished the San Remo event 'clean', which means Triumph's works team did too. Britain felt rightfully cock-a-hoop. Its teams had returned victoriously with gold medals in all the premier award classes.

Triumph celebrated by laying down the first of a lineage that was to continue for decades, especially in the USA. Turner probably, ever a man with an ear for a good name, picked up the Grand Prix tradition and dubbed his new winner 'Trophy'. No success could have been more opportune because the international acclaim (the lay-public then, starved of peacetime excitement, took much greater interest in such events) won for Triumph the even more vital reward of supplies of imported aluminium via the Ministry of Supply. Significantly, BSA, which had been campaigning iron-engined B31 and B33 based trials bikes, by 1949 had also developed lighter, all-aluminium versions, which were actually prototype ZB32 and ZB34 Goldies. These things, most especially as the eventual DB31 and DB34 big-barrelled Goldies, were to forever hound the 500 Trophies and in consequence force Triumph into building the fabulous TR6 'Desert Sled' Trophies of the classic American desert races.

It proved to be a watershed year in 1949 for Triumph. Turner's American connection was beginning to pay technical dividends. A large percentage of America's military aircraft industry was California based. When war ended its multitude of engineers were absorbed into other industries, which too few found exciting, so some of them redirected their expertise into the personally rewarding, if not very financially profitable, business of car and bike engine power-tuning. British technology was then at least the equal of American. But in the freewheeling, faster-moving California social climate, Pratt & Whitney's piston engine turbocharging and valve spring metallurgy got into the public domain while Rolls-Royce's jet engine gas flowing and turbine blade forming did

By 1966, the Trophy had become something of a hybrid, using the 5TA engine in a BSA B50 MX frame, but that year it carried (left to right) Ray Sayer, Roy Peplow, John Giles, Ken Heanes, Sammy Miller and Arthur Lampkin, to second place in the International Six Days Trial in Sweden. John Nelson

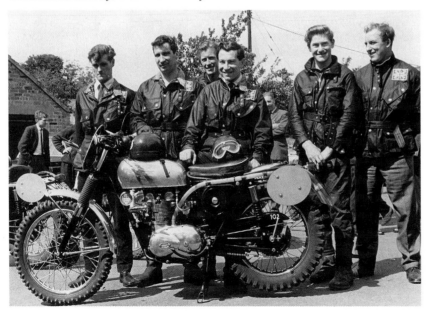

A truly great picture – 1966 and Buddy Elmore takes first place in the Daytona 200 on a T100A-based racer, averaging a record 96.38mph and setting Triumph on a road-race path to glory. John Nelson

not. By this time, JoMo was moving into the major league of motorcycle racing thanks to its new race team manager, Pete Coleman. He had dirt raced around the world and could prepare a race engine better than anyone and he knew *everyone* in the business – and way beyond. So JoMo began distributing S&W cams and valve springs. These came from the partnership of Sparks & Witham, a couple of immensely talented engineers who exploited the magnificent overspill of ex-military aircraft know-how and metallurgy to the maximum.

Because of the paucity of GPs, JoMo and TriCor by-passed them in favour of developing their own T100 racers. By 1949 these super-fast Tiger twins had proved themselves capable of taking on and beating the best of

the rest. There is little doubt that urgent American stimulation accounted for the production of the famous T100 factory 'Racing Kit' and that American technology, such as valve springs and piston design, was responsible for some of the design. By 1949, however, Meriden's Comp' Shop engineers had grown wise in the ways of tweaking their Tigers' tails and were already issuing some excellent technical bulletins on race-tuning. In these, sound guidance over camshaft types wherein E4819 and E3059R tappets were advised, and on exhaust pipe length and diameter. Carburettor type and settings, gear ratios and sprockets, valve timing and cylinder head flowing were covered in specific detail.

During this year the close-finned barrel of the all-aluminium engined

T100 was produced in readiness for 1950. The Racing Kit comprised: pistons 8.25:1 or 9:1, two racing camshafts (E3134 cam form), competition valve springs, two 1in (25mm) Amal Type 6 carburettors and single central, rubber-mounted remote float chamber, twin throttle cables, racing petrol pipes, Smiths competition 8,000rpm rev counter, 1-gallon (4.5-litre) oil tank, quick-release petrol tank, twin small-diameter exhaust pipes and meggas, one only folding footrest (to clear kick-start), one folding kick-start crank, one oval race number plate, one short rear brake rod, and one set washers and gaskets. Thus equipped a T100 would produce 24 per cent more power, up from the T100's 32bhp (24kW) at 6,500rpm to 42bhp (31kW) at 7,000/7,500rpm.

Two years later, as a concession to record-breaking demands from the USA, Meriden produced to special order a tough, cast-iron cylinder barrel to cope with the 12:1 compression ratios and the power of methanol-based dope burners.

Then there was the sprung rear hub. The first one saw the light of day following construction in 1937, when it was patented. For a variety of reasons which began with its expense, followed by a suspect performance and ending with the Second World War, it never reached production, until 1946 one year later it disgraced itself in the Czech ISDT when it proved to be not much better than a cheap alarm clock forced into the same role. Even in its 1949 Mk II form, it was rarely fitted to TR5s and often not to GPs or T100Cs simply because at 17lb (7.7kg) it was too heavy, resisted quick wheel fitting, and could not be repaired en route (they were nicknamed 'grenades' after the shrapnel effect of casually removing their spring-tensioned mechanism without the special tools). Whatever bump-absorbing advantages they possessed were invariable, and quite literally, outweighed by their bulky high-speed wanderings. As a matter of interest, Granville Bradshaw, the innovative designer behind the ill-fated (because it was never properly developed) flat twin ABC of 1914 as well some Panthers in the 1920s, designed a sprung hub early in 1937. He illustrated and described it in *The Motor Cycle* in August that year, very clearly. In principle, the Triumph design was strikingly similar, very clearly.

Not much changed until 1950 when some important technical improvements were made. By 1940, oil pressure feed to the rockers had been changed to a supply from the return side of the system. In 1950, the head was no longer drained internally but via the now familiar external pipes banjo unioned into the pushrod tunnels. An improved crankshaft carrying stronger con-rods incorporating stronger big-ends and heavier main bearings was fitted. The gearbox was uprated by the inclusion of a fixed, or

'driven' layshaft which previously had been floating, incorporating an integral top gear pinion. All the gear pinions themselves were strengthened. The consequence was a measurably more robust and quieter gearbox plainly aimed to withstand high stresses and undoubtedly a product of 6T development.

Then in 1951 came the transformation of the T100 into a serious super sportster in its own right. Plebian iron was dropped in favour of aluminium for the cylinder barrels and head. Close-finned and lightly polished it stands even now as one of the most beautiful commercially produced engines ever, and with its introduction the GP, alas, was dropped, but the Trophy continued handsomely rerigged.

Iron cylinder liners were cast in and the iron skull of the generator-adapted square fin aluminium head was replaced by iron valve seats. Low expansion 7.6:1 silicon aluminium pistons were standard. Duralumin (hard high-grade aluminium alloy) pushrods were fitted to ensure the unusually close tappet clearance of 0.001in (0.25mm) remained constant at all temperatures despite the high expansion rate of aluminium. To resist wear, tappets were Stellited and the flywheel, con-rods and rockers were polished, as were the induction tracts. A stronger clutch, borrowed from the 6T, was fitted, and, flying in the face of progress, rear suspension was limited to a Mk II sprung hub, improved by more robust sliders and proper ball-races instead of the original's flimsy cup-and-cone bearings.

Not until 1954 did much change, and then it did with a vengeance in the form of a belated acceptance that not even a Mk III, or Mk X for that matter, sprung hub could hope to remotely match the roadholding capabilities of swinging fork rear suspension. Where once TR5s had been unrivalled in America, riders like Bud Ekins on Matchless G80 and Chuck Minert on BSA Gold Stars were now winning the enduros.

Within the engine one change in particular occurred. The old crank-

shaft whipped. During testing factory engineers measured cranks 0.007in (0.177mm) out-of-true at 7,000rpm on a GP, hence the need for polishing. Then the journals had been 1.436in (36.47mm) diameter, as used on the first 6T as well. But since the advent of race-tuned 6Ts greater strength had become vital, so journal diameter was increased to 1.625in (41.275mm). Sludge traps were incorporated into the crankshaft, and a heavy duty ball-race replaced the previous roller-race on the timing side to allow for side play during expansion. Perhaps, though, and it passed almost unnoticed, was the loss of the face cam sprung, transmission shock absorber on the drive side crankshaft end. In 1953, both Speed Twin and Thunderbird were equipped with ac alternators and as these were crankshaft mounted the transmission shock absorber had to be resited. It was incorporated into the clutch body of all models as a rubber vane type and, like all of its type, was a crude device that not only coarsened performance but which also exacerbated chain wear.

While the TR5 Trophy in Britain proved its mettle as one of Britain's most successful off-roaders, winning the Manufacturers' Award for four ISDTs in succession (1948, '49, '50 and '51), in America things were a little different. To reduce a spectacular story to its fundamentals, the TR5 provided the basic rolling chassis for a GP-tuned engine. The swinging fork frame, which was to make such a difference, first appeared in public on a T110 in October 1953. It was popularly believed to have been inspired by Jim Alves's ISDT prototype, which he had developed privately. Weighing 29lb (13.1kg) complete with its McCandless suspension units it was sensibly pivoted from twin anchorage points on extended gearbox plates and a new sub-frame loop. Allegedly, Turner discovered it one day in a workshop and in a fury of righteous indignation had it ejected from the factory grounds. A few months later, Triumph's own swinging fork appeared, tragically sans Alves's strong pivot mountings.

12

Better, or just bigger?

*The parallel twin analysed, piston speeds, balance factors, bores
and strokes*

The author would like to explain that although the piston assembly weights quoted below are only approximate this does not invalidate them as typical examples of the kind of stresses involved. In fact, a bare T120 (of just one particular type) piston weighs 11.37oz (325g), but this is only half the story. Even experts disagree over the precise constituents of gross piston assembly weight. Some claim that it should include half the weight of the con-rod, others the weight of the small end alone – and calculating that is no mean feat. Some claim that the piston rings should be included while others say they should be excluded because their inertia is negated by the friction between them and the cylinder wall, although no amount of friction can negate their inertia during thrust reversals, surely? So, to avoid nit-picking, the following weights are typical estimates only, although no less exemplary for that.

Parallel twins can quake, particularly the British 650 sports twins of the 1960–70s. Triumphs were typical and, like most of their genre unless refettled by a specialist, often quite literally shook themselves to pieces when ridden enthusiastically for long. The author's *Motorcycle Sport* staff T120 Bonneville over a period of two years from 1967 gleefully fractured most of its pressed steel components, confounded its instrumentation, disgorged its shattered electrics and habitually en route lost more nuts than would a bus load of squirrels in party mood. Why should this be?

After his Ariel Square Four development, Turner knew as much as anyone and more than most about parallel twin vibration. Page's 6/1 had displayed no serious vibration for two good reasons: its engine was limited to comparatively low revs, and its construction was sufficiently massive to dampen all but severe shakes. Turner was committed to a zestful, lightweight 500.

Vibration's greatest source lies in the reciprocation of the major engine components – the piston assembly. At the top and bottom of every stroke the piston stops and reverses direction. As Turner himself often emphasised: 'The inertia stresses caused by stopping and starting the piston at the top and bottom of each stroke may be by far the most important in the whole engine, hence the importance of light moving parts.' Manufacturers negate a major part of the inertia forces by equipping the engine with a flywheel counterweighted on the opposite side of the crankpin (to which the piston assembly is secured via big-end, con-rod and small-end) to, in some measure, match the weight of the piston assembly. This is known as primary balance.

Let's take the single-cylinder T90 engine first. We will assume its piston weighs 20oz (567g), plus its attendant rings, circlips, gudgeon pin and small-end assembly, totalling a piston assembly weight of 30oz or 1.8lb (850g). To discover how much inertia force an engine creates, we use a simple formula: piston assembly weight x revs squared x stroke x factor 0.0000142 = inertia force. The author prefers to use imperial measurements with which he is familiar. For the T90 we therefore have 1.8lb x 6,000rpm x 6,000rpm x 3.5in x 0.0000142 = 3,220lb (1,462kg).

The weight of a 5T piston assembly complete approximates to 16oz or 1lb (454g). Following the same formula we arrive at an inertia force of 1,789lb (812.3kg) per piston assembly. Doubled up, of course, it amounts to 3,578lb (1,624.4kg). However, the stress on engine components is more-or-less halved by the much lighter reciprocating masses involved, although overall the inertia forces transmitted into the motorcycle itself are the same as a single-cylinder engine's of the same displacement and reciprocating mass. So far.

What we also have to account for is piston speed. When Turner designed the 5T it was a general rule that the practical limit of piston speed was 4,000ft/min (1,220m), or 67ft/min (20.4m). This has advanced to beyond 5,000ft/min (1,525m) these days but this is at the very edge of reliability. Beyond 4,000rpm, pistons and their rings begin to flutter and thence to break.

Piston speed is calculated thus: rpm x stroke over the factor 6 (imperial) or 152.4 (metric). Let's take the T90

The man who knew more about extracting torque and bhp from Triumphs than anyone else, Owen Greenwood, with regular crew Terry Fairbrother, drifting his T100 powered outfit in the IoM sidecar TT, in 1961. Brian Nicholls

first: 6,000 x 3.5 over 6 = 3,500ft/min (1,067m). Compare this to the 5T: 6,000 x 3 over 6 = 3,000ft/min (915m). This amounts to a useful 14 per cent piston speed reduction in the 5T and a corresponding reduction in engine stress. Piston speed is dictated by the distance a piston travels up and down its cylinder during each engine revolution, so the shorter the stroke of the engine the shorter the distance travelled by the piston, hence the rise in popularity of the short-stroke engine.

In fact, the T90 is a poor example of a 1930s single cylinder engine because it employs what is referred to as a more-or-less 'square' engine, in which bore and stroke (84 x 89mm) are similar. So poor Turner was actually pressed very hard indeed to prove the superiority of his twin over Val Page's progressive single. Let's take as an example a more typical engine of

the period – Norton's immortal classic, the 100mm-stroked ohc International. Using the same formula: 6,000rpm x 4in (100mm) over factor 6 = 4,000ft/min (1,220m), a 25 per cent increase in piston speed, which puts it close to the reliable limitations of the time. Assuming its piston assembly weight is a little less than the roadster T90's, at 28oz (794g), we find we still have a primary inertia force of 3,394lb (1,541kg), 5 per cent more than the 'lowly' T90. The principle reciprocating masses of the 5T (two piston assemblies) amount to 1,789lb (812kg) each and together a 'mere' 3,589lb (1,624kg).

It is frequently stated that the out-of-balance forces generated by a twin are half that of a single of the same capacity because (a): each of its pistons weighs half the amount and (b): its stroke is half that of the single. This, as you will have appreciated, in

practice, is nonsense. The reality is that depending on the engine design the measurements can vary enormously, but even so, significant stress reductions are usual.

Another out-of-balance factor has to be accounted for – secondary imbalance. Calculating it is exacting because knowledge of the engine's precise dimensions, such as crankpin throw radius and con-rod length, are required. Its origins lie in the velocity changes incurred by reciprocation of the con-rod as it responds to crankpin throw in a motion known as angular swing. While variations may be engineered through particular design, it is generally accepted that the secondary imbalance amounts to an approximate 25 per cent of the primary force. Because it acts independently of the primary force the secondary imbalance is not added to the latter and nothing, such as crankshaft balancing, may be done to negate it. Therefore we find the Norton International generates approximately 848lb (385kg) of secondary imbalance, the T90 805lb (365.5kg) and the 5T just 447lb (203kg) per piston assembly, which together may trouble the rider not much less than a single's tingles, but that individually the associated parts suffer much less stress.

Expressions such as 65 per cent balance factor do not signify an engine with 65 per cent of its primary forces negated. No engine may be better balanced than 50 per cent of its mass in static equilibrium. If an engine, whether single or a 360-degree parallel twin, develops 2,000lb (908kg) primary force, heavily counterbalancing the flywheel to wholly equal this can negate it, but only when the piston is at TDC with the counterbalance weight at BDC. Inconveniently, when the crankpin and counterbalance weight achieve notional equilibrium in the horizontal (as the piston is halfway along its stroke) there is nothing to withstand the horizontally applied free force thus developed because the piston assembly and its counterbalance weight are at 90° to each other and thus out of phase, which puts the free force in the horizontal. And if the crankshaft is balanced at what might be termed zero per cent, in which it is in balance with itself only during this horizontal phase, then once the piston achieves TDC the piston assembly would be hopelessly out of balance with the crankshaft with the free forces in the perpendicular.

The solution is a compromise. Most manufacturers opt to balance out something close to 50 per cent of the horizontally free forces. In the case of our engine this means weighting the flywheel to counterbalance half of the 2,000lb primary force with a weight opposite the crankpin, which when the crankpin and counterbalance are in the horizontal at, say, 6,000rpm, will effect a 1,000lb force against both horizontal and perpendicular forces. In the balancing of crankshafts there's nothing like experience, so manufacturers, especially in pre-computer design days, relied heavily on experienced engineers to choose the right balance factor for the correct engine

and frame partnership and intended use. The balance factor chosen is represented as a percentage of the free forces. Thus a 60 per cent balance factor means that 40 per cent of the free forces actually remain free in the perpendicular. From experience (computers now) engineers know precisely which balance factors to employ to ensure a particular engine will run smoothly over most of its practical power band. All balancing is a compromise and it is the responsibility of the manufacturer to ensure that their engines run smoothest in their most commonly used power bands.

In this, the 360-degree parallel twin is no better and no worse than the single. So why bother with it, apart from its simple structure and glamorous appeal? Turner used to regularly claim: 'A twin gives better torque – twice as good, in fact, if, as in this (5T) case, the firing intervals are equal' (*The Motor Cycle* 1951). Naughty man; his implication appeared to be that a twin intrinsically develops *more* torque. In fact, a twin does no such thing. What it does do is improve the quality of torque delivery via its combustion stroke every engine revolution, rather than the every other one of the single. Equally, a four improves the delivery quality of its torque over a twin. All multis provide smoother power deliveries, thanks to their smaller yet more frequent power impulses per engine revolution, and they should offer superior acceleration due to their lighter flywheel inertia and reciprocating parts. The more powerful out-of-balance forces of a single demand a heavy flywheel to counteract them, while a parallel twin's lower masses can be disciplined by a lighter one. Because of this and the doubled number of combustion strokes per given engine revolutions, a twin must out-accelerate a single of the same weight and power output – all things being equal, which they rarely are of course.

When Turner developed the 649 6T Thunderbird he showed great canniness in his choice of engine dimensions. A 30 per cent enlargement over the 5T may have been a disappointment to America, which was actually lusting for a 750 twin, but without the massive investment necessary to pro-

duce a completely new motorcycle of significantly greater robustness, it was the best Triumph could manage at the time within the existing 5T format. Let us assume that Turner had decided on a 750. By the standards of the day an 88mm stroke would have been about right. If we accept that its piston assembly would have weighed 19oz or 1.19lb (539g) then at 6,000rpm the inertia force would have amounted to 2,129lb (966.6kg) for each piston assembly, doubled to 4,248lb (1,933kg). It would have been practically impossible for Triumph to have retained the 5T's main components, including its crankcases and lightweight frame, with those stresses. But crafty Turner carefully tuned his new 650 twin, which thanks to its modular structure weighed almost the same as the 500, to replicate the 5T's power development through the valuable mid-range road speed, but at 2,000rpm less. With a piston assembly weight of 18oz or 1.125lb (510g), at 4,000rpm, when the ultimately 34bhp (25.3kW) 6T was producing the 5T's 6,000rpm best of 27bhp (20.1kW), it and its rider would be experiencing a mere 818lb (371kg) per piston assembly, a total of 1,636lb (742.7kg), compared to the 5T's 6,000rpm 1,533.6lb (695.6kg) per piston assembly. This amounts to an astonishing near halving of the lighter-pistoned, shorter-stroked 5T's stresses at average road speeds. Accompanying the low inertia force and similar reductions in secondary imbalance is a usefully low piston velocity of course.

Corporately these contributed virtually the entire origin of the early Thunderbirds' thoroughly deserved reputation as the sweetest natured twins ever to have left Meriden. At 6,000rpm, incidentally, each of the 6T's piston assemblies experienced an inertia force of 1,840lb (835kg). Thanks to its comparatively short stroke, as compared with the 5T, this remains manageable. Now regarded as a long-stroke engine, in fact it was the over-boring of the 5T into the 6T by 8mm, rather than an equal two-way stretch, that was to be the secret of the succeeding high-powered 650's successes. The longer stroked equivalent 5T successors – T100s and Trophies– quite literally ran out of high speed breath long before the wider bored 650s purely because the gas flow through their combustion chambers was so restricted, and they approached maximum piston velocity too soon. Probably the same cramped combustion chamber lay behind the 1947 3T's power failure.

The advantage of the 6T over the 5T may be seen in a comparison of engine stresses at 70mph (113km/h). At this road speed the 5T's engine is spinning at 4,590rpm and the 6T's at 4,150rpm. The 5T's primary inertia force amounts to 933.5lb (423.8kg) and the 6T's is 880lb (399.7kg) per piston assembly. The secondary imbalance amounts to 5T 233.3lb (106kg) and 6T 220lb (99.9kg). Piston speeds are 5T 2,402ft/min (732.6 m) and 6T 2,234ft/min (681.4m), a 7 per cent reduction for the 650. In other words, despite its 30 per cent larger engine and its 20 per cent power advantage, the 6T generates lower vibration inducing stresses than the 5T at similar road speeds, and because of its lower piston speeds measurably lowers its engine's major reciprocating component stresses.

Let's take this a stage further to racing speeds. Apart from untypical record-breaking exceptions, few 5Ts or 6Ts were ever tuned to reliably deliver power for long at more than 7,500rpm. Using the same formula as before we find that at these revs the 6T's piston speed is 4,000ft/min, smack on the limit of reliable piston velocity and the 5T's is 3,750ft/min. One of the very few people to have regularly exceeded this was Owen Greenwood, who through the 1950s and '60s was probably Britain's pre-

mier Triumph exponent of that most engine-distressing of all types of competition, sidecar road racing. A modest, good-humoured, thorough gentleman off the track, on it he was diamond hard. In a similar style to Stirling Moss, who stands as a contender for the 'Greatest Car Racer Who Never Won a World Championship' (because he insisted on racing British machinery at a time when little of worth was available), so Greenwood is to motorcycle sidecar racing. Had he used a Rennsport Beemer or even a modified Manx . . .?

Greenwood was perhaps the only man to have consistently prepared 5T engines to achieve a reliable 8,000rpm. He aimed for maximum power development at 7,600rpm but conceded in conversation that in extremis he would push his Grand Prix-based engines beyond his self-imposed 7,800rpm safe maximum, and 8,000rpm equates to 4,000ft/min with a 5T. He experimented with the 5T's successor, the unit construction, short-stroke 5TA but discarded it for its lack of mid-range power, essential for an outfit. Greenwood was quite convinced that the given the race investment of the 5TA, the 5T would have proved equally successful as a racing solo.

Could he have been correct? It must be accepted that the extraction of power alone from an engine is comparatively simple. Of far greater consequence is a need for reliability to pace power. With this in mind we will fall back to our familiar stress measurements. Their familiarity may have induced reader weariness, but clearer than any other means they illustrate

the evidence of an engine's stamina. It must be remembered that Triumph's policy was to race only what it produced for road use and that the Manx Norton, which must remain as one of the most consistently rugged competition engines of all time, had its stroke progressively reduced over the years in order that its increasing power was matched by reliability. One of its principal development engineers, and also its final one, was Doug Hele in his pre-Triumph days.

By 1956, Triumph was developing its 5TA for racing and Daytona in particular, extracting 49bhp (36.5kW) at 8,000rpm from its 490cc pushrod twin. This was a speed they maintained with impunity and during racing were often taken close to an incredible 9,000rpm. On one of those truly short-stroke engines, 8,000rpm equals a piston speed of 3,437ft/min (1,048m) and an inertia force of 2,365lb (1,063.3kg). A 5T's piston would have been travelling at 4,000ft/min (1,219m) and its inertia force would have amounted to 2,726lb (1,237.7kg) per piston assembly. Thus Hopwood and Hele in the new engine, had lost approximately 14 per cent in both piston velocity and primary inertia, with accompanying drops in secondary unbalanced forces as well. All without recourse to exotic metallurgy and design.

With this in mind it can be appreciated that while Greenwood deserves great respect for his achievements with the 5T engine and its superior mid-range power, without prohibitive cost the old long-stroke could never have equalled its short-stroke successor's racing successes.

13

Torque not talk

*No substitute for size, the Thunderbird, hurting HD, Montlhéry,
crankshaft design, 100mph and 155mpg, the T110, Daytona,
Desert Sleds*

From its launch the Thunderbird implied universal adaptability, which by record proved these first hopes had been more than justified. Arguably, BSA's range of Gold Stars are the supreme all-time competition all-rounders, but they, brave singles, were just that and no more, restricted by the impositions of one 'lung'. Sentimentality aside, they made poor roadsters. The Thunderbird did not. On any highway it was sublime, so utterly compelling it was a thing of wonder. All the more surprising when it was actually a motorcycle development out of compromise. Turner's apparently extravagant claim in 1937 for his Speed Twin – 'A twin . . . has a capacity for running at higher revolutions without unduly stressing major components, and on account of its even torque it pulls better at low speeds . . . starts more easily . . . is easier to silence, has better acceleration, better fuel consumption for the same power, increased reliability and durability and it is better cooled. In fact it is a much more agreeable engine to handle' – appeared to have been irrefutably exceeded by the bigger machine. Immediately the sport-tourer arrived in the USA it was raced, usually after T100-based conversions involving big overlap cams, high-compression pistons, re-ported gas-flowed heads and bigger carburettor(s). Typical was Walt Fulton's outright victory in the initial 100-mile Catalina GP, which to European eyes more closely resembled an enduro.

The British, who under their Government's Export or Die policy in the bleak post-war years, were lucky to even see, let alone buy, a 6T, did not really know what to do with it, apart from dream. Without Brooklands it had no venue, no class of racing that catered for anything over 500cc. By concentrating on international road racing it was bound by the FIM's capacity ceiling of 500cc, scrambles (moto-cross) had barely got under way and production racing (stock machine) in which the progeny of the 6T was to eventually thrive, had yet to arrive.

Turner had since the late 1930s been regularly visiting the USA and was acutely aware of its huge commercial potential. That he was equally aware of its people's need for some kind of American relationship to the brands to which they gave their loyalty is proven by his naming of the new 650. Whether Turner himself or his California distributor, Bill Johnson, actually thought of the name Thunderbird will never be known. Legend has it that it arose during a drive Turner made with Johnson on the US West Coast in 1948. Without doubt the new 650 had been under serious discussion because Johnson, speaking on behalf of his franchised retailers, had long been urging Turner for a bigger bike. Something was wanted that would accelerate to a genuine 100mph (161km/h), prefer-

ably a 750 with which to compete on even terms with American metal.

A 750cc engine was impossible, at least within Turner's commercial strategy. The greatly increased engine power would have necessitated engine and frame components of sufficiently increased strength and weight to have excluded the modular adoption of the existing 5T production operation. Wisely, in the short term, Turner decided to use what was available, so 650 it had to be. Besides, Triumph engineers had a great deal of 650 twin experience behind them in the form of the 6/1.

So closely did the 6T replicate the 5T that component interchangeability was commonplace, although this stopped short at the 6T's crankshaft, which was longer in its throw by 0.079in (2mm). In 1966, the author met a London dealer, Jack Gray, who in 1949, had slipped a pair of 6T pistons into his overbored 1938 5T without major modification and enjoyed the sweetest natured yet potent roadster twin, of 633cc, he could recollect using.

What Turner did not seem to grasp was the fundamental difference between British and American perspectives. What British motorcyclists wanted, even by proxy in those years of wearying scrape, was an agile, docile, economical, comfortable large-capacity tourer with more than one cylinder and the high speed stamina of a Manx Norton. What Americans

wanted, quite simply, was something with which to waste Harley Davidson's racing primitives. The former presented a mighty potential complex of desirable utilities, while the latter indicated a much more elemental animal. Yet Turner, for all his US familiarity, launched the Thunderbird in a blaze of publicity which fascinated British and European enthusiasts yet left Americans so unmoved as to barely register on their consciousness.

To announce its new 650, Triumph arranged a high-speed demonstration of a 6T trio at Montlhéry Autodrome near Paris in September 1949.

The three machines were reputedly standard, the very first from the production line. However tempting it may be to imagine that they had been secretly blueprinted by engineers, in all probability they were not, although they were undeniably power-tuned. Triumph motorcycles then were built with great pride by skilled assembly craftsmen in what was probably the most modern motorcycle factory in the world. What was remarkable was the extraordinary speed and stamina of three near-standard 650cc tourers which owed their existence to what was an irrefutably hasty (six months from drawing board to production) yet inspired cobble-up of a stretched 500 – with its roots in a 250 single of the early 1930s. Whether by luck or judgement, the Thunderbird was to prove to be Triumph's finest motorcycle, the company's springboard to greatness and Turner's signature to immortality.

Now, these early 6Ts were equipped with ¹⁵⁄₁₆in (23.5mm) carburettors and 7:1 pistons. When they arrived in the USA, which is where most of them went to boost exports, American dealers were unimpressed by the performance. They saw no advantage in a Thunderbird with torque superiority over the Speed Twin if its 23 per cent larger engine was no faster than a Tiger

Opposite: *A carefully posed picture of Alex Scoby (left), Neil Shilton and Len Bayliss (right), three of the team who, in 1949, hurled the three first production Thunderbirds around Montlhéry circuit near Paris for 500 miles (800km) at a mean 90mph (145km/h) plus. The monument behind them is the Arc de Triomphe. VMCC*

Jim Alves in a relaxed mood on a late works TR5 Trophy at a mid-1950s ISDT. Cyril Ayton

100, which it was not (5T 27bhp/6,300/85–90mph, T100 30–34bhp/6,500–7,000rpm depending on specification 95–100mph, 6T 34bhp/6,300rpm 95–100mph). When the complaints arrived in Britain, Meriden's engineers did similarly to the 6T what they had to the 5T's T100 conversion by increasing carburettor size by ¹⁄₁₆in (1.6mm) up to 1¹⁄₁₆in (27mm) and lifting compression to 8:1. By way of cosmetics they also brightened the model, unintentionally made drab by Britain's utilitarian wartime mental overspill, with brighter blue paint and some chrome-plated trim. The extra top-end kick lost no mid-

range torque, gave it much more useful top-end zest and pleased everyone.

While most reports of the time emphasise the standard British specification of the three Montlhéry bikes, there is some evidence that these machines may have been equipped with US carburettors and pistons. Certainly they pulled higher gearing, their standard 24-tooth engine sprockets being replaced by 25-tooth. This lifted top gear from 4.57 to 4.38 and afforded a very useful 300rpm drop from standard at the 100mph/5,700rpm at which they were circulating. It was 600rpm from peak power and 1,300rpm from safe maximum, all

The occasion is unknown, but as the standing motorcyclist is Neal Shilton, Triumph's fleet sales manager who loved nothing better than forcing the pace over huge mileages, this is probably a France-targeted blast co-sponsored by The Motor Cycle *magazine. One of its journalists, John Ebrell, is in the Watsonian 'chair'. Cyril Ayton*

indicative of a mightily generous torque plateau.

Triumph's aim was for all three Thunderbirds to average 90mph (145km/h) for 500 miles (806km) around Montlhéry. For the sake of safety, Dunlop racing tyres were fitted, while to cope with the unremitting high combustion chamber loading, KLG racing spark plugs were used. A hint of the tune state of the engines may be discovered in the exchange of the standard (Amal) 140 main jets for 210s. Within a few months the factory recommended that for maximum engine power the air filter should be disconnected and a 190 jet fitted, but these were bigger still. The only possible conclusion is that Triumph engineers had pushed the term 'standard production model' to its limit because no ordinary 6T could have conceivably pulled a 4.38:1 top gear on over-rich carburation to circulate at over 100mph. Besides, the clutches were strengthened with harder springs, presumably to cope with the extra power, which by implication must have been close to 40bhp.

One other probable source of these early twins' magnanimous engine per-

formance lies in their cylinder heads. Turner was insistent that their valves were fitted precisely at 90° to each other and not, as so often assumed, to match the radii of their combustion chambers' skull. In those days, the craftsmen who assembled Triumphs took great pride in ensuring this was so. In later days, sadly, this was not the case, as best exemplified by all-too-familiar and irresolvable performance disparities between otherwise identical models. While neither hemispherical combustion chamber skulls nor 90 degree valve angles are currently regarded as ideal, they were then the best that auto-engineering had to offer.

Be that as it may, all three 6Ts succeeded handsomely – No.1: 92.23mph (148.42km/h), No. 2: 92.48mph (148.82km/h) and No. 3: 92.33mph (148.58km/h). However, a portent of future problems was to manifest itself in the vibration-induced breakages of No. 3 which caused it to be the only one of the trio not to average 90mph-plus including pit stops. These times were, No. 1: 5hr 32min 11⁹⁄₁₀sec, 90.30mph (145.79km/h); No. 2: 5hr 29min 55²⁶⁄₁₀₀sec, 90.93mph

(146.33km/h); No. 3 5hr 48 min 32 7/10sec, 86.07mph (138.51km/h). No. 3 split its petrol tank, which was replaced, running its engine dry, then the rear chain guard lost a mounting bolt, and its rear mudguard split. Apart from hints of overcharged batteries and the odd damp patch of oil mist seepage, all three finished in fine mechanical fettle. The riders were Jimmy Alves, Allan Jefferies, Alec Scobie, Bob Manns and Len Bayliss under the general management of Neil Shilton and the technical direction of H. G. Tyrell-Smith. Edward Turner 'hovered'.

Turner, doubtless, must have been a happy man, having freely admitted the design of that which worried him most – the crankshaft – had absorbed as much development time as all the rest of the machine combined. Obsessively cost-conscious, Turner refused to buy the necessary machine tooling for the one-piece crankshaft the engine deserved. But the cranks held for the duration. While British adulation over the achievement spread far beyond the confines of motorcycling, as proved by widespread BBC and national press reportage, only a handful of the most fanatical Triumph buffs in the USA even

According to motorcycling lore the Thunderbird engine was simply, 'a Speed Twin with bigger holes in it.' Ergo, it should therefore have weighed and cost less. VMCC

A 1911 3½hp (499cc) free engine model. The clutch of these revolutionised motorcyling by allowing their riders to start the engine at a standstill and to stop without stalling. Garry Stuart

The Reverend Helmfried Riecker on his 200cc TWN trials model, a very distant relative of the 200cc Tiger Cub, because TWN was founded as a sister Triumph company in Germany prior to the First World War. Brian Nicholls

One of the world's great motorcycle engines, the Model H. Author

A 'Riccy' at Source in Ricardo Engineering's museum in Sussex.

The drive side of a fine yet undeveloped single, a 1936 Tiger 80. Garry Stuart

The bike that captured American, as well as British hearts, minds and wallets, a 1939 Tiger 100. This one sans its optional, and rare, bronze competition cylinder head. Garry Stuart

Triumph brochure illustration for its 1939 flagship. Author

Immediately following the Second World War, Triumph, in its new factory returned to production with the trend-setting Speed Twin. This surviving 1946 model was quickly superseded by models bearing the 'trademark' headlamp nacelle. Garry Stuart

Often regarded by classicists as representing the art of the motorcycle at its peak, a first-year swinging fork T100 of 1954. Garry Stuart

Few motorcycles, if any, have through form, example and record, resonated through the eternal halls of fame like the Bonneville. This is the first of its type from 1959. Garry Stuart

Beloved of modern collectors, but cursed in its time for its frame fractures, a 1961 duplex-framed Bonneville. Garry Stuart

By 1970, the Bonnie had ascended to its 650cc technical climax, but was no longer the undisputed master of either highway or track. Garry Stuart

What might have been. Despite the BSA badge, this triple originated from Meriden's experimental shop in 1971 and, against expectation, was not designed for extra power. Its toothed belt-driven sohc top end was developed to minimise mechanical noise as a means of coping with anticipated sound level reductions. The engine found its way to Ireland, where it was installed in a replica Rob North frame and raced. The bike is now owned by British triple guru, Phil Pick. Apart from the cam box and timing chest, the engine is standard Trident. Author

Tests were made at Meriden with a variety of frames to carry the ohc engine, including this rare Egli, or Egli-type model, which is the only survivor of a batch of six. Tony Page

When NVT took control of the BSA Group, it dabbled in the possible rather than the probable. These two views show a Trident engine cradled in the hated T140/A65 oil-bearing frame, and even more improbably, the 'Trisolastic' – a T160-powered Commando. Tony Page

Above: *The last of a long line of award-winning off-roaders, a 1970 5TA-based Adventurer, probably the sole Tribsa of any real virtue. Simon Everett*

Left: *One of the last of a 25-year lineage, the 1978 744cc version of the Bonneville in the form of the T140V. Simon Everett*

Doug Hele in retirement, c1998, with the experimental P1 triple rescued from undoubted extinction by the (British) Triumph Owners Club and restored to its original condition and specification. Most people agree that its Bonneville appearance would have been better retained in favour of the slabby style of the production models. The only non-original item is the dummy distributor; ignition is Boyer electronic. Author

You will not find a greater memorial picture to the Seventies. From left to right: Rob North, Steve Brown, Jack Shemans, Arthur Jakeman, Ray Pickrell and Les Williams, all astride ex-works triples. Tony Page

In the early 1980s, a batch of T140 racers were built to compete in Britain's first flat track championship. Despite an excellent start to the series, it faded out. This is one of the machines. Tony Page

Fast touring on a fast tourer, the author reeling in the miles from the saddle of a 1200 Trophy. Simon Everett

Produced by the Meriden Co-operative, the 8-valve TSS could have been the best ever twin, but lack of development made it undependable. TOC

The T140 Executive – a Meriden promise of Hinckley's heavyweight Bonneville to come. TOC

Towards the end of the decade, 1998, the range included the Thunderbird Sport which, with a new perimeter frame and 'tweaked' engine transformed the T'bird into a supremely understated, surprisingly fast and agile roadster . . . Author

. . . the Speed Triple had been uprated with the new fuel-injected engine and 'curly' frame until, in the hands of most mortal men, even as a sport-roadster it could just about hold its own in super-sport company. Author

TT600 rider Andi Notman at Oulton Park in the 2000 British Supersport Championship. Dave Sykes

The current Bonneville in US cruiser style. Luxury and refinement unimaginable with its forebear. And weight . . .

Up with the world's best sportsters, Hinckley's top of the range flagship scratcher, the Daytona. Triumph

Right: *A Sprint with its clothes off –
the RS, a bold, bad and ultra-nimble
roadster.* Triumph

Below: *The tourer, as proved by its
panniers, the current Sprint, which goes
like a sportster.* Triumph

The modern Triumph that with good reason has probably won a greater cult following than any other, the traily-styled but quite unclassifiable, super-torquey Tiger. Triumph

After its first year's minor engine performance hiccups, Hinckley's first venture into middle weights with the TT600 has demonstrated equality in all things with the Japanese Big Four's sport four 600s. Triumph

blinked. The measure of a good motorcycle to them was in its race winning capability, nothing more or less. The high-speed stamina of a roadster was an irrelevance.

Typical of the British reaction was *Motor Cycling's* reportage: '. . . and, indeed, cruising is dependent on weather and (rider) stamina rather than the speed at which the Thunderbird will travel. No difficulty was experienced in keeping the speedometer above 80mph (130km/h), and on one road average speeds were high enough to produce a firm resolve that, other than in the company of close friends, no mention of them would be made.' The magazine extracted a top speed of exactly 100mph (161km/h), acceleration of a standing quarter-mile (403m) at 16 seconds and 82mph (132km/h). That this was no fluke was amply demonstrated to the author when, in 1995, a friend using his wholly original, and somewhat scruffy, 1952 6T held the pace of accompanying modern machines on a 4,000 mile (6,500km) high speed round-Britain coastal fund-raising blast.

To escape the high cost of capital investment, Triumph/Turner had finally settled on what was then an unusually fabricated crankshaft which, more than any other single factor, was to set the power, speed and stamina limits on the sons of the Thunderbird. Parallel twins, Turner all too well appreciated, could be assembled with single cylinder production plant. While Turner was understandably proud of his first twin, the 5T, he actually held the T100 in higher regard, invariably quoting its specification and achievements and incorporating into the 6T what had been learned from the T100's ultimate development, the Grand Prix, despite his publicised distaste for the racer. To this end he incorporated the GP's Hidinium RR 56 light alloy connecting rods in the 6T. Each of the two crankshaft 1⁷⁄₁₆in (36.5mm) pins were forged in manganese-molybdenum with a 55-ton tensile strength and by way of six-bolt webs were fastened at 360° either side of the close-grained cast-iron central flywheel.

To put it bluntly, Triumph lacked the machine tools to forge and/or

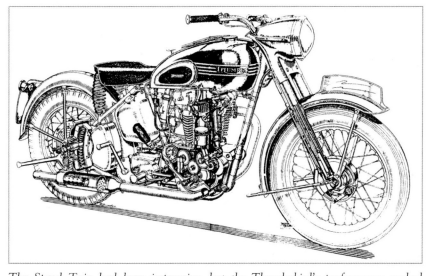

The Speed Twin had been impressive, but the Thunderbird's performance rocked motorcyclists of the day back on their heels. VMCC

machine the unified crankshaft the 6T and all its descendants would have benefited from, and Turner refused to invest the capital necessary for such plant. So Triumph compromised with bolt-coupled overhung cranks.

By the time the 6T made its appearance, Triumph had exchanged the original 5T's white metal plain big end bearings for superior split thin-wall shell bearings. In what appeared to be contradictory engineering practice, the crankshaft relied on a drive side ball-race bearing and timing side a double-lipped roller bearing, yet the roller bearing had a load capacity 2.5 times that of the ball. The reversal of ideal roles perfectly illustrates commercial craft because the roller bearing was designed to absorb crankshaft material creep during heat expansion and also to resist heavy side loading in use, both of which were beyond the scope of a ball bearing. Equally canny, Turner rejected a three-bearing crankshaft because the central bearing would have largely denied Triumph the simple single cylinder production methods that were the greatest attraction of the parallel twin to its makers. As AJS/Matchless was to discover to its cost with its own parallel twins a few years later, a central main bearing demands the most meticulously jigged crankcase alignment if the crankshaft is not to suffer breakage from stressed misassembly.

Between 1951 and 1954 the Thunderbird reached its peak. A mag-

neto supplied the sparks and it breathed through a special constant velocity SU carburettor (which it shared with the Ariel Square Four), while a 60W dynamo charged the battery. For all its treachery in competition, on the road the Mk II sprung hub, while technically a futureless quirk, was acceptable. In this specification the Thunderbird was everything a fast tourer should be – incomparably elegant in form and motion. For all the competition prowess of T120s, Triumph would never again approach such high standards. In 1954, the Thunderbird was equipped with a crankshaft alternator and, thus, lost its face cam transmission shock absorber to the now familiarly inferior rubber vane type. A coarser natured motorcycle now, it also lost its impeccable reliability, thanks to its wretched ac electrics. Its new swinging fork rear suspension was, in truth, an improvement. Then, in 1956, another cheapskate movement further degraded it by the exchange of its sweet breathing SU for one of the new Amal Monobloc carburettors, a crude instrument by comparison. Over the next six years the 6T put on a few pounds and a few bhp, but it was never the same again and in 1962 was mercifully withdrawn from the range.

So pleased was Triumph with its SU-equipped 6Ts that in July 1952 it invited the motorcycle press to participate in a strictly observed economy run on a standard 6T. Well, 'standard' insofar that it was taken from the production line, run in, then geared up from the normal British top of 4.57:1 to 4.24:1, tyre pressures were raised from the recommended 18psi (1.24 bar) front and 17psi (1.17 bar) rear (yes, these figures are correct!) to what was then an astonishing 35psi (2.41 bar) front and rear. A leaner SU needle was also fitted and at a steady 30mph (48km/h) in top gear the machine logged a satisfying 155mpg (1.8 litre/100km). Americans, once more, ignored it, but in Britain, wherein the motorcycle was still regarded primarily as a means of transport, however exciting, the notion of a motorcycle which encompassed the ability to cruise at 100mph and also (if unrelatedly) sipped a mere gallon of petrol every 155 miles, bordered on the fantastic. The British rediscovered a devotion to Triumph which had disappeared with the loss of the 3½HP racer's prowess prior to the Great War.

But in the USA, the T'bird had made Triumph great and set the 650 standard flying high. Within the bike's first year in America, JoMo (Johnson Motors) was offering a race kit comprising 8.5:1 pistons, ¹⁄₁₆in (1.6mm) oversize inlet valves, greatly improved valve springs which were not simply stronger but progressive and better resistant to 'flutter' and heat and measurably more durable, plus a variety of cam forms and partnering tappet reprofiles. With this as the foundation, 6Ts began race winning and record breaking. One of the earliest was JoMo's own, which in 1950, in the hands of mainly Bobby Turner and Blackie Bullock, recorded 135.84mph (216.99km/h) at Lake Rosemund, California. One year later the same twin-carburettor Thunderbird set a 132.26mph (212.84km/h) seven-year record for petrol-powered modified standard machines (Class C) at Bonneville.

So well did 6Ts respond to power tuning that, in 1953, at the demand of both British and American dealers, racers and enthusiasts, a brand-new model was produced. This was the T110 (Tiger 110), made legendary in Britain by *Motor Cycling's* 117.2mph (188.6km/h) and 93/96mpg (3/2.9 litre/100km) road test report of 1954. Years later the author met an ex-

Meriden road tester who claimed that in fact the high speed had been obtained by factory testers following meticulous engine tuning including substantial recarburation. *The Motor Cycle's* report of 100mph (161km/h) under ordinary highway conditions and an absolute maximum of 109mph (175km/h) with the rider prone in a strong tail wind was much more representative of the 40 or 42bhp (30/31kW)/6,500rpm 650 sportster (depending on source).

With the introduction of the T110, Triumph at last relinquished its stubborn grip on its anachronistic sprung hub by introducing swinging fork rear suspension. Alas, it was to prove to be the Achilles heel of asphalt-domiciled Triumphs because its pivot point, anchored centrally only, was in consequence insufficiently resistant to lateral warpage under duress at high speed. Woe betide the fast-cornering T110 pilot who did not keep his bike's wire tight. Thus, in Britain especially where road racing ruled, the marque's notoriety for treacherous instability with its sprung hub was further reinforced by the equally weak swinging fork. To be fair, off-road competitors rarely complained, presumably because the upsetting effects of mud, sand or rocks camouflaged unwarranted deviations of the rear wheel.

On the other hand, the new 8in (203mm) air-scooped front brake was a real sweetie, probably the best of its period and certainly one of the most handsome offset drum brakes ever, even now a classic hub prized as few others are.

With the advent of the 6Ts it is all-too-easy to overlook the 5Ts. These things in their class were more than keeping their ends up. In the Daytona 200 races of Spring 1951, 44 HDs, 20 Nortons, 16 Triumphs, 15 BSAs, 10 Indians, four AJSs and one each Vincent and BMW competed. This was prior to the AMA-introduced 750 sv–500 ohv rule. Dick Clamforth on a Francis Beart-prepared Manx won at 92.81mph (149.35km/h), followed closely by another Manx and hard in its heels a third placed T100. The first HD was eighth and British machines filled eight out of the first 10 places. It was this meeting more than any other factor which instigated the AMA's unsuccessful attempt to persuade the USA's Tariff Commission to raise import duties from 10 to 40 per cent.

For all the 1959 T120 Bonneville's greater fame, Triumph's foundation rested on the 1954 T110. Its origins lie in America's demands for greater power and speed, as well as British ones to comply with demands for a machine suited to the rising popular-

Turner and the three T'birds at Montlhéry. The tank-top tummy pads and bum-stop pillion seats were necessary during the record-breaking ride. John Nelson

ity of production machine racing. Much of the power tuning that had been learned with the T100 variants and then employed in the 6T was adopted by the T110. Its potential was often foiled during the first two years of its life because the cast iron cylinder head failed to radiate sufficient heat and, combined with poor oil circulation, the excessive heat from sustained high speeds caused grave combustion problems, warped the head, blowing gaskets and losing either lubricant or compression, or both. A redesigned iron head in 1955 helped little.

For all that, it was a potent, if well-mannered, sportster for road use, so long as the rider used the manual ignition advance/retard lever intelligently. Its 42bhp (31.3kW) at 6,500rpm would return for the first time a genuine top speed of over 100mph with an over-suited rider, albeit lying prone. Despite rumours, few if any British 650 twins would get far into three figure maxima with a touring-seated rider. The T110 however, had been developed for toughness and thanks to its improved robustness revealed a potency that went much further than potential.

The crankshaft was further stiffened by increasing its journal diameters to 1⅝in (41.2mm), the con-rods were widened, the main bearings were increased in diameter and the flywheel balance factor changed from 64 to 70 per cent. Perhaps because it retained a single carburettor the T110 managed a low and medium speed pleasantness never equalled by its twin carb' young brother, the T120. Once above 5,000rpm (80mph/129km/h in top) however, it displayed what was virtually unknown on the Thunderbird, which was to plague all sports parallel twins much over 500cc and was to eventually bring them down – vibration.

In 1956, Triumph gathered together most of what it had been learning, particularly in the USA. For all the spectacular performance of its TR5 desert racer, the opposition on BSA Gold Star and Matchless G80 500cc singles were proving its equal. So, taking a leaf from riders who had been mixing TR5 chassis and T110 engines, Triumph did the same itself. Turner, brilliantly, announced that this new 650cc model was the first to be designed specifically for America and sold it as the TR6 Trophy. He was probably correct because it was actually a child born largely from the demands of its own eastern-based company, TriCor, although most of the development work was carried out by Henry Vale, head of Meriden's competition department.

An inch (25mm) shorter in the wheelbase than its roadster relatives, and at 365lb (165.7kg) it weighed just 5lb (2.3kg) more than the TR5 yet developed 42bhp (31.3kW) compared to the 500's 32bhp (23.8kW). A 21 per cent power/weight ratio advantage plus a much broader spread of torque gave it an advantage no Goldie or G80 competitor could live with over desert terrain. The TR6 became an immediate American legend. Its basis was the T110 although with the iron cylinder head thankfully replaced by a brand-new aluminium component dubbed the 'Delta'. At a stroke the overheating-originated unreliability that had plagued this engine was cured. Along with the new head came a new carburettor – Amal's Monobloc, a slim 3-gallon (13.6-litre) off-road tank and dual seat, fiercer new E3325 cams, 3.50 x 19 front and 4.00 x 18 rear trials tyres, a siamesed exhaust system and small competition silencer, a QD lighting system, either a Lucas competition (racing) or 'Wader' (trials) magneto. Compression was lifted to 8.5:1 but the following year this dropped by a half atmosphere. The factory claimed it was to improve low speed torque and, while it may well have improved it, most people believed it was a hasty attempt to inhibit the cylinder head cracking which was plaguing this particular model.

Already distrustful of Lucas's deplorable ac electrical systems, American dealers demanded that magneto ignition and dynamo lighting were retained, which could be removed quickly.

The TR6 quickly developed a reputation for toughness and speed, but British engineers lacked American experience over filtration, so in the interests of reliability and engine longevity standard ones were exchanged for US filters which did keep out sand dust. Curiously, against British off-road experience, California racers began extending the TR6's wheelbase by up to an astonishing 5in (127mm) to 60in (1,524mm), some 4in (102mm) longer than a T110, and increasing steering head rake by approximately 5° over the previous 27°. This pulled it back to roadster and longer. Why? Simply to retain steering stability over the flat yet irregular deserts of the Western states' races when top speeds of 100mph-plus were common among the race leaders who, with eyes focused 400 yards (366m) ahead to deal with the general route, needed a bike that would negotiate itself safely across underwheel treachery. Sand-washes at the ton needed the kind of skills that few Europeans then had ever met in either moto-cross or trials. Yet in 1957, to accommodate American requests for quicker off-road handling, Triumph steepened the steering geometry of the TR6. In all probability this curious contradiction was little more than evidence of the fast growing diversification of Eastern enduro and Western desert racing demands.

Whatever, Trumpet's new Desert Sled hit the spot like nothing before or since, filling the first 12 places in America's Big Bear Run the first time out.

If Americans loved 'their' 650 in 1956, the British went wild in 1959 at the release of the T120 Bonneville.

14

Power politics

*One-piece cranks, land speed record breaking, Vincent and NSU,
Johnny Allen, the FIM farago, good ole American know-how,
T120C TT and the T120R Thruxton, the 500-miler, birth of the
Bonneville, Lucas 'Prince of Darkness'*

The appearance of the T110 in 1954, with swinging fork rear suspension and a single carburettor, surprised few people. The cylinder heads of competition machines, especially those popularly modified in T100C twin-carb fashion, tended to crack. Not that T110's were anything but fast, as proved by Bill Johnson's record time of 147.32mph (237km/h) on a C class (modified road machine) at Bonneville at August 1958.

As previously explained, Turner insisted upon crankshafts fabricated from three parts – a central cast iron flywheel to which each of the two crankshaft halves were flange-clamped by six ¼in (6.4mm) high-tensile steel bolts. Increasingly, and despite meticulous zero-tolerance fitment, component creep was occurring at high engine speeds on the 42bhp/6,500rpm T110. Not even Turner could ignore what plainly spelled technical humiliation and ultimate commercial disaster ahead. Barely in time he allowed his engineers under Frank Baker to design a one-piece forged steel crankshaft with 1⅝in (41.3mm) journals to which a 2¼in (57mm) wide, heavy cast-iron steel rim was secured by three ⁷⁄₁₆in (11.11mm) high-tensile bolts. It did the trick.

Almost immediately power-tuning experiments leapt ahead on a twin-carburettor T110 equipped with E3134 cam forms and old-style Type 6, 1⁷⁄₁₆in (27mm) remote float racing carburettors. This first of the legendary 'Splayed Head' 650s produced on test a reliable, and non-cracking, fraction under 49bhp (36.6kW) at 6,800rpm. When it was tested at MIRA (Motor Industries Research Association) test track at 128mph (206km/h) by Percy Tait, it attained an untypical 6T-founded velocity common only to blueprinted experimental models. In October of that year Triumph announced the 46bhp/6,500rpm T120 Bonneville.

Now let us go back a few years to the mid-1950s when there was a mighty tussle between New Zealand's Russell Wright with ex-Scot Bob Burns (using a modified 1,000cc Vincent Black Lightning), the impressive technical might of Germany's NSU and its 500cc ohc supercharged parallel twin in the hands of Wilhelm Herz, and America's 'Stormy' Mangham with his Triumph 650cc 6T-based projectile (better known as the 'Johnny Allen streamliner'), Allen

Tony Godfrey (standing) and John Holder, partners in Triumph's 1961 Thruxton 500-mile endurance race victory on a Bonneville. The name Thruxton for the works-prepared PR Bonnies had yet to be adopted. Behind the headlamp is ex-racer Alec Bennett and in front of the bike is The Motor Cycle's *editor, Harry Louis. Brian Nicholls*

being the rider. At this time, pride in the achievements of one's nation was not derided as xenophobic by the spiritually bereft disciples of political correctness now crippling Western nations. The world far beyond two wheels watched spellbound the record breaking heroics that occurred between 1955 and 1966.

NSU in 1951, at 180.1mph (289.8km/h), wrested the MWLSR (Motorcycle World Land Speed Record) from BMW's 1937 173.6mph (279.4km/h) grasp. Then, on 2 July 1955, New Zealanders Wright (rider) and Burns (tuner) achieved a mean 185.0mph (289.6km/h). They were limited as much by venue as power and decided that Utah's salt flats were vital if they were to exceed the 200mph (322km/h) that was their ambition.

Despite their best one-way run of 198.3mph (319.1km/h), the Vincent team was beaten by the Triumph team on 6 September with a mean speed of 193.72mph (311.7km/h). Then in 1956 the same Mangham-Allen team broke through the fabulous 200mph two-wheel 'barrier' at the same venue with an astonishing mean of 214.17mph (349.2km/h).

Herein lay the inspirational origins of the T120 Bonneville.

Mention has been made previously of the isolationist attitude of the USA and its effects on that nation's motorcycle sport. In 1955 the AMA was not a member of the FIM (then FICM), having withdrawn membership in 1922 following disagreement over its, the AMA's, 'Race From the Crate' policy. The FIM has its headquarters in Geneva, Switzerland, a tidy-minded little country so utterly committed to the preservation of human life that it has banned road racing (although encouraging mountain climbing and skiing, which are no less injurious although conveniently out of 'the public gaze).

When Mangham and Allen's record-breaking victories were first registered with the FIM in 1955 and '56, the FIM accepted them despite the AMA's non-membership, which was pretty magnanimous all things considered. Then all Hell broke loose. Or it did early in 1958 when the FIM reversed its decision and rejected

Buddy Elmore winning the Daytona 200 on a T100A-based racer in 1966 at a mean of 96.38mph (155km/h), 46.5bhp and maximum of 125mph (201km/h). TOC

the speed recorded by Allen on his Triumph.

Why? Because, the FIM claimed, the AMA's timing equipment had not been FIM approved and no FIM observer had attended to ensure fair play. By-and-large American protests centred on the superior quality of its timing equipment to any available to the FIM. The FIM countered that had the AMA equipment been checked against FIM equipment it may have sufficed. To which the AMA pointed out that, as its CIT (California Institute of Technology) 'clocks' were accurate to within 1/1000sec while the FIM's were limited to just 1/100sec, such a test would have been meaningless. Remarkably, considering the FIM's final decision, the AMA's equipment had been manufactured by one of the FIM's approved horological institutes – the CIT! The British, on the other hand, equally furious and lead by Triumph, rested their case on the fact that the FIM's own regulations stated that any protest or objection had to be placed within three months of the registered record claim. In the event almost eight months had passed.

In 1958, ducking and weaving against what had become a general howl of protest at its suspect redecision, the FIM defended its action by identifying NSU as placing a protest

in October, immediately following its unsuccessful attempt to wrest the prestigious title back from Triumph within the three-month period, and also, by claiming that the CIT's timing apparatus certification was made invalid by imprecise identification. Unsurprisingly NSU retorted that it had not protested at all but simply 'Requested further information' about various technicalities involved with the Triumph team.

All-in-all the mucky business largely persuaded the world's motorcyclists, media and other interested sportsmen and women to view the FIM unfavourably. After protracted litigation Triumph lost its case against the FIM solely on a technicality through poor legal representation. On 11 February 1959 the High Court of Justice, London, decided that Triumph should have first bought the matter to an FIM Tribunal and if still unsatisfied should have bought the FIM to court. Instead of which, Triumph had bought the case against Augustin Perouse, late FIM President, and the then current President, Pieter Nortier. The court decided that FIM officials could not personally be sued and their names were ordered be struck from the records of the court proceedings. Despite a public consensus vindicating Triumph, the FIM withdrew Triumph's FIM licence for

Floodlit flat tracking; Triumph-v-Norton. TOC

two years. Not that it mattered much at all, especially in the USA.

One amusing consequence of all this occurred in 1958. Mangham, who was perceived by the motorcyling world as a clean cut all-American hero fighting heroically, and successfully, against overwhelming Teutonic odds, gave NSU a final black eye. NSU, actually one of the world's truly great manufacturers whose technology exceeded that of rivals by decades and which lay behind Honda's early success, had not escaped unscathed from the debacle. Although barely recognised at the time, the company was already in the early stages of a tragic decline from which it never recovered. Mention has already been made of the limitations imposed on the 5T/T100 power maxima by its cramped combustion chambers. In

1956, modifications introduced to strengthen the 'long-stroke' 500cc (71 x 82mm) engines alloy barrels; their spigots were reduced in height from $\frac{3}{16}$in (4.8mm) to $\frac{1}{8}$in (3.2mm), which resulted in a minor combustion chamber shape improvement that led to increased valve exposure. And a new cylinder head with improved porting was fitted. With these tiny efficiency rises to help him, Mangham built a 500cc record breaking streamliner and Jack Wilson prepared the engine. Employing the same inspired 80 per cent nitro fuel mix the 650 had burned, rider Jeff Thomas sped through the traps at 212.3mph (341.5km/h) to set a new MWLSR for 500cc machines.

Good ole American know-how had indeed triumphed over unlimited funds and technical sophistication,

apparently. This, though, was record breaking at the cross roads. Where previously empiricism had lead engineering, as exemplified by Burns and Wright, the application of science was taking over, as exemplified by NSU. Mangham also, for all his countrymen's beloved folk-culture mythology, was in truth a scientist, or at least an engineer, as well as a pilot, in the aircraft industry. The difference between NSU and Triumph-Mangham was that whereas NSU's technology was corporately sourced from NSU's unique research centre, Mangham's was garnered from widespread expertise around American industry, mainly aircraft, as well as immense assistance from Meriden's team of engineers, lead by the committed Frank Baker, and race-engineered by the peerless skills of Jack Wilson.

One of America's aces, the great Dick Hammer TT racing (flat track with a couple of artificial jumps) on what appears to be one of the fearsome T120TTs. TOC

Probably the world's greatest Triumph twin endurance racing exponent, Londoner Dave Degens, participating in the 1966 Barcelona 24-hour event on a unit T120. Degens' concentration on endurance racing began in the early 1960s when he started analysing mechanical retirement causes. Most, he decided, were due to transmission failure, followed by valves and piston problems. With this in mind, he constructed his famous T120-engined, Norton-framed Triton (which he still has) with which he became the first all-British winner of the famous Spanish event, in 1965. Since then, Degens above and beyond any other engineer, has continued to develop Triumph twins to an astonishing level of efficiency, generally exceeding that of any modern engine. Dave Degens

The vital factor was the machine's highly penetrative aerodynamically stable shell, because its 100bhp (74.5kW) was 10bhp (7.4kW) less than the 500cc NSU and very similar to the Vincent's. The reality of the German machine's technical complexity was owed as much to NSU's greater, if eventually terminal, commitment to Wankel rotary development, of which the supercharger was a vital and secret experimental proto-motor, as to the actual speed record itself.

From thereon aerodynamicists rather than engine tuners ascended to the MWLSR premier role. For the next few years Triumph men dominated. Lead by Johnny Allen, in 1962 Joe Dudek, an engineer working on the 4,000mph (6,437km/h) Bell X-15

rocket-powered research aircraft, built what was to become the fastest-ever Triumph at an FIM-approved mean 224.5mph (361.3km/h) maximum – the 667cc Bonneville based streamliner. It lives in history as the 230mph (370km/h) Trumpet twin and it has never been bettered. Almost.

Triumph-powered record breakers reached their zenith with Gyronaut X-1 in 1965. The development story of this twin 650-engined motorcycle is too comprehensive to report here. The author recommends the excellent *Triumph Motorcycles in America* by Lindsay Brook and David Gaylin for all the details. Built by Bob Leppan, who also rode it, and his business partner Jim Brufoldt, it was designed by Alex Tremulis, one of America's most influential and progressive car

designers, to exceed 250mph (402km/h). Employing quite conventionally race-tuned engines for the sake of reliability, each of 70bhp (52kW), later 75bhp (60kW) Leppan recorded 229mph (368km/h) before losing control on a flooded section of the salt flat strip.

The following year Leppan rode an improved Gyronaut with 820cc 90bhp (67kW) engines to record a mean 245.67mph (395.3km/h) but without FIM approval, about which deficit no-one gave a toss. More than any other motorcycle it proved conclusively, thanks to its unprecedently low drag factor, that penetration, quite as much as power, was the answer. Then, at a calculated 280mph (450km/h), the gremlins in the front end snapped a suspension arm and the whole plot took off before landing to slide through the lights at 264mph (425km/h) *on Leppan's left arm!* He, and one of the most beautiful and influential streamliners in the history of two and four-wheeled record breaking, thankfully survived.

Triumph had one more serious attempt at the MWLSR in 1973 when Denis Manning campaigned Bonneville Speed Week with another 750cc/100bhp twin Triumph engined streamliner by aerodynamicist Lyn Yankel. On a bad surface Manning crashed at 280mph (450km/h), but still managed to slide across through the traps at 277mph (446km/h). Then Don Vesco eventually capped MWLSR attempts for Triumph by exceeding the awesome 300mph (483km/h) target in 1975 on a twin engined TZ700 Yamaha. With the coming of the strokers, somehow, the greater part of the Salt Flats glory seemed to fade a bit.

In 1958, the year of the T110, the weary old Thruxton Nine-hour event was revived as the Thruxton 500-mile endurance race. Those present will never forget the spectacle of the young Mike Hailwood partnered by Dan Shorey on a T110 holding off the 'Flying Scotsman', Bob MacIntyre backed by Derek Powell, on a 700cc Royal Enfield Super Meteor. On that cracked-up old airfield peri-track Hailwood and Shorey won at an average speed of 66mph (106km/h), a bare two laps ahead of Bob Mac' and Powell.

The T120 differed from the T110 by its 1½in (38mm) exhaust pipes, its 8.5.1 compression ratio, its twin 1⅟₁₆in (27mm) 'chopped' (sans float chamber) Amal Monobloc carbs fed via a remote rubber-mounted 'matchbox' float, E3134 inlet and E3325 exhaust cams and, most important of all, the new one-piece forged crankshaft. Its handsome engine developed a claimed 42bhp (31.3kW) at 6,500rpm, it weighed 404lb (183.4kg) dry, although fully tanked and equipped with 37lb (16.7kg) of fuel, tools, and battery it grossed 441lb (200.2kg). And everyone believed, or wanted to believe, that its model designation would be reflected in its speed which, of course, is what its maker anticipated.

An average T120 in the hands of a typical enthusiast normally seated would accelerate to approximately 105mph (168km/h). Beyond that lay a more rarefied region wherein all manner of factors influenced power and speed. An absolute maximum, with leather-clad rider prone, lay in the 110–115mph (177–185km/h) region, as verified by *The Motor Cycle's* 'Riders' Reports' survey of May 1965 when a mean average of 113mph (182km/h) was collated. This more-or-less coincided with the author's experience of his own 1966 model.

For all the changes made to the Triumph's prestigious 650, including a 6bhp (4.5kW) power boost throughout its 15-year production life, the standard model's top speed rose very little.

Although continuously developed the T120 underwent three main periods. The first was the brief 1959 phase, when the electrics were by magneto and dynamo, the frame was 6T single-loop, the engine's twin chopped Monobloc carbs drank through a remote 'matchbox' float chamber and the headlamp was within Triumph's trademark nacelle. These rare and lovely first editions, with their execrable high-speed cor-

nering manners, may have been flawed but they were superbly assembled, satisfyingly reliable, very fast and have rightly become treasured amongst connoisseurs of fine motorcycle art.

The second phase ran from 1960 to 1963. Apart from minor styling changes, the most visual alteration was from nacelle to exterior headlamp and the exchange of tele-fork metal shrouds for rubber gaiters. As these alterations had become standard production racing format, in which the majority of participants rode Triumphs, they were far from mere cosmetics sops.

In a vain attempt to cure the Bonneville's notoriously poor high-speed handling (in fairness a skilful rider could by the judicious use of progressively opened throttles sans cog-swapping largely circumvent the swingeing yaw, while an exceptional chassis engineer could, through meticulous preparation keep the wheels more-or-less in line) at minimum cost to existing production systems, Triumph engineers introduced the duplex frame.

Now highly collectable, the twin-tube frames won a reputation no less infamous for breakage than their forebears' had been for collywobbles. Any

Gary Nixon at speed on the half-mile, Ohio. John Nelson

American West Coast champion, Eddie Mulder in the desert. John Nelson

number of cures were attempted, of which an additional stiffening under-tank rail plus changes to frame tube material appeared to be the final answer. The cause lay in harmonic resonance, which, as Triumph discovered to its near cost with No. 3 6T (JAC 770) at Montlhéry in 1949, was to dog the T120 and its variants for their entire life.

Equally troublesome, was over-rich carburation rooted in the same vibration (fuel frothing pressurises a float chamber to force excessive fuel through the jets into the carb mixing chamber) so Triumph, doubtless with relief, surrendered the rubber-mounted remote float system *et al* in favour of conventional twin Mono-blocs, which in road use performed satisfactorily, and cheaper. The chopped carbs in modified trim with anti-frothing jet collars continued to be listed as a vital option for racing however. Portentously, a Lucas crankshaft alternator supplied the lighting power.

Then, in September 1962, the third significant chapter in T120 history opened. Doug Hele left Norton for Triumph and things were never the same again. Under Bert Hopwood, who had taken over responsibility for motorcycle engineering at Meriden,

Hele did what Turner demonstrably had been either incapable of understanding or executing – he tackled Triumph frames' lack of axial stiffness. When the unit-construction Bonnie appeared in 1963 it was a revelation. Hele revised the entire design, transforming the engine and gearbox into a unified bloc then employed this as an anchor contributing to swinging fork pivot spindle security. Where previously the swinging fork had been fixed mainly on the previous frame's 'saddle tube', the new frame clamped the swinging fork pivot at its extremes in heavy gauge steel plates that clamped together the gearbox and the rear frame tubes.

Above and beyond all other developments this rear suspension improvement saved the T120, because in 1962 appeared the only model that was to seriously challenge the Bonnie's racing prowess, being Norton's 650SS. This magnificent mileater was based on Bert Hopwood's 1948 497cc Model 7 and developed eventually by Doug Hele into the 650SS. With a claimed 49bhp (36.5kW) at 6,800rpm, a blueprinted maximum speed of 115mph (185km/h) or so and suspended on its Manx-bred rolling chassis, it would have swallowed the original Bonnie

whole and spat out the pips. In the hands of riders such as Phil Read and Brian Satchell, the 650SS, with victories in the Thruxton 500 Mile and IoM Production TT, more than any other model hit the new Bonnie where it hurt. Fortunately Hele, the man who more than most had been responsible for the 650SS, was also responsible for the post-'63 T120.

Where the 'pre-unit' Bonnie's weakness lay in its chassis, the 'unit' Bonnie's flaw lay within its engine. By this time Lucas's warning of magneto production cessation was finally in operation. Turner especially was enthusiastic about ac coil ignition, so much so he vigorously, and with deplorable success, had long championed Lucas against mounting criticism from the rest of the entire British industry's outrage. It was cheap. Theoretically it held every advantage, its low speed spark energy being greater and its timing more accurate than any high-volume-produced magneto could manage, theoretically. In practice however, the new ignition pack was doubly crippling. The contact breaker point mechanism was manufactured to such abysmal quality that obtaining accurate timing on both cylinders was impossible. Accurate timing on one was guaranteed to upset the other. Not until 1968, five years after the adoption of coil ignition, did Lucas belatedly solve the root cause of so many break-downs, which took the form of its highly self-celebrated 6CA individually adjustable twin c/b set.

So damaging was the ignition system that BSA engineers, driven to desperation, designed their own remote, or 'quill' driven c/b set for competition purposes. These, although strictly a BSA works speciality, quickly found their way out by the back door and were adopted by eager Triumph race teams.

The second equally severe consequence of the ghastly new ignition was manifest in huge numbers of burned pistons returned under guarantee claim. In this case BSA's A65 twins suffered even more. Combustion chamber overheating was after an agonising period eventually traced to the existence of a rogue spark incited by contact breaker point bounce effecting pre-ignition. British production race entrants were quick to develop their own strong c/b springs and then to grind the trailing ramp of the c/b cam into a more progressive decline. Equally disastrous was the melting of the nylon heels, or cam followers, of the contact breaker points.

By this time electronic ignition was making an appearance and Stan Shenton, the dynamic proprietor of Boyers of Bromley, had backed electronics engineer Ernie Bransden's replacement spark system. After three decades of igniting Triumphs (and most other old British twins) with unfailing accuracy it has earned itself a reputation as the premier electronic pack. It was offered to Triumph for £9. Bert Hopwod rejected it because Triumph was paying Lucas an alleged 15s (75p) for its ignition system.

From this point on, the BSA Group, including a reluctant Triumph, in what appeared to be a Satanic triumvirate rite with the British Leyland car group (Austin, Morris, MG, Wolsely, Triumph, Riley, Jaguar, Rover) and Lucas, worked with tireless vigilance transforming what had once been a prestigious reputation for British vehicles into the butt of Western auto-jokes. As demonstrated by the high quality of its commercial vehicle and aircraft equipment, Lucas could design and manufacture with the world's best, but British car and motorcycle manufacturers saw cheapness as their products' sole attraction and demanded minimal cost, therefore quality, from their subcontractors. Lucas was myopic enough to comply, with the result it earned itself the richly deserved sobriquet 'Prince of Darkness' for its services to auto-electrical systems. None of the main proponents involved in this insane business ever fully recovered their reputations and all three (Lucas, British Leyland and BSA) entered the opening stages of what would eventually be resolved in tragedy.

One other oddity arose from the unit construction T120. Any innocent who dismantles a Triumph 650 twin will find himself faced by the paradox of a ball-race main bearing on the highly stressed drive side of the crankshaft and a roller bearing, with its 2.5 times greater load bearing qual-

ities, on the timing side. While not ideal it was a satisfactory compromise that allowed for heat expansion on the timing side crankshaft end thanks to lateral bearing tolerance, impossible on the drive side because of the vital need for unfailing chain alignment. When, with the introduction of the unit-construction T120s, drive-side main bearings began failing the natural assumption was that the ball races were finally overstressed.

In reality, the problem lay in the much stronger crankcases of the one-piece engines. They no longer flexed and through their strength allowed the crankshaft no flexure, so the bearing broke up. Quietly, Triumph adopted a ball-race with greater inbuilt tolerances and by so doing simply resolved the problem.

One often reads that prior to Doug Hele's final selection of 62° for the steering angle of the 1966 T120, Triumph had experimented constantly as it attempted to overcome its bikes' handling difficulties. Not so. The first change in 1959 was a steepening of 3°

from 64° to 67°, by which 2.5in (63mm) was lost on the wheelbase, all at the request of American track racers who wanted quick, light steering. Then, in 1961, it was reduced 2°, back to 65° to suit the needs of American desert racers who wanted high speed stability. The British, as always, quietly coped.

Also at this time, Triumph adopted BSA's tele-fork. It may well have signified the beginning of a component-sharing operation that rightly was to so enrage Triumph owners in particular, but the BSA fork proved more equable to the two-way damping the fast rising cornering speed of the new T120 demanded. Triumph had for some years identified a compression damper (as well the familiar rebound) in its elegantly slim tele's hydraulics but it was unsatisfactory. BSA's Hele-originated two-way damped fork encompassed its worthwhile and conveniently tuneable shuttle-valve damping system perfectly.

Nor was the crankshaft balance factor always changing the way tradi-

Wilbur Ceder (left), president of Johnson Motors, who backed it; Bill Johnson (no relation), who rode it; Joe Dudeck who designed it, and Earl Flanders, right, the AMA observer who gave it his blessing. This established the world record speed for motorcycles of 230.069mph, averaged two-ways over a measured-mile course. The 667cc T120 engine was prepared by Pete Coleman and the time was confirmed by Helmut Bonsch representing the FIM. In 1962, Johnson achieved a mean two-way speed of 224.57mph and a one-way best of 230.27mph. John Nelson

A rare sight in the Isle of Man, a Le Mans start for the first PR TT in 1967. T120s far exceed all other entries. John Hartle won at a mean of 97.10mph (156km/h) and managed a fastest lap of 97.87mph (157.5km/h), on a Bonnie of course. Stan Shenton

tion remembers. It remained at a constant 50 per cent until Spring 1962 when the T120 altered to 71 per cent, then in July of the same year the familiar and unchanging 85 per cent was adopted.

The Bonneville was sold in the USA in a variety of forms, most of which employed the familiar 47bhp/6,700rpm engine. America's standard Bonnie was the T120R, which barely differed from its British counterpart. Then came the T120C which varied in detail between East and West Coasts but was designed specifically for racing and benefited from special racing pistons, although to the same 8.5:1 compression ratio, bigger valves, different cams (E3134 inlet and E3059R exhaust) and wide radius tappets, 1⅛in (28.5mm) twin Amals and remote float, close ratio gears and stronger clutch springs. These modifications lifted power to a

claimed 52bhp (39kW), which was considered by many to be over-modest and, until the advent of the T120TT Special with its unit engine and superior frame, gave best to nothing else.

In 1963–65, arrived the brutal T120C TT Special with short open 'pipes, 11.2 or 12:1 racing pistons, 1³⁄₁₆in (30mm) Amals breathing through meticulously tapered inlet ports, ET ignition, and 55bhp (41kW) on tap at up to 6,800rpm. No more potent 650 ever left Meriden and, while a flat tracker, it owed its power tuning almost solely to American record breaking experience at Bonneville, particularly Bill Johnson's 1962 224.5mph (361.2km/h) MWLSR missile, engineered by Pete Coleman. Just under 1,000 were built; few survive. Those that do exist in purdah. They were vicious motorcycles, as hard to start, and no less injurious to the timorous than a badly

set-up G85CS Matchless, and with an explosive power step once in use.

Britain had its own special, the T120R Thruxton, named to celebrate Triumph's victories in the prestigious Thruxton 500 production race. This reached its zenith in 1969 when Percy Tait and Malcolm Uphill came first, John Cooper and Steve Jolly second and Len Phelps and Chris Carr third, with Bonnies also filling fifth, sixth and seventh spots. As the Bonneville had become legendary so the Thruxton entered the realms of living mythology. As far as the author is aware, the first time the association was made public by Triumph was the appearance in a *The Motor Cycle* advertisement following the Thruxton 500-mile production race when Tony Godfrey and John Holder rode their T120 to victory in 1962. 'Thruxton Triumph by Bonneville' was the statement.

In order to placate the twin demands of the ACU (Auto Cycle Union) over production race machine homologation, and its dealer race teams clamouring for works replica T120 production racers, in 1964 Triumph's experimental shop was given leave to build the racers.

In exactly the same manner as their T120C TT American counterpart, the T120R Thruxton was meticulously assembled by Triumph's most dedicated technicians using hand-selected components taken from the assembly line.

Where aluminium castings were concerned, such as cylinder heads and crankcases, these were received as blanks and precision-machined in the experimental department. Turner's, and by this time the controlling BSA Group's, denial of the wholly profitable Triumph factory the modern production plant it needed was beginning to have a cumulative effect, as increasing numbers of less skilful assembly workers were expected to operate increasingly old-fashioned and labour-intensive machinery.

Typical was the cylinder head machining operation, which relied almost wholly on the skill of the operator to overcome the weaknesses of a badly worn and outdated machine. Many, maybe even most, standard Triumphs left the factory with semi-pocketed valves because of the difficulty of easily measuring, and thus machining, valve seat depth. This, combined with equally formidable problems of accurate valve angle placement, which were vital, was equally as responsible as Lucas's coil ignition for the depressed performance of so many standard T120s. Experimental department technicians placed every valve precisely at its required 90° (to each other, 45° to the cylinder axis) and seating on the face of the combustion chamber skull. Unless this symbiosis occurred further power tuning would be unlikely to achieve a cohesive optimum.

Crankcases were impeccably paired and machined, as were crankshafts, immense care being taken over securing with Loctite the three $\frac{7}{16}$in (11mm) through-bolts which secured the dense

cast iron rim flywheel to the steel crankshaft. Loctite was used on all standard crankshafts but even then a few flywheels worked loose under the unexpected rigours of competition.

Equally meticulous, was the porting operation, which was finished with a slight taper towards the inlet valve. Carburation was by twin 1$\frac{5}{32}$in (29.3mm) chopped Amal Monoblocs with either a remote 'round' or 'matchbox' float chamber and linked by a balance pipe. Beloved by Americans in particular, the splayed carburettors and porting were actually a power depressant. Parallel ports and carbs returned a superior performance, as experiments had amply proved, but the standard head stud arrangement precluded parallel ports without loss of material and subsequent cracking.

It must be appreciated that two of the inbuilt requirements of any production racer are a good low engine speed torque delivery and enduring reliability, because most of them back in the high-days of sport bike racing were expected to double up as endurance racers. Thus, one of the

In a typical British short circuit race of 1967, Dave Nixon follows Paul Butler around Druids bend at Brand Hatch, both on T120s.
Stan Shenton

Thunderbirds got everywhere. Here, one rests beside a milestone somewhere in the Far East. Author

material signatures of the Thruxton was its pair of Thunderbird camshafts. Apparent aliens in a racing engine, when paired with Triumph's 'Big-Foot' wide radius competition tappets, and *nothing* else, they return the strong mid-range torque that is vital for nursing both man and machine over a half-day's continual racing, as well as high revving bhp.

All genuine Thruxtons were equipped with close-ratio gear clusters, initially four-speed Triumph and latterly five-speed Quaife.

Every engine was bench tested to deliver between 52 and 54bhp (38/40kW) between 6,500 and 6,800rpm. The maximum safe racing revs was quoted as 7,200rpm, but in extremis, when last-lap honour was at stake, 7,500 revs was a pretty safe risk. And there was power all the way, so possibly these engines did give more than their quoted safe best.

Approximately 55 T120R Thruxtons were manufactured. About three left Meriden in 1964, the majority in 1965 and nine or so were built in 1966, with rumours of the odd one as late 1967, but records are vague. Originals survive only in cloistered precincts, guarded by angels.

How to recognise the genuine article these days when so many standard Bonnevilles have undergone pretty authentic race conversion? Check that the exhaust balance pipe is waisted down to 1.25in (32mm) from its 1.5in (30.5mm) connections. Most models are equipped with an external tappet oil feed although some were blanked off. The rear sub-frame should be adapted to accept the slightly longer racing suspension units. Six-pint (3.3-litre) oil tanks are standard. The offset front brakes are equipped with an air scoop.

Why were the works T120s so much faster than even a Thruxton? Rod Gould's 140mph (225km/h) in the IoM Production TT of 1968 is usually quoted as the timed maximum, although another 10mph (16km/h) is considered to represent the absolute limit for a true road race twin. Quite apart from meticulous blueprinting, Meriden employed special racing 'silencers' with consequential carburation changes, and it favoured for its works racers not the 6T cam but cam forms borrowed from BSA's A65 twins, where it was known as the Spitfire, and eventually listed by Triumph as the E6897 inlet and E6988 exhaust. Great care was also employed in further gas flowing techniques and into the adoption of even higher compression ratio pistons of 12:1, sometimes remachined and polished down to 11:1 to favour gas flow.

Then, in 1971, the whole Triumph edifice began to crumble. BSA, with no more feeling for brand loyalty or marque traditions than should be expected from a golf club-besotted executive board without a motorcycle between them, began badge engineering. BSA's powered by Triumph engines left Meriden and identikit Triumphs powered by BSA engines left Small Heath. The insanity of Umberslade's inmates had spilled over the walls and infected everyone.

15

Little twins and a tiny single

Hip baths and T21s, BSA's early death-grip, twins at Daytona, Gary Nixon, Percy Tait and Giacomo Agostini at Spa, Daytona sportster, Honda in the IoM, the T20 Cub, a final US-backed ISDT fling

Triumph had throughout its life as a motorcycle manufacturer been vainly endeavouring to profit by Britain's preference for 350cc models. Most motorcyclists knew by either popular opinion or experience that unless it was to be hitched to a 'chair', a 350 returned 95 per cent of the performance of a 500 for about 70 per cent of the gross cost involved. But for all its brave attempts Triumph had never managed to capture the valuable 350 market.

Then, in 1957, came the T21 Twenty One, a £175 350 twin designed specifically to bring the glamour of its £270 T110 650 sportster into go-to-work-Joe's budget. That was the plan. In practice, however, the 18bhp 350 was dropped from production in 1966, although the sportier T90 continued for three further years. As with its predecessor, the 17bhp 3T, the T21's charm lay solely in the sweetness of its engine, and that alone was insufficient. Try as it might, Triumph could convince neither trade nor public in Britain or America that its cumbrous mudguarding and 'hip-bath' bodywork was anything but inelegant. Moreover, try as they might, engine tuners could no more produce any more mid-range torque from a notoriously puny engine, than they could usefully boost its bhp. Those who did attempt to race-tune it found that the best power revs always seemed to lie at the start of the bloodline.

Given a ruthless pilot, a hard-pressed T21 would manage 70, maybe 75mph (113/121km/h) but any attempt to change direction hard and fast, or even hold line along an undulating road, would cause the kind of nasty loss of stability that can only ever be a consequence of a weak frame.

This was Turner's baby through and through. Fortunately he was saved from eventual humiliation by his engineering team, headed by Frank Baker, and the introduction of the greatly over-squared 5TA Speed Twin in

1959. The T21's frame was closer related to its diminutive brother, the 200cc T20 Tiger Cub than to anything bigger, with a steering head projecting outward from a skimpy, single-loop frame and a swinging rear fork no more securely anchored than the traditionally unsatisfactory big twins. With the extra 27bhp (6,500rpm) of the 490cc engine behind it, the frame warped unforgivably, and unforgivingly. The petrol tank had been over-optimistically designed to act as an auxiliary stress

Percy Tait's 1968 T100A-based IoM TT racer. Note the attention paid to oil capacity and cooling. He did not feature on the winners' rostrum, but the following year (see telegram) . . . Brian Nicholls

member and unsurprisingly it frequently split.

By the time the 34bhp T100A arrived in 1960, both British and American off-road competitors were beginning to enthuse over the potential of the model as a time-trial/enduro/desert racer, and most especially as a road racer in Britain, but the cheapskate frame simply was not up to it. Even so, not until 1964 did Triumph do much about it. By this time Edward Turner had retired and Bert Hopwood had returned from Norton to take his place and he, unsurprisingly, head-hunted his old development engineer, Doug Hele, to partner him at Meriden. As an interim measure a single top tube was bolted in triangulation beneath the petrol tank to run between the steering head and the main frame; it helped.

Not even the formidable partnership of Hopwood and Hele could,

```
TRICOR TIMO

TRUSTY COVENTRY
MSGTBY 31305 11TH JULY 1969

ATTENTION ROD COATES

PERCY ON LATES 500 WAS SECOND TO AGOSTINI IN BELGIAN G.P.
HANDLES AS GGOD AS OLD MACHINE SINCE USING NEW TYRES. OLD MACHINE
WITH ALLY BARREL ENGINE NOT SO FAST AS BELGIAN G.P. MACHINE
SUGGEST SENDING THIS LIGHT MACHINE COMPLETE FOR GARY ON UNDERSTANDING
IT MUST BE RETURNED IN TIME FOR ULSTER GRAND PRIX PRACTICE
WEEK 10TH AUGUST 1969 . CONSIDER IT AN ADVANTAGE TO SEND PERCY
OVER TO CONFIRM MACHINES PERFORMANCE IN PRACTICE AS BEING SIMILAR
TO BEHAVIUOR OVER HERE. ALSO TO ADVISE ON ANY PECULIARITIES AND TO
GAIN EXPERIENCE OF U.S. RACING PRACTICE . ASSUME FRAME WIL L CONFORM
WITH YOUR REGULATIONS .


PLEASE RING EARLYMV
TRICOR TIMO


TRUSTY COVENTRY    EITHER RING OR TELEX    ++++++ FIN TKS  SC +++++
```

. . . in 1969, Tait excelled himself, as explained in this telegram from Meriden to Tricor. Doug Hele

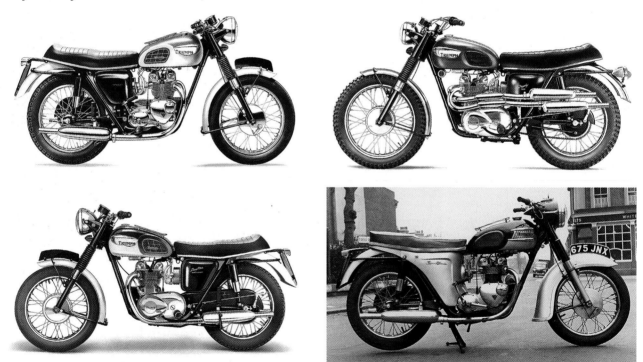

Top left: *The standard T100S, 1968.* TOC

Top right: *The T100 Trophy never matched the competition success of its illustrious TR5 Trophy, principally because by 1969 the competition had become too fierce.* TOC

Bottom left: *The Daytona may well have demanded excessive TLC from fast-riding owners, or given sooted spark plugs to gentle ones, but in the right hands one of these formidable sportsters was agile enough to give a T120 the slip.* TOC

Bottom right: *After the debacle of the appalling 'bathtub' Trumpets, these 'min-skirt' alternatives helped to cool some criticism, but still not enough. This is a Speed Twin.* Cyril Ayton

Comparatively unusual as a trials chair tug because of its modest torque, the short-stroke T100 found favour with the evergreen all-rounder, Arthur Wheeler, seen here in the 1964 Sidcup Trial. Brian Nicholls

however, overcome the inertia of the BSA Group executive. The mills of the new chairman, Eric Turner and his insufferable BSA Motorcycle Division managing director, Lionel Jofeh, ground slow but, unlike those of God and the law, exceeding unsure. So not until 1967, 10 long years after the new model had been laid down, was the means for its potential to be realised.

By this time, the BSA Group was beginning to reel confusedly in its death agonies, although practically no-one appreciated it at the time. Its

American executives and their distributors were utterly confounded, as were British middle management. Despite the appalling decisions reached by the BSA board, its devoted middle management and engineers on both sides of the Atlantic continued to work miracles. In 1964 we saw a hint of the future as America entered the ISDT on Triumphs, two TR6s and three proto T100Cs. The team comprised the great Bud Ekins and brother Dave, their friend Steve McQueen, with John Steen and Cliff Coleman. Bud Ekins

uncharacteristically injured a foot and McQueen less uncharacteristically crashed, but Dave Ekins and Coleman went home with Golds and Steen a Silver.

Then the following year George Montgomery came home third and Gary Nixon fourth on T100 racers behind Roger Reiman and Mert Lawill on ohv 750 HDs in the Daytona 200. HD twitched. By this time even the seemingly impenetrable arrogance of the BSA Group board had been wakened to the importance of American

Top: *The T20 Cub of 1954. Pretty, lively and economical, but too many years were allowed to pass until it became reliable (electrics) and durable (bottom end).* Cyril Ayton

Middle: *Inspired by off-road competition success, by 1962 Triumph announced the T20S/H Sports Cub. Against all expectations in the right hands (slim and light) it proved to be surprisingly fast, capable of 80mph (129km/h) and was immense fun to use fast.* TOC

Bottom: *A complete range of off-road Cubs was turned out, from trials to scrambles, enduro to trail. This is the RT20S scrambler of 1960, which more-or-less set the pace.* Author

sales, so for 1966, BSA, as well as Triumph, entered works teams at Daytona, which by this time rivalled the IoM TT for prestige. Clive Bennett of BSA took with him six BSA A50 Wasp-based racers (50.1bhp/8,150rpm), and Doug Hele six T100T-based specials. Triumph won; HD came in third.

Gary Nixon took first place and team mate Buddy Elmore followed him home. Perhaps it was not so surprising after all, because Hele's parallel twin racing nous had been honed on the astonishing 100mph+ (161km/h) 1961 Senior TT lap of Tom Phyllis on the Hele-prepared Norton Domiracer. All the Triumphs finished, even though a crash knocked leader Nixon down to seventh place. As these twins were lapping Daytona at 136mph (219km/h), it stands to reason that their ultimate top speed would have approximated to 150mph (241km/h). This equals the velocities achieved by the 25 per cent larger T120-based racers. Without American assistance however, even Hele would have been lost, because during practice a variety of mechanical breakdowns caused by lubricant starvation and faulty cam followers plagued the Meriden twins.

Hele's aim was not limited to maximum power. In an engine which had been tested up to 10,000rpm and which, unlike its long-stroke forebear the 5T, was unrenowned for torque, he aimed for mid-range usability and, thus, reliability. Adoption of twin 1³⁄₁₆in (30mm) Amal GP carburettors, 9.75:1 compression pistons, and reverse cone megaphone exhausts were familiar of course, but only a small part of it. Gas flow into the cylinder heads was painstakingly studied resulting in 39° valve angles and 1½in (38mm) inlet valves, including a cross sectional porting reduction of ¹⁄₁₆in (1.6mm) so as to accelerate gas velocity into the combustion chamber, crankcase breathing was completely reworked – which measurably improved thermal efficiency – the lubrication system was redesigned to include an American-developed oil radiator from a Chevrolet car, and a special remote-mounted contact breaker ET ignition set was fitted.

The Mountain Cub was an American development of the T20s. It was quickly turned into a formidable desert racer in its own right.
TOC

In the days before skidoos, bikes were adapted. This Sno-Cub was modified with great success by JoMo, US West Coast distributors.
TOC

While maximum power was 50bhp between 8,000 and 8,700rpm, much greater significance was placed on the 44bhp at 6,500rpm. Generously, Hele identified Jack Shemans, of Triumph's experimental department, as the prime engine developer. Thanks to its superb combustion chamber and low reciprocating stresses, the engine responded magnificently to race-tuning, while the frame did not, and this was Hele's five-month-long commitment. To reduce a protracted tale to its fundamentals, Hele, who with Brian Jones had already redesigned the T120 frame for the 'unit' Bonnie and awarded it with high-speed stability to equal the Norton 650SS, wisely

decided to opt for the same again. The brand-new T100A-type frame was in effect a reduced T120 one, complete with the same strongly reinforced steering head and swinging fork pivot braced by engine unit, main frame and rear sub frame tubes.

With Percy Tait as chief development rider rolling chassis development progressed until the final dimensions were perfected. These were: wheelbase standard at 54.25in (1,378mm), steering angle 27°, trail 3.88in (98.5mm), fork deflection 5.62in (143mm) reduced from standard by 0.75in (19mm). Tait was later to achieve what may well be the short-stroke 490 twin's greatest achievement

when, in the 1969 Belgian Grand Prix he finished second to MV Agusta-mounted Giacomo Agostini in the 500cc event. Spa-Francorchamps is a notoriously demanding grand prix circuit, combining extreme speed with closed road twists and turns. That a pushrod road-based twin could contest an event with any specialist grand prix machinery is remarkable in itself, but on that circuit of all, is astonishing and reveals Tait's rare talent. A hard-headed and shrewd business man, Tait in his younger days could be a clown when the mood struck him. He was also over modest. When questioned about his success, he shrugged and put it down to a batch of unusually potent petrol.

So occurred a motorcycle which, before the legendary 750 triples arrived in Daytona, came, saw and conquered. Further improvements for the 1967 Daytona 200 brought wholesome reliability, improved power and winning glory. Gary Nixon won, Dick Hammer chased him home and HD's George Roeder had to make do with third place, a complete lap behind the Trumpeteers.

Thus the Daytona sportster was born in 1967. It proved to be so successful that it remained in production until the cessation of Meriden in 1974. Thanks to a weight of just 340lb (154kg), some 40lb (18kg) less than a Bonneville, while no faster than the 650 although it maximised at around 112mph (180km/h), over a twisty road it was undeniably quicker. At least it was in the hands of a skilful owner, because for all its nonpareil agility, the Daytona was a much more demanding sportster. If used for long in traffic it sooted its plugs with cracking vengeance and, while tractable enough, the engine did not climb on the cam until it was spinning at 5,000rpm (65mph/105km/h), which necessitated pretty intense concentration. Regrettably the bike suffered from two defective adjuncts of fast riding. It lost tune quickly, needing more-than-average maintenance and, although it felt sweeter than most parallel twins to ride, unless given lavish TLC rewarded a hard riding owner with destructive high frequency vibration.

Nevertheless, the Daytona was a fine motorcycle. In Britain it dominated the 500cc production racing class not much less thoroughly than the Bonneville did its. In its first year out David Nixon on a Boyer-entered model grabbed third place in the IoM 500 PR TT. Then, in 1968, Daytona-mounted Ray Knight, production racer and journalist extraordinaire, won the same race at 90.09mph

Two of Britain's finest trials Cub exponents, Roy Peplow picks a path over the rocks of the 1958 Clayton Trial, while Gordon Blakeway takes a muddy section of the 1960 British Experts Trial at full bore in second. Brian Nicholls

Hardly a Trumpet, but a BSA single with the wrong name on the tank. But Comefords, major sporting dealers in Surrey, turned them into top-hole trials bikes, as witnessed by this 1969 Scottish Six Days Trial model. It was Comefords who, in 1967, also began turning out serious trials Cubs. Brian Nicholls

(145km/h). But in 1968, just as the BSA board was beginning to smugly relax into lethargy again, something nasty happened.

The year previous at Daytona in Honda's brash display of rev-happy nonsense, a brace of 450cc Black Bombers had been swept aside by the charging sextuplet of Meriden's best. Someone had forgotten that only a decade earlier, in 1959, Naomi Taniguchi and his chums on 125cc twins won the IoM Ultra-Lightweight TT Team Prize for Honda. As the disdainfully pinstriped executives of the British industry crawled ever further up their corporate dark tunnel of warm security towards stagnation, calloused-thumbed Sochiro Honda smiled respectfully. So, in 1969, what had failed in Daytona succeeded in the IoM: Bill Penny won for Honda the IoM 500cc PR TT on – you might have guessed – a 450cc Black Bomber. For the next five years, until the PR TTs ceased, Daytona riders fought a valiant rear guard action against Suzuki, Kawasaki and Honda, but the mould was setting.

By this time Triumph's little-un, the T20 Tiger Cub had won itself a reputation as a smashing little ultra-lightweight competition machine. As a roadster it enjoyed a reputation for a lively, fuel-sipping performance in which a cruising speed of 55mph (88km/h) and 100mpg (2.8l/100km) were satisfyingly compatible. But the wee beast was flawed, although not quite fatally enough to terminate it, by an ac electrical system of unmitigated devilry; thanks be to Lucas whose chronic unreliability could always be relied upon in times of stress, and an equally notorious big end.

Its life began in 1952 as the 149cc T15 Terrier. Sometimes credited as a development of Triumph's similarly sized model XO of 1933, largely on the strength of its ohv 'sloper' engine, in fact the Terrier was no such thing. It

Triumph engines have always been popular with special builders. The best were the world renowned Metisse off-roaders, which are still venerated, 'Grumphs' (Greeves rolling chassis) have always been popular with DIY engineers. Bob Pearson's is unusual because it employs a 350 3TA engine, rather than the usual 5TA. Author

Doug Hele (right), Triumph's engineering guru, was by nature a quiet gentleman. Sid Lawton, a contemporary who favoured Aermacchis as well as Triumphs, was not. Brian Nicholls

issued fresh from Turner's post-war drawing board as utility starter to the Triumph range, in which the 3T should have been the next step up. A mechanically noisy and underpowered model, in 1955 the Terrier was dropped unmourned in favour of its improved protégé, the 1953 T20 Tiger Cub. Without going into nut-by-bolt detail, its engine had been improved by the adoption of a plain bearing big end, alas. Long before Triumph had returned to a properly lubricated roller bearing big end in 1966, the Alpha bearing company had made itself a handsome living out of bottom end roller bearing conversions.

A range of Cubs no less as broad in scope as the twins was eventually produced, ranging from trials models through enduro to the fastest 15bhp (11kW) 80mph (129km/h) road sports models. A special Mountain Cub was exported to America incorporating the engine of the Sports Cub in what amounted to the rolling chassis of the TR20 trials model, complete with wide ratio trials gears. It proved to be one the company's most popular machines and in this trim won itself a fine reputation as a formidable lightweight desert racer.

From the Cub engine was developed BSA's 250cc C15. This in turn was continually enlarged and improved in stages until what had begun life as a utility 150, in the form of the B50 MX in the hands of Jeff Smith and motocross crew was winning world championships for BSA.

What has this to do with Triumph? For the 1973 ISDT, despite the fact that the BSA Group was dead on its feet and bringing down Triumph with it, America decided to field its own team. The event was to be held for the first time in the USA, initially in Texas until the desert venue was scrubbed as unsuitable, so the AMA transferred it to Massachusetts's damper climes in the mountainous Berkshire region. Remembering past glories with the old TR5 and in full knowledge of the potentially competitive new TR5T, Triumph America decided to have a go.

Had it not been for the highly respected BSA B50 MX developed frame with its renowned fine handling, it would not have happened, but it was hoped that this would in some way counter the poor power-to-weight ratio inflicted by the single carb 34bhp/7,000rpm T100A engine, by this time showing its age.

A solely American project, the parent factory gave no help whatsoever, largely because of bitter internal politics caused by impending closure,

The Triumph Tina scooter. It was simply a decade too late for the scooter boom, because technically it performed well, especially the constantly variable automatic gearing. Cyril Ayton

By the time the Adventurer appeared, it too was obsolete. Based on the BSA B50 MX rolling chassis and ISDT-developed, it performed superbly, but by 1973 it lacked competitive zip. TOC

but under Triumph America's Bob Tryon, the Americans dismantled then blueprinted a total of 12 machines in standard 490 and 650 class-eligible 504cc capacity. To make them competitive the bikes were heavily modified with Betor tele-forks, Rickman QD rear wheels and any amount of weight-saving dodges, which reduced them from 340lb (154.5kg) to little more than 300lb (136kg). Against all odds, and much more competitive machines from Europe, they did not win but the team finished well up. Another from the same batch was supplied to the British team which came home second to the Czech CZ team, which earned the US builders huge respect amongst the more experienced, and somewhat surprised, Brits.

Given further development time there seems little reason to doubt that with wholehearted Meriden co-operation the TR5T could have lost another 30lb (13.6kg) and put another 6bhp at least into a torquey power style. A 275lb (125kg), 40bhp (30kW) Trophy could well have put Triumph back amongst the off-road leaders again. All that remains of that final fling is the 1973/74 TR5T Adventurer trail bike. For all its fun-in-the-sun (US) and lug-through-the-mud (UK) aims, the Adventurer is a remarkable motorcycle to ride hard and far off road. While slightly old-fashioned, compared with Husqvarnas and Kawasakis of the same period, its perfect balance of power and handling return a rare safe pace across hazardous dirt tracks. The pedigree shows.

16

Into the maelstrom

*The other Turner, Jofeh, 'Slumberglade', BSA's death grip tightens,
the insanity of badge engineering, old school ties, the squandering
of talent, the Bandit/Fury debacle, Hopwood and Hele ignored*

Following active wartime service, Eric Turner joined the Blackburn Aircraft Company in 1946 as an accountant and by 1950, at 32 years of age, he was managing director. Nine years later he joined the board of the BSA Group and by 1961 had taken over from Jack Sangster as chairman as well as retaining his position as chief executive. He knew nothing whatsoever about the motorcycle industry and even less about its products. How and why an accountant was chosen to run a group of such diverse and highly specialised products, where for the sake of progress sagacious decision had of necessity to be partnered by promethean action, for motorcycle production with its increasingly volatile commercialism in 1961 contributed 34 per cent of the Group's total, is unclear. He may well have been recommended by BSA's worried auditors following Sir Bernard Docker's dismissal in 1956 and the consequential executive restructuring. The year prior to his chairmanship the BSA Group's profits had been a healthy £3,418,000.

The rot probably began when, during Turner's 1962 position as president of the British Cycle and Motor Cycle Association, Britain made a gift to Japan of virtually unrestricted export facilities into the UK without equally concessionary rights for British exports to Japan, although he did have the good grace to remark that such trading practices were 'inhospitable'. This, despite the fact that by 1960 Honda was making and selling 1,400,000 motorcycles annually, far in advance of the entire British industries' 155,523. The rot accelerated when, in 1967 Turner head-hunted Lionel Jofeh, chairman of Sperry Gyroscopes, (instrument makers to the aircraft industry) to take over BSA's motorcycle division (including Triumph) from Harry Sturgeon, also ex-aircraft industry, on Sturgeon's untimely death.

Triumph was much more dependent on exporting to the USA than was BSA. Triumph built a total of 32,144 machines of which 24,917 (77.5 per cent) went to America; BSA built 40,435 and sent 23,302 to the USA (57.6 per cent).

None of the three earned the respect of the existing management, who were experts in the business of making motorcycles. Jofeh in particular, also Turner, seemed to go out of their way to alienate their vital and dedicated middle management. Rather than concentrate on the core business of increasing motorcycle production at a time when the American market was howling for more, Turner turned his interest to the expensive introduction of non-contributory ancillaries, such as unsuitable computerisation. He also decided to lose BSA/Triumph's unparalleled storehouse of engineering know-how in the sinkhole of Umberslade Hall by the simple expedient of throwing money at it, to the tune of £3–4 million a year.

Here, in the grounds of this converted mansion, which quickly earned itself the byname 'Slumberglade', 300 largely newly engaged engineers committed themselves to fulfilling Jofeh's ambition of reinvigorating motorcycle design. Practically none of them had any experience of two powered wheels. When questioned Jofeh arrogantly proclaimed that this was a 'Very Good Thing', because his bright new engineers would ensure unprecedented rapid progress untainted by antiquated tradition. In June 1974, the author spoke to a retired BSA accountant and learned that by the accountant's reckoning the new tele-forks that had been adopted to partner the oil-carrying frame had cost in excess of £60,000 to develop. This equates to a current approximate £360,000! The fork itself was by no means exceptional (it leaked hydraulic fluid), so why had it cost so much, when any back yard special builder could have cobbled together a fork of superior quality from a half-decent selection of proprietary units? Because, in the opinion of the retired accountant, the greatest cost involved had been educating aircraft engineers into the mysteries of suspension. So much for the advantages of untainted progress.

It must be grasped throughout this story that despite its appalling man-

There is something ironic, surely, about one of the Monty Python *comedy team members, Carol Cleveland, pillion posing on the misconceived 1971 350cc twin-cam Triumph Fury. The man up front is Tony Lomas, Coventry speedway (stadium dirt-track) ace and Triumph technician.* TOC

agement by BSA, including the refusal to install new production machinery, Triumph at Meriden continued to show remarkable profitability, earning for itself a gross profit of £128,800,00?? in the two decades preceding 1970. But in 1969 BSA's motorcycle division had all but collapsed when thousands of unsold BSAs hung around in dealers while suppliers such as Lucas in dreadful irony declared no further interest in catering for such a small market. BSA

Group shares fell from 47s 3d to 6s 4d and no amount of old-school-tie golf-clubbing by BSA's top management (which until then, it was joked in the City of London, alone had been sustaining confidence in the old Small Heath hulk) could any longer forestall the inevitable.

To cap it all and despite the widely publicised installation of a brand-new computer-controlled production line into BSA's near-Dickensian (circa 1913) factory in 1970, production too

had gone belly up. In a debacle of wasted money and time, BSA witlessly and against the good advice of its existing engineers, attempted to modernise with computers a production system relying largely on its hopelessly antiquated machine tools. Production fell from 33,000 in 1970 to 7,200 a year later.

Lord Shawcross, who in 1968 had been brought in by BSA's bankers, Barclays with a guarantee of a new £10 million credit facility, sacked Jofeh in July 1971 and Eric Turner quickly followed. It was, though, too late. Shawcross commissioned the auditors, Cooper Bros & Co., for a company analysis. The findings for the imminent collapse were thus. 1) A lack of production and design harmony between Small Heath and Meriden. 2) Unexpectedly aggressive Japanese competition. 3) Insufficient statistical and costing information. 4) Inadequate budgeting leading to poor forecasting. 5) Lack of proper marketing data. 6) Poor co-ordination between marketing and production departments. 7) Lack of comprehensive information on inventory situation at home and abroad. 8) Particularly bad communications with American and home market dealers.

Then it was discovered that BSA and Triumph were incapable of supplying more than 73 per cent of their after market spares! Even so, Cooper Bros decided that Meriden promised greater future prosperity. Its premises were newer, more compact, at one level and therefore suitable for modernisation. More significantly, its workforce, as truculent as ever and still comparatively highly paid, radiated a high morale, unlike BSA's. Besides, the BSA motorcycle division had anticipated a 1972 profit of £782,000 but had recorded a £426,000 loss. The BSA Group's loss amounted to a staggering and insupportable £8,500,000 in 1971 and £3,300,000 in 1972.

By this time, BSA at Small Heath was manufacturing the three-cylinder engines, wheel hubs, fork yokes and innumerable other parts and shipping them to Meriden for assembly. What previously had been friendly, if fierce rivalry, turned to outright antagonism. A typical example was the discovery by Triumph that BSA was shipping scrap, or rejected components, to Meriden and invoicing Triumph for authentic components.

Brian Eustace, the new chief executive appointed by Barclays, after deliberation in his Report on the British Motorcycle Industry to the Department of Trade and Industry (DTI) recommended a new, modern, smaller factory at Small Heath with Meriden continuing to be used for manufacturing until Small Heath's completion. The new machines would be Bert Hopwood's series of modular machines built on his 22bhp (16kW) 200 or 250cc-based ohc single and which would rise by increments of additional cylinders to a 1,000 or 1,250cc V5.

Alas, this most long-term practical of all solutions was dropped when a querulous DTI approached Dennis Poore, who at the time appeared to be the saviour of the British motorcycle industry. He had turned Norton around after all, albeit with an engine almost as old in concept as the 5T, and only after asset stripping AJS, Matchless, Villiers, James and Francis Barnet. As the DTI has assessed the immediate export potential of BSA/Triumph at £10 million annually, and as there were approximately 3,500 employees involved plus huge numbers of subcontractors, the DTI was only too glad for Dennis Poore, representing Manganese Bronze Holdings (MBH), to take over the responsibility.

Poore agreed to form a new company, Norton Villiers Triumph. The British government, through the DTI, agreed to subscribe £4.8 million, MBH £3.6 million plus the whole of the £1.6 million existing share capital of Norton Villiers – a total share capital of £10.3 million.

Suspicious of their traditional enemy BSA, fearful of the DTI's preference for a rebuilt Small Heath and alarmed by unofficial warnings that Poore with the DTI's agreement wanted Meriden solely for its value as a building development site, the 1,750-strong Triumph workforce took over their own factory, claimed all rights to the marque and denied entrance to all and sundry.

Perhaps as a reaction to its almost

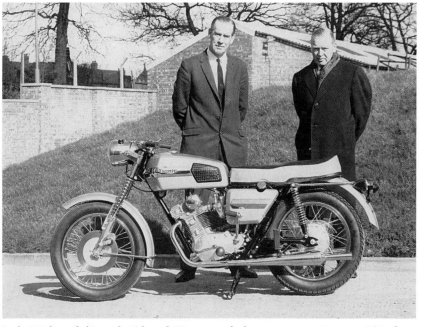

Jack Wickes (left) with Edward Turner and the prototype twin-cam 350 (later Bandit/Fury). It took 10 months to reach this stage from the blueprint. John Nelson

incalculable losses accumulated in the First World War, the Great Depression and the Second World War, Britain lost it head in the 1960s. While cultural lunacy seemed to benefit the entertainment and fashion industries, which flourished as they had not since the Reformation of the 17th century, practical crafts such as manufacturing and town planning received scant attention and reeled, dwindling into rough-handed decadence. No-one on the board of Great Britain Ltd,

seemed to care very much that its industrial division was in terminal collapse.

So an embittered and beleaguered Triumph workforce at Meriden for 18 months resisted all attempts to negotiate a commercially feasible solution. Dennis Poore was identified as the Devil's Disciple and the inheritor of all Meriden's woes. In reality the man, while as ruthlessly objective as any of his breed must be, would have been wise to have hired a diplomatic

Meriden in the 1970s. Of the 15 cars seen clearly, 14 are British . . . John Nelson

The final task in the Meriden production line was to set the ignition timing. John Nelson

spokesman because he frequently spoke so thoughtlessly that it appeared he was without humanitarian virtue. But he was trapped three ways between a government which wanted to be seen to do no wrong in the public eye yet was unwilling to provide sufficient aid for Triumph, his own employers Manganese Bronze Holdings whose resources were strictly limited, and by Meriden's implacable workforce. This irresolvable situation eventually destroyed all British government patience, and thus the financial establishment's, confidence in British motorcycle production forever.

In mid-1964, BSA hired an American management consultancy, McKinsey and thenceforth adopted its advised strategies. In doing so it almost completely ignored two men who were probably more suited to the task of advancing both BSA and Triumph's interests through pragmatic design and development, because of their grasp of all involved, than any others. They were, of course, Bert Hopwood and Doug Hele. Tragically, the business of modernising BSA's lack-lustre A65 and Triumph's ageing T120 twins went to Umberslade Hall under the tutelage of Stephan Bauer, who had headed the Norton Commando design team.

How much influence McKinsey had on Cooper Bros' analysis of BSA/Triumph's situation is anyone's guess, but Bauer's solution was the disastrous P39 spine frame, into which improperly developed geometry was hastily crammed both BSA and Triumph twin engines.

With few exceptions everyone hated it: BSA and Triumph fans because it destroyed marque individuality and therefore confused loyalties, riders under 5ft 10in (1,780mm) could not touch the ground with their

John Nelson, right, Meriden service manager, at the last stage of Triumph production – in the service area with one of his staff. Nelson has become one of Meriden's greatest historians. John Nelson

One of Triumph's dynamometers in Meriden's development department. In the dynamometer is a T20 engine, which because of its competition carburettor and air cleaner, appears to be of US desert racing specification. John Nelson

feet when seated, BSA and Triumph dealers for the same reason, plus the fact that its appalling build quality piled up warranty claims to a degree that not even Lucas's early ac electrics could match, competition riders because the over-high frame was weak and cracked, and its oil-carrying capacity was insufficient. The out-moded drum brakes were poor, the five-speed gearboxes weak, the switchgear sloppy.

To cap all that, BSA had, in 1970, launched its Ariel 3 moped trike in a blaze of costly publicity. To be fair it was reliable, thanks to its dependable Dutch-built Anka two-stroke engine, but BSA had forgotten during its development in the big hands and powerful legs of its test riders, that its target buyer would be female – house-wife or commuter. As practically no women had the strength necessary to heave the weighty little monster into life it flopped as surely as a hot beached flounder.

Then the following year, the world's disbelieving motorcycle press and more gullible media saw the final spasm of a dying pachyderm – the brand-new 350cc dohc twin BSA Bandit/Triumph Fury – announced at a reprehensibly costly reception in one of London's palatial hotels in Hyde Park.

When, in 1964, Edward Turner retired as BSA/Triumph's managing director, although continuing as a non-executive director of the Group, he continued to take a lively interest in motorcycle design. Through his own design company he began draw-ing up a brand-new model designed to challenge the Japanese. The BSA Bandit/Triumph Fury 350 was smooth, fast and powerful and the frame suspi-ciously light. In fact the entire model was very light because of Turner's brief to produce a 350 that would beat the

Japanese on performance and price. But further testing revealed an insuffi-ciently robust motorcycle. So the pro-ject was handed to Doug Hele, who, a loyal gentleman to his core, when questioned by the author denied he had to do much more than 'clean it up a bit'. According to Percy Tait, who did most of the test riding, the Hele Bandit/Fury, although stronger, would not manage 100mph while the Turner prototype managed 117mph.

In the event, Hele, with Hopwood's blessing, utterly transformed the machine. He rejigged the crankshaft and crankcases, cam drive, valve layout and lubrication system until the essentially brand-new engine pro-duced a healthy 34bhp (25.3kW) at 8,500rpm in complete reliability and ran smoothly. The spindly Turner frame was changed for one frequently likened to a Rob North Daytona triple item. Maybe, but in 1951, shortly after he left Norton for the first time, Hele had been one of the design team behind Hopwood's ill-fated (but tech-nically and dynamically impressive) single-cylinder 250cc BSA dohc racer, whose 33bhp (24.6kW), 248lb (112.5kg) was enough to circulate the British Motor Industries Association (MIRA) test track 130 times at an average of 100mph (161km/h). That racing Beesa employed a full loop duplex cradle frame by Hele himself, very like a Rob North item but pre-ceding it by two decades, and similar in all fundamentals to the final Bandit/Fury's, apart from the latter's commercially enforced compromises.

They built 100 pre-production models and all who rode them loved them. By this time the Group's losses were such that BSA's bankers had taken over and regardless of its quali-ties or its Meriden origins, no new motorcycle warranted further capitali-sation. After all, it was yet another Triumph 350 . . .

17

The twins bow out

In view of the 30-year production life of the bigger Triumph twins, it is impossible to comment at length on all model variations in a book, let alone a single chapter. For this purpose, Steve Wilson's recent book *Bonneville T120/T140* (Haynes) is recommended. Here though is the chronological genealogy in brief.

Triumph Meriden 650cc models, 1950 through 1974

6T Thunderbird: 1950 through 1966. The original 650 and up to 1958 probably the sweetest natured tourer Triumph, maybe Britain, ever produced.

T110: 1954 through 1961. The first sports 650, 42bhp single carb and tractable yet fast, but in its first two-year production with an iron cylinder head easily overheated at speed.

TR6 Trophy: 1956 through 1970. A T110 engine in a TR5 Trophy frame. Possibly the most vivacious motorcycle ever made. Thanks to its American desert racing success it was the bike that made Triumph its fortune. Unforgivably in Britain after 1963, it lost its competition edge entirely.

T120 Bonneville: 1959 through 1970. 46bhp. The first twin-carb sportster based on a T110 engine employing a T100C-type 'splayed' head. Innumerable variations, but the best is probably the 1968-on model with its individually adjustable twin c/b assemblies. Legendary scratcher of Olympian nature and record.

T120R Bonneville: 1963 through 1973. 46bhp. Standard American Bonneville.

TR6R Trophy: 1966 through 1970. 44bhp. Single-carb American-styled desert racer, west coast. Mercurial.

TR6C: 1966 through 1967. 42bhp. As above but East Coast trail/enduro style. Docile dynamite.

T120C: 1963 through 1965. 48bhp. American desert racing Bonneville. *The* 'Desert Sled'. Lusty.

T120TT: 1964 through 1967. 50/55bhp. Works-prepared American flat track racer. Evil.

T120R Thruxton: 1965. 50/55bhp. British production racer works prepared. Mythic.

TR6R Tiger: 1971 through 1973. Undistinguished single carb spine frame Beezumph. Gauche. Low production quality. Poor handling.

TR6C Trophy: As above with trail bike styling.

TR6CV Trophy: 1972 through 1973. As above. V = five-speed gearbox.

TR6RV Tiger: 1972 through 1973. As above, road styling.

T120R Bonneville: 1971 through 1973. Beezumph Bonneville.

T120V Bonneville: 1973 through 1974.

Triumph Meriden 750cc models, 1973 through 1974

T140V Bonneville: 724cc (first batch only) 744cc consequent, 52bhp twin-carb sport tourer. Better received in America for its competition potential than in Britain. Low production quality but smooth.

T140RV: As above, single carb.

Triumph Workers Co-operative models, 1974 through 1983

T140V Bonneville: 1974 through 1978, as previous.

T140RV: 1975 through 1975, as previous. T140 Silver Jubilee Bonneville: 1977. Glamorous cosmetics with royal pretensions.

T140D Bonneville Special: 1979 through 1980. Stylistic with cast alloy wheels.

T140E Bonneville: 1978 through 1982. Left-side gear lever, electronic ignition and electric starting as extra.

T140ES Bonneville: 1980 through 1983. As above but alloy wheels and electric starting as standard.

T140 Executive: 1980 through 1982. As above but with touring fairing and panniers.

T140TSS: 1982 through 1983. 57bhp eight-valve adaptation of 1960s Weslake conversion. Potentially the best of all Triumph twins let down by inadequate development and material quality.

T140TSX: As above with US styling.

Harris-built 'Devon' Triumphs, 1985 through 1988

T140 Bonneville: as previous models but incorporating a multitude of unavoidably imported components.

TECHNICAL DATA

MODEL	Tiger Cub (T20)	Sports Cub (T20S/H)	Twenty-one (3TA)	Tiger 90 (T90)	Speed Twin (5TA)	Tiger 100 (T100S/S)	Thunderbird (6T)	Trophy (TR6)	Bonneville 120 (T120)
Engine Type	O.H.V.	O.H.V.	O.H.V.	O.H.V.	O.H.V.	O.H.V.	O.H.V.	O.H.V.	O.H.V.
Number of Cylinders	1	1	2	2	2	2	2	2	2
Bore/Stroke, m.m.	63×64	63×64	58.25×65.5	58.25×65.5	69×65.5	69×65.5	71×82	71×82	71×82
Bore/Stroke, ins.	2.48×2.52	2.48×2.52	2.29×2.58	2.29×2.58	2.72×2.58	2.72×2.58	2.79×3.23	2.79×3.23	2.79×3.23
Capacity, cu. cms.	199	199	349	349	490	490	649	649	649
Capacity, cu. ins.	12.2	12.2	21.2	21.2	30	30	40	40	40
Compression ratio	7:1	9:1	7.5:1	9:1	7:1	9:1	7.5:1	8.5:1	8.5:1
B.H.P. and R.P.M.	10@6,000	14.5@6,500	18.5@6,500	27@7,500	27@6,500	34@7,000	37@6,700	40@6,500	47@6,700
Engine Sprocket Teeth—Solo	19	19	26	26	26	26	29	29	29
Clutch Sprocket Teeth	48	48	58	58	58	58	58	58	58
Gearbox Sprocket Teeth	17	17	18	17	20	18	20	19	19
Sidecar (G/Box Sprocket)	—	—	—	—	—	—	18	17	17
Rear Sprocket Teeth	46	48	46	46	46	46	46	46	46
R.P.M. 10 M.P.H. Top Gear	986	955	790	808	711	763	616	634	649
							Solo / S/C	Solo / S/C	Solo / S/C
Gear Ratios—Top	6.84	7.13	5.70	6.04	5.13	5.70	4.60 / 5.11	4.84 / 5.41	4.84 / 5.41
„ „ —Third	9.04	8.56	6.95	7.36	6.26	6.95	5.47 / 6.08	5.76 / 6.44	5.76 / 6.44
„ „ —Second	14.05	13.37	9.18	9.71	8.26	9.18	7.77 / 8.64	8.17 / 9.15	8.17 / 9.15
„ „ —First	20.40	19.8	14.14	14.96	12.71	14.14	11.43 / 12.48	11.81 / 13.40	11.81 / 13.40
Carburettor—Make	Amal	Amal	Amal	Amal	Amal	Amal	Amal	Amal	Twin Amal
„ —Type	32/1	376/272	375/62	376/300	375/35	376/273	376/303	389/97	389/203
Front Chain Size	⅜"×.225"×.25" Duplex	⅜"×.225"×.25" Duplex	⅜"×.225"×.25" Duplex	⅜"×.225"×.25" Duplex	⅜"×.225"×.25" Duplex	⅜"×.225"×.25" Duplex	⅜"×.225"×.25" Duplex	⅜"×.225"×.25" Duplex	⅜"×.225"×.25" Duplex
Rear Chain Size	½"×.205"×.335"	½"×.205"×.335"	⅝"×⅜"×.40"	⅝"×⅜"×.40"	⅝"×⅜"×.40"	⅝"×⅜"×.40"	⅝"×⅜"×.40"	⅝"×⅜"	⅝"×⅜"
Tyres—Front, ins.	3.25×17	3.00×19	3.25×17	3.25×18	3.25×17	3.25×18	3.25×18	3.25×19	3.25×18
„ —Rear, ins.	3.25×17	3.50×18	3.50×17	3.50×18	3.50×17	3.50×18	3.50×18	4.00×18	3.50×18
Brake Diameter—ins. (cms.)	5½" (13.97)	5½" (13.97)	7" (17.78)	7" (17.78)	7" (17.78)	7" (17.78)	8" F (20.32) 7" R (17.78)	8" F (20.32) 7" R (17.78)	8" F (20.32) 7" R (17.78)
Finish	Hi-Fi Scarlet/Silver	Hi-Fi Scarlet/Silver	Silver Beige	Pacific Blue/Silver	Black/Silver	Burnished Gold/White	Black/Silver	Burnished Gold/White	Pacific Blue/Silver
Seat Height—ins.	29"	30"	29½"	30"	29½"	30"	30"	30½"	30½"
„ „ —cms.	(73.7)	(76.2)	(74.5)	(76.2)	(74.5)	(76.2)	(76.2)	(77.5)	(77.5)
Wheelbase—ins.	49"	50"	52¾"	53½"	52¾"	53½"	55"	55½"	55"
„ —cms.	(124.5)	(127)	(134)	(136)	(134)	(136)	(139.6)	(141)	(139.6)
Length—ins.	77"	78½"	81"	83¼"	81"	83¼"	84"	84½"	84"
„ —cms.	(195.5)	(199.3)	(206)	(211.5)	(206)	(211.5)	(213.5)	(214.5)	(213.5)
Width—ins.	25"	26"	27"	26½"	27"	26½"	27½"	27"	27"
„ —cms.	(63.5)	(66)	(68.5)	(67.3)	(68.5)	(67.3)	(70)	(68.5)	(68.5)
Clearance—ins.	5"	8¼"	5"	7½"	5"	7½"	5"	7⅛"	5"
„ —cms.	(12.7)	(21)	(12.7)	(19)	(12.7)	(19)	(12.7)	(18.1)	(12.7)
Weight—lbs.	215	223	340	336	341	336	369	363	363
„ —kilos	(94)	(101)	(154.6)	(152.8)	(155)	(152.8)	(167)	(165)	(615)
Petrol—Galls.	3	3	3	3	3	3	4	4	4
„ —Litres	(13.5)	(13.5)	(13.5)	(13.5)	(13.5)	(13.5)	(18)	(18)	(18)
Oil—Pints	2¾	2¾	5	5	5	5	5	5	5
„ —Litres	(1.55)	(1.55)	(2.8)	(2.8)	(2.8)	(2.8)	(2.8)	(2.8)	(2.8)

Details of high performance equipment for certain models published separately

TRIUMPH THE GOLD MEDAL RANGE

In the 1964 International Six Days' Trial held in East Germany, the Triumph Team won four gold medals and a Manufacturers Team award. All the Triumph factory riders were chosen for the British Teams, and finished without loss of marks in this, the most arduous event in the motorcycling competitions calendar.

The U.S.A. Vase 'A' Team competing in this event for the first time ever, gained along with their new Triumph machines, two gold and one silver medals.

A SELECTION OF TRIUMPH SUCCESSES IN 1964

Of the many Triumph successes during 1964, the following results were achieved in events officially approved for factory entries.

Victory Cup Trial

Premier Award	Ray Sayer	Tiger Cub

Bemrose Trophy Trial

200 c.c. Award	Scott Ellis	Tiger Cub
500 c.c. Award	Roy Peplow	Tiger 100

Scottish Six Days' Trial

200 c.c. Award	Ray Sayer	Tiger Cub

Welsh Three Days' Trial

Premier Award	John Giles	Trophy TR6
Gold Medal	Ken Heanes	Trophy TR6
Gold Medal	Roy Peplow	Tiger 90
Silver Medal	Ray Sayer	Tiger 100
Manufacturers Team Award	John Giles	Trophy TR6
	Ken Heanes	Trophy TR6
	Roy Peplow	Tiger 90

Army Three Days' Trial

Premier Award	John Giles	Trophy TR6
Manufacturers Team Award	John Giles	Trophy TR6
	Ken Heanes	Trophy TR6
	Roy Peplow	Tiger 90

International Six Days' Trial

Gold Medal	Roy Peplow	Tiger 90
Gold Medal	Ray Sayer	Tiger 90
Gold Medal	John Giles	Trophy TR6
Gold Medal	Ken Heanes	Trophy TR6
*Gold Medal	Dave Ekins	Tiger 100
*Gold Medal	Cliff Coleman	Trophy TR6
*Silver Medal	John Steen	Tiger 100
Manufacturers Team Award	Roy Peplow	Tiger 90
	John Giles	Trophy TR6
	Ken Heanes	Trophy TR6

*U.S.A. Vase 'A' Team Members.

World Speed Record quoted in this catalogue was attained at Bonneville Salt Flats, Utah, in September 1962.

This page from a 1965 brochure, lists the range's technical specification and a summary of the factory's remarkable achievements in international competition. Author

From a factory brochure of 1955, a cut-away illustrating the salient features of what was then the world's fastest high-volume produced sports bike (Vincent Black Shadow excepted), the iron-engined T110. Author

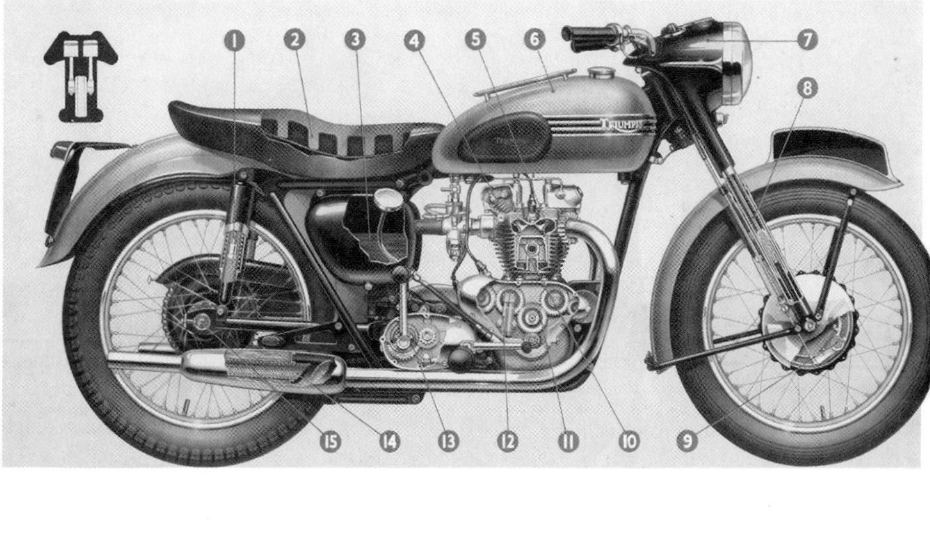

POPULAR FEATURES OF TRIUMPH DESIGN

1. Swinging Arm rear suspension with hydraulic damping readily adjustable for varying loads.
2. Triumph "Two Level" Twinseat. Soft latex foam covered with black waterproof Vynide. Specially shaped steel base rigidly mounted. The ideal seat solo or with passenger.
3. Combined unit exclusive to Triumph—incorporating oil tank, air cleaner, battery and tool box. Smooth full width exterior, easy to clean and neat in appearance.
4. Fully enclosed overhead valve gear lubricated under pressure. Alloy rocker boxes with accessible threaded valve covers for easy tappet inspection.
5. The famous Triumph hemispherical cylinder heads with large diameter inclined valves. Remarkable performance proves the outstanding efficiency of this design.
6. Shapely 4 gallon Petrol Tank with plated quick release filler. Useful tank top luggage grid. Chromium styling bands and rubber knee grips.
7. Triumph Nacelle (Patent No. 647670) encloses headlamp unit in neat streamlined shell integral with top of forks. All switchgear and instruments rubber mounted.
8. Triumph Telescopic Forks, long action with hydraulic damping. Ensure a comfortable ride and accurate steering at all speeds.
9. The Triumph Front Brake has always been renowned for its power, smoothness and safe operation. Large diameter cast iron drum with polished alloy anchor plate. Finger adjustment.
10. Alloy full skirted pistons with internal strengthening ribs. Two scraper and one oil control rings. "H" section connecting rods of RR56 alloy with massive plain big-end bearings.
11. Drives to the camshafts, magneto and dynamo are by a selectively assembled train of gearwheels. Accuracy in manufacture ensures silent operation and complete reliability.
12. The specially designed double plunger type oil pump driven from the inlet camshaft spindle delivers, under pressure, a constant supply of oil to the engine bearings and overhead valve gear, returning it subsequently to the oil tank.
13. The famous Triumph 4 speed Gearbox with positive foot operated gearchange. Multi-plate clutch with cork inserts operating in oil, sweet in action and light to handle. Polished alloy outer cover. Rubber pad type shock absorber in clutch.
14. Exclusive to Triumph, barrel shaped silencers heavily chromium plated. Particularly efficient in use, providing a very subdued but pleasing exhaust note.
15. The Triumph Q.D. Rear Wheel ends the bogey of difficult wheel removal. The wheel can be extracted by withdrawal of the spindle leaving the rear brake and chain untouched.

EXTRAS

PROP STAND. Retained by spring, out as a prop or folded back. For all models.
PILLION FOOTRESTS. For all models. Folding type, rubber covered.
TWIN CARBURETTERS. For Tiger 100 only.
QUICKLY DETACHABLE REAR WHEEL. For 5T, 6T, T100, T110, TR5.
TWINSEAT for "Terrier".

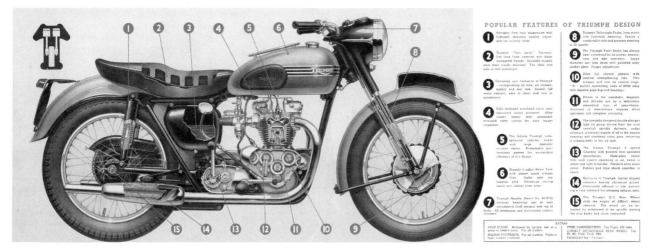

TRIUMPH

The Best Motorcycle in the World

The Triumph "Bonneville 120" offers the highest perform-ance available today from a standard production motorcycle. Developed from the famous Tiger 110, the 650 c.c. two-carburetter engine is individually bench tested and produces 46 BHP at 6500 r.p.m. This is the motorcycle for the really

Bonneville 120

knowledgeable enthusiast who can appreciate and use the power provided. At the same time it is tractable and quiet in the Triumph tradition and is a worthy addition to the range.

TRIUMPH ENGINEERING CO. LTD., MERIDEN WORKS, ALLESLEY, COVENTRY, ENGLAND

Printed in England   Ref. 444/58

TRIUMPH

Bonneville 120

SPECIFICATION

Engine 650 c.c. o.h.v. vertical twin with two gear driven camshafts. Alloy splayed port cylinder head with two carburetters, cast iron barrel, high compression pistons. New one piece forged crankshaft with bolt on central flywheel. "H" section RR56 alloy connecting rods with plain big-ends. Dry sump lubrication with plunger type pump and pressure indicator. Gear driven dynamo and magneto with manual control. Polished aluminium oil bath primary chaincase.
Gearbox Triumph design and manu-facture. Shafts and gears of hardened nickel and nickel-chrome steel. Positive stop footchange. Multiplate clutch with indestructible Neolangite linings and rubber pad shock absorber.
Frame Brazed cradle type frame with swinging arm suspension,

hydraulically damped and adjustable. "Easylift" centre and prop stands (latter optional extra). Provision for anti-theft lock to steering head.
Forks Triumph design telescopic pattern with hydraulic damping and steering damper.
Fuel Tanks Handsome large capacity all-steel welded tanks. Quick release fillers. Oil tank in "one-piece" unit with battery and tool container. Froth tower on oil tank.
Nacelle (Patent No. 647670) Triumph design integral with top of forks enclosing headlamp instruments and switchgear. Instruments intern-ally illuminated.
Brakes Front: Full width hub, heavily finned, incorporating efficient 8 inch brake. Rear: 7 inch diameter with cast-iron drum integral with rear sprocket.

Wheels & Mudguards Triumph design wheels with plated spokes and rims. Fully valanced rear guard and side lifting handles.
Lighting Equipment Lucas 6 volt 60 watt dynamo with ball bearing armature. 12 a.h. battery, powerful headlamp with combined reflector/front lens assembly, "pre-focus" bulb and adjustable rim. Wide angle rear/stop light with reflector.
Speedometer Smiths 120 m.p.h. (220 Km.p.h.) chronometric type with r.p.m. scale, internal illumina-tion and trip recorder.
Handlebar Comfortable shape with quick action twistgrip and adjustable friction control. Integral horn push. Ball ended clutch and brake levers with cable adjusters.
Twinseat Triumph design, Latex foam cushion covered in black water-proof "Vynide".
Tools Kit of good quality tools and tyre inflator.

TECHNICAL DATA

Engine type	O.H.V.	Front chain size	½ × ·305
No. of cylinders	2	Rear ,, ,,	⅜ × ⅜
Bore/Stroke mm.	71 × 82	Tyres, Dunlop —front ins.	3·25 × 19
ins.	2·79 × 3·23	rear	3·50 × 19
Capacity cms.	649	Brake dia.—ins (cms) front	8 (20·32)
ins.	40	rear	7 (17·78)
Compression Ratio	8·5 : 1	Finish	Pearl Grey/
B.H.P. and R.P.M.	46 at 6500		Tangerine/
Sprocket teeth—Engine	24		Black
Clutch	43		
Gearbox	18	Seat height ins. (cms.)	30½ (77·5)
Rear wheel	46	Wheelbase ,, ,,	55¾ (141·6)
R.P.M. 10 m.p.h. top gear	594	Length ,, ,,	85½ (217)
Gear ratios—Top	4·57	Width ,, ,,	28½ (72)
Third	5·45	Clearance ,, ,,	5 (12·7)
Second	7·75	Weight—lbs. (kilos)	404 (181·8)
First	11·2	Petrol—galls (litres)	4 (18)
Carburetters (2)	Amal	Oil—pints ,,	5 (2·8)
	376/204		

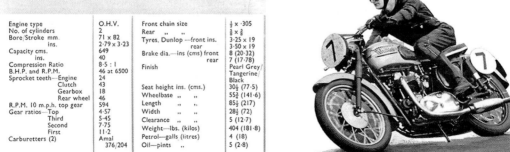

The first T120 Bonneville of 1958 is now a rare and valuable collector's item and differs in many details from later models, such as the headlamp nacelle and the twin carburettors' remote float. Author

Technical Information
Bulletin No. 2

PREPARATION AND ASSEMBLY OF

5T, T100, TR5, 6T, T110, TR6 & T120 ENGINES FOR MAXIMUM PERFORMANCE

A number of special high performance components are available for the above Triumph machines which may be fitted to increase the power output. This Bulletin tabulates and co-relates all the necessary technical information that is available, so that the owner who wishes to increase the performance of his machine may do so, starting from a point experience has shown to be the best. These alterations are not suitable for machines which are to be retained for normal road use.

If he follows the sequence outlined he will achieve the optimum for the particular chosen condition, after which the maximum will be gained by his own experience and endeavours.

WORKSHOP TOOLS

It will be assumed that the following items are in the owner's possession and that he has both the experience and necessary workshop facilities :—

Piston ring clips.
Engine timing disc and pointer.
Dial test indicator.
Set of Feeler gauges.
Camwheel remover and replacer Z.89.

Crankshaft pinion remover Z.121.
Clutch and magneto gear remover DA.50/1.
Triumph Instruction Manual for Twin
Cylinder Models (appropriate for the year
of the machine's manufacture).

For all dismantling and assembly procedure follow the instructions as detailed in the Instruction Manual. The procedure detailed hereafter is in respect of the non-standard high performance equipment only.

Once Edward Turner had been forced by overwhelming public consensus to accept that by winning races Triumph twin sales improved, factory engineers prepared a series of engineering instructions that have never been bettered. This is part of the opening page of the most highly regarded. Author

By the mid-1960s, the British TR6 had changed into a wholly road-going single-carburettor 'Bonneville'. In many respects, thanks to improved carburation under 6,000rpm, it offered a superior highway performance. This is a 1968 version. TOC

The American TR6 remained much truer to its origins, even though by 1969 its dominance of flat track and desert racing was in decline. TOC

The American Tiger 650 was what the British knew as the TR6 road version, 1969. TOC

Arguably the last of Meriden's home-developed, the Doug Hele-framed Bonnevilles were the best ever. This is the American T120R, but the British was the same although with lower, narrow handlebars. By this time the ignition system was reliable! TOC

Arguably the first of the 'Slumberglade' (Umberslade Hall) Bonnevilles were the worst ever because they had lost their pedigree through unforgivable dilution with identikit BSAs, 1971. TOC

This mess of improbable potage is what the BSA corporate mind saw as a Triumph ISDT/desert racer, the degenerated 650 Trophy of 1971. TOC

Although unsympathetically styled, once the Umberslade Bonnevilles had been developed, they performed excellently. Their oil-in-frame chassis may have been too tall, but it was torsionally stiff, the suspension was excellent and the conical drum brakes superb (but only if prepared by a brake expert); 1972. TOC

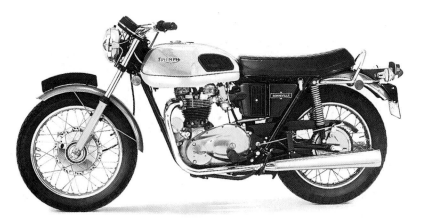

In 1973, the first 750cc T140s appeared. They were widely acclaimed by American motorcyclists who appreciated their strong torque characteristics for flat track and the greater material robustness of their engines for the drag strip. The British preferred the greater nimbleness of the Meriden T120s and the vastly superior speed and stamina of the triples for road racing. TOC

The engine of John Giles's TR6 which, in 1956, carried him to an ISDT gold medal. This was in 1965 when Triumph still had the wit to leave ignition reliability well alone in the form of a Lucas Wader magneto (trials competition quality) with its moisture trapping breather. Note also the waterproofed Amal carb', the armoured fuel line, the chain oil lubricator, the rubberless footrests, the heavy knee pads, the wired-on-and-sealed cylinder head, and the compressed air cylinder for tyre inflation. Brian Nicholls

Despite being little more restyled TR7Vs, the 750 Tiger Trails could give a good account of themselves off road, but by 1981, they were two decades too late. Author

18

The last post

T100 triple experiments, the PI, the TT100, two modular ranges,
Jack Wickes, Daytona racing, Percy Tait, Gary Nixon, Rob North
and the frame, Slippery Sam, The Quadrant, Vetter, NVT.

The story of the Trident, and its BSA counterpart the Rocket Three, is one without parallel in motorcycling's rich history. Primarily it is one of high romance, involving as do all the finest romances, the secret endeavours of devoted loyalists, a leadership riven by jealousies, disintegrating empires and the chivalric battle of brave yeomen against blighted knights. Eventually though, it exemplifies the triumph of sheer, damned, blundering, corporate imbecility of a magnitude against which no individuals may survive.

By the early 1960s, American demands for a multi-cylinder 750 were persistent. While the 650 twins still ruled flat track and desert, record breaking and road sales needed something with greater potential. As early as 1963 Hopwood and Hele, then subordinate to Triumph's managing director Edward Turner, began low-key experimenting with a 750 triple, the P1. Despite its unexpected success as an experimental machine, when Turner learned of it he, in his inimitable style, rejected it out of hand. By 1963, Turner had become aware of the inherent flaws of his 650 twins. In fact, he had always known of their weaknesses, disliking power tuning much beyond the Thunderbird's modest output and submitting to it solely, and always fearfully, on the strength of American persuasion and the competition-focused US market's profitability.

Smitten by America and with one eye on the future, Turner by this time had begun attempting to sell his own multi-cylinder range, even to the extent of approaching American companies as possible manufacturers within the USA. No-one, least of all the BSA Group, seemed impressed. His range would be modular but based around a 750cc four, which was the American Trade desire too. It should not be confused with Hopwood's own modular design aspirations.

It will be remembered that the old 5T-based T100 was dropped because its cramped combustion chambers restricted breathing and its long stroke induced excessive piston speed at high engine revs. Old fashioned though the engine was, its mere three-year obsolescence ensured adequate parts availability and the exercise was in any case mainly exploratory on the nature of what Hele especially saw as the most promising compromise engine type for a new Triumph – a transverse three. Both Hopwood and Hele were all-too aware of Turner's, as well as the BSA Group board's, myopic attitude regarding other than minimal research and development investment.

To everyone's surprise the cobbled-up 63 x 80mm 750cc machine went like the wind, to such an extent that, rather as the 1937 500cc 5T had surpassed the sum of its 1932 250cc 2/1 origins, so the triple's performance far exceeded the sum of its T100 donors. So much so that even in its primitive state it was capable of 124mph (200km/h): on every fast test run by tester Harry Woolridge it chewed up its Dunlop K70 tyres, which led to the development of Dunlop's TT100. It also boiled its engine oil, being equipped with an iron cylinder head. But it did turn out 58bhp (43.2kW) at 7,250rpm at its crankshaft, and that was not to be taken lightly because the T100 made do with 32bhp (24kW) at 6,500rpm. 45 per cent more power from a 33 per cent capacity increase is a marvellous bonus not often given to engineers.

In BSA Group history, 1964 was to be more of a headstone than a milestone year. Edward Turner retired, Harry Sturgeon replaced him and news broke of Kawasaki's dohc 750 four, later to become the 900cc Z1, and of Honda's CB750 Four. Sturgeon panicked – a not too strong a verb. Hopwood allayed his fears with news that he had an experimental three-cylinder engine ready for development and was given the instruction to get it into production without delay.

Hele in particular was thoroughly alarmed because when he and Hopwood had initiated experimentation it was with the understanding that the transverse three in production would, for the sake of economical and accurate assembly technique, require a horizontally split crankcase. They also had in mind a short-stroke, toothed belt-driven sohc layout. The 750 would form the spearhead of

Hopwood's proposed new modular range. Alas, the perceived efficaciousness of the experimental triple proved too tempting to executives with neither knowledge of nor much interest in motorcycles or engineering.

Turner's brilliant pragmatism had enabled him to perceive that in the design of the 5T lay the simple assembly method of the existing singles. Both, after all, employed a single crankshaft supported by two main bearings in each of the two crankcase halves. Sturgeon, however, for all his energy and wit, was not an engineer, and was unable, or maybe unwilling in the view of new plant capitalisation, to appreciate the significance of the technicalities involved. These were stupendous, as time was to reveal, beyond the scope of commerce and its mortal servants to overcome.

A Trident engine's lower part comprises seven main aluminium castings, of which the crankcase forms three parts. These, unlike a single or most parallel twins, necessitate that proper crankshaft alignment is achievable only following the most meticulous matching of crankcases, machining, jig-boring and alignment during final assembly.

To the immense chagrin of Meriden, BSA built all the three-cylinder engines because of what was supposed to be, but never was, its modernised assembly line. All manner of vital production techniques were mismanaged. They caused transmission failures and vibration from misaligned sprockets caused by incorrect sprocket machining; similar carelessness and consequences from crankshafts; the familiar unreliable performance from Lucas's cheapskate

Top: *A standard Trident of 1970 in British specification. The 'Dan Dare' silencers, often despised for their appearance, remain unrivalled for performance and sound.* TOC

Middle: *Following a tidal wave of protest over the Trident's angular styling, from US trade and enthusiasts alike, Meriden 'Bonnevilised' the American triple. This is a 1973 model.* TOC

Bottom: *And this is the 1973 British version.* TOC

The author enjoying the novel experience of a true multi-cylinder British machine shortly after the Trident's launch. Author

Left: In its final form the Trident was developed by NVT and the Meriden Co-operative into the electric-started, BSA-originated sloper engined T160 of 1976. Author

Below: Rivals! Two of the greatest production machine racers of the period. Peter Williams on a works 750cc Norton Commando chases Ray Pickrel (wearing Percy Tait's helmet) on a works 750 Trident around one of the most evocative bends, Creg Ny Baa, on the world's greatest ever road racing course, the IoM TT Mountain circuit. The event is the 1971 PR TT. Williams put up the fastest lap at 101.06mph (162.63km/h) but Pickrel eventually won at 100.07mph (161.03km/h). Brian Nicholls

triple contact breaker ignition; premature shock-absorber rubber wear; diaphragm clutch simultaneous drag and slip, as well as the usual leaky Triumph pushrod tunnel seals.

By 1975, NVT at Kitts Green had modernised the entire package with an electric starter and five gears, but by this time all hopes for a bright future had gone. The bike always had been obsolete because of its four-decade-old design origins, which could no longer cope with increasing government demands for low exhaust emissions and sound levels coupled to a parallel buyer's one for greater power. Nor could it adapt to the modern assembly techniques needed to keep the price down. One great irony of regression was witnessed in the construction of the T160's crankshaft. BSA's iron foundry was one of

A motorcycle which like no other in the history of racing, won the hearts of British enthusiasts, the legendary Slippery Sam, which through the 1970s utterly dominated the 750cc class of production machine racing. Here, Tony, one of the Jefferies motorcycling dynasty, urges Sam to first place in the 1973 IoM 750 PR TT, at a race speed of 95.62mph (153.87km/h). Brian Nicholls

the best in Britain and staffed by craftsmen of the highest calibre. They, more than any other contributing team, gave the Trident its single most valuable feature – its one-piece, hot-twisted, 120 x 3 crankshaft. Like all truly great developments, the simpli-city of this unique technology seemed unimpressive until much later in the engine's life when, after years of victorious racing and expansion into 1,000cc conversions of double the power output, did it dawn on most of us that these cranks never, ever broke.

Few racing motorcyclists in the history of motorcycling have displayed greater talent or courage than America's Gary Nixon, here seen on a Trident scrapping titanically with Tony Jefferies on a Commando at Mallory Park's 1970 Race of the Year. Brian Nicholls

But when Small Heath was sold by NVT they forgot about the crankshaft forge, so from thereon the 'shaft had to be built up at ludicrous cost for the Workers Co-operative workforce at Meriden by a specialist engineering company employing over 50 separate assembly operations.

Hele's other great contribution to the Trident's stamina, invariably over-looked, was his replacement of Triumph's plunger oil pump with its ruinous penchant for cavitating under stress, by an Eaton-type rotary pump with three times the capacity and guaranteed flow under all conditions.

Hele, moved from Meriden to Kitts Green by NVT, found great irony in his appointed task. He was offered the job of developing the 750 Norton Commando into an 850 (actually 830cc). When he inspected its crank-shaft he saw it was the same over-stressed item that he had so disliked back at his time with the old Norton company and now they had wanted him to turn its 650 into a 750. Instead of which he moved to BSA/Triumph and began to modern-ise the T150. Without access to modern production methods he realised his task was thankless, but always a loyal man, he set to. The T160 he drew up was a fine machine, albeit one penalised by the additional 40lb (18kg) weight of an electric starter and its associated parts, and a very high price indeed. Certainly its high-speed stability was a further improvement over the T150's already fine handling.

Once Sturgeon had given the pro-ject his blessing, the P1 was taken out of hiding and the P2, the first true prototype triple, was built. Among innumerable modifications, its bore and stroke were changed to 67 x 70mm. Hopwood by this time was working on a new 500 twin and 250 single of modular intent, so under-standably the new 750 would follow suit. The 250 was BSA's C15, to develop in 1968 into Triumph's TR25W range. Unfortunately, by the time the 500 twin's plans were announced, the Americans had started campaigning T100As at Daytona and complained that having just got them AMA homologated, they had no desire to start all over again for the Hopwood modular twin. So it was quietly dropped, by which time the P2's 67 x 70mm cylinder dimensions had been established.

Dennis Poore was completely disinterested in Hopwood and Hele's modular package for Triumph's future, being under the spell of Cosworth's new four-cylinder F1 car engine which he saw adaptable by Norton as replacement for Norton's 30-year-old twin. Soon after that Hopwood retired, Hele turned in his final working days to British Seagull, a British manufacturer of utility boat outboard two-strokes and Triumph's great unsung hero, Jack Wickes, found his skills were welcomed in America.

One can only wish that the Trident had adopted the T100A's 69 x 65mm dimensions, which is more-or-less what the progressive and far-sighted Hopwood and Hele had planned at 70 x 64mm, because its free breathing combustion chambers would have released even more power. Moreover, at 7,500rpm its piston speed would have been a stress-free 3,200ft/min (975m), rather than the Trident's 3,437ft/min (1,048m). Even at 8,500rpm, it would have been a mere 3,895ft/min (1,187m), when the Trident would have been beyond that vital 4,000ft/min (1,200m) safety limit. Despite its power style the Trident had its fair share of problems, one of which was high cylinder bore wear and oil consumption, cured only with difficulty and the use of newly developed piston rings. As many a modern long-suffering Trident owner has discovered after buying low cost replacements, apparently identical BSA C15 pistons and rings simply don't cut the mustard.

Despite its 1963 birth, two years were to pass before serious development was to begin. Even so, the Trident's protracted gestation period effectively killed it at birth because by 1968 Honda's faultlessly engined 750 Four was in America's showrooms. Too much of the Trade had simply lost patience, and, along with the Beezumph twins, the angular, slabby styling of both BSA and Triumph triples raised an absolute furore of criticism from American and British enthusiasts accustomed to the classic aestheticism of the T120 twins. The styling originated from David Ogle, whose odd-looking sports cars and Reliant's scullery-cultish three wheeler car should have been a portent to Umberslade Hall's directors of his equally lacklustre two wheeler forms.

The responsibility for what history is beginning to regard as some of the most handsome vehicles, let alone motorcycles, ever built – Triumph's twins – is usually attributed to Edward Turner, and rightly so. He was an artist in his own right and his eye for balanced form remains probably unmatched and exceeded even that of the great Turin design studios. He was a poor engineer whose impatience with all the time-consuming but essential minutiae of engineering draughtsmanship and its translation into a functioning material form was notorious, but he knew form – style – as no-one else and his eye for detail in this respect was fearfully exacting. When the photographers of Triumph's advertising agency arranged a photoshoot, Turner was always present to insist upon a total purity of line uncluttered by cables, wiring, clips, incorrectly positioned controls, bracketry and all the familiar paraphernalia of any motorcycle's composition. Nothing would be removed but everything, however insignificant, had to be subordinate to the overall appearance of sleek and righteous unity. Wheels would be turned until their inner tube valves were hidden from sight and switchgear knobs positioned just so.

The man to whom greatest credit should be given was the great Jack Wickes. He was an engineer/draughtsman of supreme talent whose grasp of Turner's ideals was so complete it enabled Triumph achieve that which Turner alone could not. Wickes was responsible for translating his impossible boss's notions into blueprints that craftsmen could translate into components. He is also credited by innumerable Triumph ex-employees with contributing a great deal of original design, for which Turner was acclaimed, and without Wickes, Turner would have floundered helplessly. How he put up with Turner's tantrums for so many years is one of life's great mysteries. If he had a fault it was a surfeit of modesty, because when Turner retired in 1964, Wickes was overlooked. If only he rather Ogle had been consulted then the style of the Trident would have pleased, rather than peeved, everyone.

Before passing on to the racing triples, one other model deserves brief mention. This is the Craig Vetter-styled BSA Hurricane/Trident X75 of 1973. In the late Sixties and early Seventies, Vetter was America's fore-

The one that got away. In the final days of Meriden, its engineers lead by Doug Hele, developed a potent dohc triple with which to challenge the two-stroke Yamahas at Daytona. It was track tested to great effect and runs to this day, but it came too late to resurrect the dead-on-its-feet BSA Group. TOC

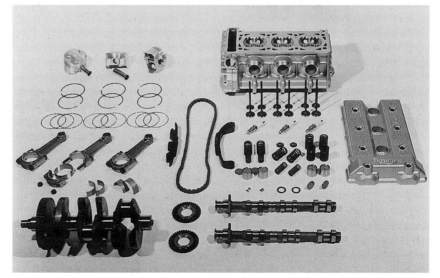

Meriden also developed the 987cc Quadrant. This was a purely experimental Trident with an added fourth cylinder and, while smooth, powerful and fast, it was excessively wide, heavy and somewhat unwieldy. This is the Quadrant under test by a factory development rider. Doug Hele

most fairing manufacturer. The material and dynamic quality of his products defied serious criticism. Shocked by the sales stasis of the triples, BSA's US executives secretly contracted Vetter to sculpt a radical redesign. This wholly American project was completed by 1970. When it was revealed to Eric Turner he delightedly agreed BSA would initiate production. In fact it was handed to Meriden because Small Heath's finances were in a parlous state.

Now highly prized collectors' items, the Vetter triples were not-too-well received by the press, which found them wanting in both build quality and performance. Vetter himself, an open-minded, highly creative craftsman heading an immensely successful company and with an honest man's head for business, suffered badly. While BSA claimed to have settled his original contractual fee as agreed, in reality Vetter had to fight bitterly over an extended period for the approximate £7,000 fee he was owed and the experience hurt him. Even then because of 'confusion' over the production run, which should have stopped at an agreed 500 models but which ran to a probable 1,200 by cessation in 1972, no more fees were paid despite Vetter's expectations.

Even worse from designer Vetter's point of view, BSA/Triumph had retained only the basic outline of the machine – its exhaust pipes, body shape and so on – while actually destroying the essential spirit of the machine by riding roughshod over his explicitly Edward Turneresque instructions about the necessity for exquisite detailing. Vetter had given them a clean form, resplendent in flowing lines and sensual curves uncluttered by ancillary bits and pieces. BSA/Triumph's contribution was raggedness. Vetter never quite got over his disappointment.

In 1969, people began racing the Trident (as well as the Rocket Three). Not until Doug Hele and his Meriden race team buckled to, however, and turned their attention from the race-winning T100As, did the big triples shine. At Daytona, with Gary Nixon on a Trident and Mike Hailwood returning to racing with a Rocket Three, the world held its breath as the national heroes vied for supremacy. But those same damned Lucas contact breaker points that so often destroyed British hopes, did so again. First Hailwood's then Nixon's machine broke down from rogue sparks, pre-ignition and piston failure. Veteran Dick Mann, on what could hardly have been a legally homolo-

gated Honda Four evidently equipped with magnesium engine cases, won, followed by Gene Romero and Don Castro on Tridents.

A great deal of respect was afforded to the famous Rob North-designed and built Daytona frames. Hele had approached Ken Sprayson to supply racing chassis. Sprayson declined because the two months working time would have been barely enough for jig design and construction, let alone the six frames themselves. Percy Tait had been impressed with a Royal Enfield GP5 250 road racer he had been campaigning with a Rob North frame, as he had with a North-framed overbored 750 T120. Tait approached North, who agreed to save time by manufacturing each frame individually without a jig. They were completed within six weeks.

Despite Tait's lifelong profession at Triumph as a development rider and his equal prowess as a racer, his advice over necessary modifications went unheeded. So Tait ensured that when Gary Nixon visited Britain, the right people heard Nixon voicing the same critique. This time those up top listened and thus the second generation 'Low Boy' frames were born for 1971.

In that year, there was no mistaking BSA/Triumph's intention to win. They fielded 10 bikes and riders, American and British, including Hailwood (who retired with a broken valve) and Nixon (who finished but whose bike was plagued by a misfire and broken clutch mechanism), as well as Dick Mann who took over from near-winner Paul Smart while Gene Romero and Don Emde followed him home. This time, the engines were equipped with the BSA-developed remote-mounted, quill-driven, American contact breaker assembly. In 1970, the racing triples had developed up to 71bhp (56kW) at 7,800rpm while up to 85bhp (63.4kW) at the same revs was the best of the 1971 models thanks mainly to redesign work carried out on the cylinder heads and combustion chambers.

Whether or not the racing triples could have responded to further intensive development for the 1972 Daytona 200, will be a point of contention evermore. Certainly Hele believed they could and had developed new race gear to suit. But the twin devils of rapid Japanese race development with much more modern engines, mainly in the form of Yamaha two-stroke fours and Kawasaki's own manic two-stroke triples, and BSA's impending collapse signalled by the sale of Umberslade Hall, stopped the racing triples in their tracks.

What might have been was signalled by Britain's John Cooper who, in 1971 in the race of The Year at Mallory Park and at the Race of The South had the gall to beat 500cc Grand Prix World Champion Giacomo Agostini on his GP MV Agusta. Then Gary Nixon did much the same against Yvon Du Hamel on his Kawasaki triple at Ontario. They were heroic times.

One real hero remained – the all-conquering, retired-unbeaten, immortal PR Trident, *Slippery Sam* that so terrified the Japanese in production racing classes they effectively had it banned, by the simple means of excluding all machines over five years old. It was so beloved of almost the entire nation of British motorcyclists that to this day it remains as the single most famous racing motorcycle to have ever existed in Britain. Not even George Brough's full race SS80 V twin of the 1920s, *Old Bill*, nor Sammy Miller's 1960s trials Ariel HT5 'GOV', can match it.

The Quadrant engine. Due to a hasty need for simple drive chain alignment the engine was offset to the right side (astride). Doug Hele

Slippery Sam was built specifically for the IoM PR TT by Triumph's race engineers. It won outright at the second attempt in 1971 and again in 1972 piloted by PR specialist Ray Pickrell. Tony Jefferies, son of the great all-rounder Allan, got the laurels in 1973. Mick Grant, better known for his Kawasaki GP exploits, claimed the prize in 1974. Then in 1975 came what proved to be the great old PR triple's eternal monument, Dave Croxford and Alex George's victory in the gruelling 10-lap PR TT, when they averaged 99.60 mph (160.2km/h) over that tortuous road circuit's 377.30-mile (542.8km) race total.

By 1972, as a consequence of the BSA Group's financial troubles *Slippery Sam* (nicknamed after untypically coating itself almost beyond hand-grip with blown oil at the French Bol d'Or 24-hour endurance race) was sold to Les Williams, the almost equally legendary British Triumph engineer.

19

Resurrection

History unrepeated, Meriden abandoned,
John Bull rides again

What precisely stimulated John Bloor to enter that most risky of British businesses – motorcycle manufacturing – must remain conjectural because the man himself remains the enigma he has so resolutely engineered. His business acumen places him towards the peak of British industrialists, quite the equal of, say, Richard Branson, who with the wholly justified aims of boosting his company image cheerfully admits to being a self-seeking publicist. Bloor, though, operates from an equally sincere belief that the 'cult of personality' detracts from the image of the product itself. As recent events are proving, however, this philosophy cuts both ways.

By the start of 1983, the Meriden Co-operative had ceased manufacturing because it had run out of operating capital. Ten years previously investigation by NVT had revealed that a further £15 million was necessary if profit were to be realised, and that only following another five years trading. After assurances of Government financing in March 1975 following enquiries and then promises by Anthony Wedgwood Benn MP in August 1995, the Government's Export Credit Guarantee Department withdrew its £4 million offer. Dennis Poore, NVT's managing director, bereft of cash after all this time, lost patience and signed away all claim to Triumph rights. GEC lent the co-operative £1 million on the strength of 2000 unsold T140s and the newly

independent Meriden hoped this would be its springboard to success. Far from it. As usual with insufficient funding, the money served only to finance further crises. Neither bankers, distributive trade, or suppliers had sufficient faith and Triumph at Meriden went under.

These had been desperate years but not idle ones for Triumph's R&D department in the charge of Brian Jones. He knew full well the T120/T140 in practice had for two decades been dead on its wheels. He was equally convinced that Triumph's future must be securely founded on its parallel twin heritage. With this in mind he and his colleagues buckled to and outlined the 900cc ohc, balance-shafted, water-cooled Diana. It never ran but the design was promising, perhaps too promising because its eventual rejection was to permanently influence John Bloor's design policy.

Exactly how much Bloor paid for Triumph late in 1983 is not known but it is assumed by most people with fingers in the British motorcycle industry pie that it was close to £200,000. This included all rights to the name, logo and trademarks, all intellectual property and all existing projects. The most promising of these was the Diana engine, which because it had been actually designed by Weslake with a grant from the West Midlands Development Board, was assumed by Bloor to be ideally prepared for material development. By

the final years of the 20th century Bloor had sunk an admitted £100 million of capital into Triumph and did not anticipate recovering it through motorcycle sales. Such investment, Triumph spokesmen said, was what Bloor regarded as nothing more or less than a 'ticket' or 'licence' to start motorcycle manufacturing.

The money did not come from the British commercial establishment, which originally viewed the Triumph project with disdain, but has since become frantic in its (vain) efforts to become involved, but Bloor's own existing land development and construction companies.

Precisely why Bloor decided to build motorcycles is known only to the man himself. It is said that he considered other businesses but was determined to diversify into something disassociated from construction and that would be globally prestigious. He had no enthusiasm for motorcycling or for motorcycles in the particular, save as production units. It is sometimes said that in wanting the old Meriden factory for development, Bloor stumbled across the Triumph marque. Maybe, but even in those early days the man foresaw that during the 1990s the yen would collapse and as a result the decline of Japan's auto-industries promised opportunities for European motorcycle manufacturers. How right he was proved to be.

His business acumen is legendary,

as is his ability to identify the elemental truth in any projected plan and its presentation. He makes no bones about his lack of engineering skills but has the remarkable ability to recognise both talent in engineers and the righteousness of their designs.

A new Triumph factory was constructed at Hinckley in Leicestershire, barely 15 miles from Meriden, and within a matter of months it had been completed. This was home ground to him because Bloor was above all else a builder, and a very good one at that, whose houses when sold on were invariably advertised proudly as 'Bloor Built'.

No more than a dozen staff were installed, of whom only three were ex-Meriden. Most were engineers. They persevered with the experimental Diana engines but the basic design was seriously flawed in various details, including balance shaft operation and engine bottom end. On top of this it was ineradicably down on its projected power output without major redesign. After nine months Bloor decided to call a halt to further Diana development and to switch his commercial policy.

He had decided that twins were of minor significance to the world at large, and by this time he had formulated a plan to build a range of modular machines that would prove attractive to a global network of dealers. In company with some of his most important engineers by this time he had visited three of the Japanese Big Four, all of which had proved unexpectedly hospitable and helpful. They had the foresight to appreciate that a home-based British manufacturer's industrial, political and social influence was more valuable to them in the maintenance of British/European motorcycling than their small, perhaps insignificant, loss of market share

Above: *Brian Jones (left) with the ill-fated Diana modular engine he drew up at Meriden for the Co-operative work force.* Author

Right: *This is the 1200 Trophy's role — touring, in this case in the hands of the author, and overlooking the small town of Ludlow, Shropshire. The panniers are non-standard.* Simon Everett

Left: *The first one. Hinckley's 1200 Trophy of 1990.* TOC Right: *From Hinckley's first catalogue in 1990, the rare and collectable Daytona 90bhp (67kW) 750 model. Despite a few flaws, it remains as an icon of one of the world's most remarkable renaissance manufacturers.* TOC

to the new, and small, manufacturer. Moreover few, if any, Japanese then believed it was possible for a brand-new company to arise and survive.

From Japan Bloor learned his automated production techniques and from Japan he bought most of his computerised machine tool systems.

As soon as the Diana had been dropped, work started on a new engine, the basis of which would be a 400cc single suited to the Japanese market's cheap licensing regulations. Then would come an 800cc modular sports twin and a 1,200cc flagship three. Work on this plan started but Bloor intervened: he wanted a 1,000cc four, which as he had grown to appreciate was by then dominating the Japanese-lead world market. With that in mind, a 1,000cc four was laid down, which would make a 750cc three. The single and twin were buried.

At this early stage of Triumph at Hinckley, John Bloor was all-too willing to take the advice of his experienced motorcycle engineers. They were mightily concerned over the apparent lack of a new Triumph identity, something which Bloor was either unwilling or unable to recognise as vital for survival. They saw a big triple as the answer, one dedicated to torque rather than bhp alone. Bloor resisted but eventually agreed to its development.

His reluctance was due to Japan's ignorance of triples, apart from Kawasaki's two-strokes. By this time Bloor had unequivocally decided on a policy of following popular Japanese design trends. Triumph bought a complete selection of popular, pacesetting machines, such as Kawasaki's GPZ900, Suzuki's GS1100, Yamaha's FJ1100 and even a BMW K1100. They were studied and, while never copied, their design trends were noted and the most popular trends adopted. Thus, if out of four engines three were wet sump types incorporating balance shafts and all-chain drive, then so be it for Triumph too.

Why? Because in utterly rejecting all that had gone before, Triumph at Hinckley lacked all the building blocks so familiarly essential to design and development engineers. They had nothing to fall back on. Although it is popularly believed that Triumph 'lifted' technology, absolutely no design features from other manufacturers were copied. Nor were Japanese manufacturers involved with any design or development aid. Against that, of course, by adopting benchmark design patterns of others' transverse fours, your own transverse four is unlikely to achieve anything remotely approaching uniqueness if hard-nosed commerce is one of its cornerstone qualities.

Such a design policy was vital because Bloor's capitalisation of Triumph was limited and, in exactly the same manner as Harley-Davidson's resurgence following its management buyout from AMF in the early 1980s, Hinckley's engineers had no option but to operate a right-first-time development policy. So not only were Triumph's design principles familiar and proven, its construction techniques were those of calculated overbuild. They were also those of uncompromising high quality.

For instance, the cylinders employed a wet liner construction, more common among high quality car manufacturers for its light-weight superior heat dispersing qualities, but practically unique in motorcycling. Aluminium cylinders had been attempted but the very high revs (beyond 10,000rpm) demanded of the so-called 'long-stroke' engines pushed piston speeds above the safe limits of piston ring technology and the consequential ring fluttering encountered at extreme revs/piston speeds broke the cylinders' nicosil-type bore coatings. Improved technology since then has lead to the development of the ultra-lightweight and thin or 'wire' rings safe up to as much as 5,000ft/min (1,500m).

Great care was applied to reducing the frontal area of these big motorcycles – the experimental machines being 1200 fours – to a minimum. The major problem was the rider.

Nothing much could be done about head and shoulders without a radical reshaping of the fundamental motorcycle outline and Bloor's mainstream design philosophy ruled that out. But the legs could be tucked away.

In order to keep the rider's knees inward some manufacturers, such as Yamaha, tilted their engines forward and lifted the carburettors high. In designing a big tourer with a minimum 200-mile (320km) range, fuel tank capacity could not be sacrificed. So Triumph's engineers decided to place the engine as far forward as possible, taking account of the radiator of course, which also gave a good weight distribution. They then narrowed the cylinder head to an absolute minimum by employing inverted bucket-and-shim tappets rather than rockers (popular then) and also by water-cooling the engine with an across-flow, rather than the usual rising-flow system needing large diameter internal plumbing, which also improved heat dispersal. Great care was applied to developing straight, rather than splayed, induction tracts as a means of pulling the carburettor in, with the added benefit of improved engine efficiency. Further engine narrowing was achieved by running the cam drive chain and clutch on the same side of the 1200. This enabled the rider's knees to be pulled inward.

The assumption that a long-stroke engine was chosen as an aid to slimness is incorrect. In fact, of course, at 76 x 65mm the long-stroke was no such thing. Once the decision was taken to produce a 900 three as the foundation model, actual development proceeded first with its 1200 big brother four. One oddity remained however, the 1,000cc Daytona sports four, which for the sake of prestige remained as a challenger to Japanese superiority. Its bore and stroke were 76 x 55mm. Stroke, not bore, changed cylinder dimensions.

Triumph's engineers managed to persuade Bloor that in a race for pure bhp the Japanese, with their incomparably greater resources and capital, must win. Triumph's mark of distinction should be useable, simple-to-apply, top-gear acceleration, impressive torque from an unusual engine, yet one within Bloor's mainstream parameter. Hence the 900 triple.

All engines can be measured in the amount of gas they can induct and exhaust. Within road-going practicability they can be made to pass air through them in lots of quick or fewer deeper breaths. The Japanese preferred the former, Triumph engineers saw possibilities in exploiting the latter. All else being equal, a long-stroke engine will always develop greater torque than will a short-stroke engine at the same engine speed because its greater piston speed will induce higher gas speeds and, thus,

improved combustion efficiency.

That Triumph was correct in its choice of engines is indisputable, but one of the original short-stroke engine survived until as late as 1999 in the form of the overlooked and under-rated Trident 750. One of these, road tested by the author in 1996, convinced him that despite the 90bhp (67kW) 750's 11 per cent disadvantage against the 98bhp (73kW) 900 Trident, the short-stroke 750 was undeniably smoother as well as demonstrating an indefinable yet most positively recognisable quality of virtue missing from the gutsier 900. Why did everyone prefer the 135mph (217km/h) bigger bike even though in practice the 127mph (204km/h) 750 was not a whit slower over nip-and-tuck riding? Because the 900's torque was so much stronger. At 61lb/ft (83Nm), its 18 per cent torque advantage over the 50lb/ft (68Nm) was even greater than the amount indicates because the 900 peaked – and that on a flat plateau that seemed to begin at not much more than tick-over – at 6,300rpm and the 750 at 8,700rpm. These equate to top gear speeds of 94mph (151km/h) and 125mph (201km/h) respectively, so it may be seen that the attraction of the 900 lay much less in its absolutes than in the manner it delivered them, albeit more roughly that the 750. So, Triumph was correct in its assessment of its public's preferences.

Those early Hinckley Trophies have won themselves a fine reputation for durability, most of which these days is attributed to the rugged overbuild of the models. This is true in part and was effected to ensure maximum reliability as a means of enhancing the range's reputation. But there was more to it than that. For instance, one of the great destroyers of modern engines is what is termed lubricant 'ratcheting'. It occurs when oil passing between very high temperature engine internals and oil radiators is alternately overheated and overcooled, destroying its lubricity. Triumph engineers took great pains to eliminate this all-too-common phenomenon.

One of the great mysteries surrounding the Trophies is their crude final drive method of exposed chain.

In part it was unavoidable, even though disliked by a great many at Hinckley.

In the first place Triumph had decided on a modular range in which all but an absolute minority of parts were common to all. So successful was this that until the new 5-series engines arrived in 1997 a dealer would find that 30 major parts alone fitted all models. It was vital to keep retail stocking simple to keep down stocking costs because breaking into a fiercely competitive global business with a brand-new network had involve minimum agent investment.

Shaft-drive Trophy transmissions were admittedly preferable but the cost and complication involved was beyond short-term commercial expediency. Experiments with toothed belt drive revealed that these wore fast when subjected to high-powered hard riding (as Buell has found). Draughtsmen attempted to arrange an enclosed chain pivoting under constant tension around the gearbox shaft/sprocket, Hesketh style, but the geometry involved widened the frame precisely where it needed to be narrow – at the rider's ankles.

Triumph's commitment to the advantages of a higher penetration of a minimised frontal profile may be best exemplified by the experience of the early years' testing. The prototype long-stroke Hinckley Triumphs were 1200 Trophies but in naked format, albeit disguised as unrecognisable 'Yawondukis'. These 143bhp (106kW) fours were turning in maximum velocities of up to 140mph (225km/h) in the hands of race-leathered test riders, which, at 10mph (16km/h) above the reality of their over-the-counter production brothers, is pretty typical of the best of blueprinted prototypes. When the first triple was tested, to everyone's surprise it turned in a higher maximum speed. Why? because it was turning out a nominal 96bhp (71.6kW), and was equipped with Triumph's first fairing shape. Also worth considering is the fact that the triple's short-stroke engine, which in the opinion of some engineers, had a better high-speed capability.

After a couple of years the novelty of a resurrected Triumph, and all the emotional baggage involved with the establishment of a large scale, hot-metal British manufacturer, settled. Enthusiasts, and most especially road-testing journalists with a desperate need to find fault as a means of declaring their analytical credibility, found that, after all, Triumphs *were* flawed! Their observations centred mainly on the Trophys' (fours mainly but triples as well) *mal de terre* when subjected to fast direction changing. The new Triumphs' reliance on the engine and a pressed steel spine sub frame for support became the focus of criticism, all of it as misplaced as similar observations on Vincent before it and Moto Guzzi after it, both similarly secured. In fact, during tests both on track over MIRA's variety of surfaces and in the laboratory, on board material creep sensors recorded that against other more conventionally framed motorcycles the Triumph engine/spine arrangement was a mean 30 per cent torsionally stiffer and more resistant to stress-induced material failure.

No, the unsettling waywardness of a fast-cornered Trophy, lay in its suspension. Fortunately for riders the immense torsional stiffness of the massive frame and the spine sub-frame together quite literally held the shenanigans in perpendicular line.

Unfortunately for riders Triumph exploited this very strength by at the last moment prior to production, buying cheapjack suspension systems at low cost. When the author queried this seriously unsettling, although never threatening, behaviour with Triumph people he learned that, as market research had revealed this performance was acceptable to 80 per cent of Triumph owners, Hinckley was satisfied.

More criticism was aimed at the high centre of Triumph gravity, although this was no greater than that of any other comparable model. It was all in the eye, thus mind, thus interpreted dynamic.

The models appeared high from the bulk of their engines combined with the apparent bulk of their big fuel tanks, which at 5.5 gallons (25 litres) was singularly capacious. At a fast touring mean of 42mpg (6.8 litre/100km) on the 1200 model, this returned Triumph's aim of 200 miles (322km) between refuelling stops. The engines looked bulky for three simple reasons, these being their calculated overbuild, their wet sumps and their balance shafts.

We know about the reasons for the overbuild and the wet sump, but the balance cranks seem to defy logic, for

other three and fours have run smoothly enough without them. Modern motorcyclists, however, demand turbine smoothness, and where once a Trident's or Laverda 3C's tactile output may have satisfied, they will no longer. Rubber engine mounts were considered but these would have required a bulky frame. An engine/spine chassis denied rubber mounts for the obvious reason that axial stiffness would be sacrificed. Reluctantly, because of their weight and complication, the compromise of balance shafts became inescapable.

As Les Harris had discovered before Bloor, one of Triumph's greatest difficulties was in overcoming the disappearance of British suppliers and subcontractors, at least those of any worth. When, for instance, tenders were requested to supply aluminium engine castings, the best British foundries could supply were within 1.5mm of machined finish, while the Japanese guaranteed 0.5mm. Moreover, the Japanese more than any other nation were willing to supply specialist components such as electrics, suspension and brakes in small quantities. Even that was not made simple because when British design engineers went to Japan they found themselves talking to production engineers. The two rarely see eye to eye, the former's idealism contrasting with the cost-dominated regime of the latter.

This may well account for the otherwise unaccountably low grade damping of the Trophy's suspension. When Bloor set the standard of his new Triumphs it was of the very highest order. Nothing would be second rate. Yet once production was under way, it was obvious from substandard damper performance that British accountants, rather than design engineers, and Japanese production-oriented engineers had been communing.

A variety of models were produced, all conforming to the modular pattern with the partial exception of the 1991/92 998cc, four-cylinder, 120bhp, 140mph (225km/h) Daytona 1000. It was probably the most remarkable motorcycle Triumph at Hinckley has produced to date. From a company entirely without practical foundation it amounted to what must be an

Rightly, one of Triumph's best-loved models, the naked and unadorned Trident roadster, which continued right through the 1990s, barely changed. TOC

unprecedented technical achievement and deserves to be recorded as one of the most remarkable British classics of all time.

Then came the 885cc 509, T595 and 955cc Daytona of 1997. By this time annual production had risen from the 2,000 units of the first year (1991) to 15,000, which was sufficient to free Triumph from the economic necessity for modular construction. These 5 series bikes were brand-new in every sense, although still recognisably of the triple family. Where the original Sprint sport triples had weighed around 500lb (227kg), the 5s were around 455lb (206.5kg). Triumph was learning fast and had gained enormously in confidence. What had previously taken six years to design and develop, this time took just two. Or it would have done had not the 5's launch been delayed by a year following interminable troubles with fuel injection development. The new engines were much more compact as well as being constructed from much less metal. All appeared to be perfect, but Triumph made some serious design mistakes.

The 'new' lightweight gearboxes, which were actually modified existing ones, broke up by the score, as did the new aluminium frame. Why this particular design was selected is anyone's guess, but it was probably a symbol of its maker's arrival in the high-tech big league combined with a declaration of alternative intent away from the often but erroneously criticised spine frame. It too cracked, costing Triumph dear in terms of recall, warranty and reputation. It was a peculiarly complex design, full of curves, welded sections and bracing, often criticised by experienced frame engineers and which must have been a production engineer's nightmare. By a massive investment of work through its dealers Triumph did overcome these problems and one year later, the new range had established itself has the equal of most.

Certainly a new frame was required. Room had to be found within all new models' body work for an unavoidably large plenum chamber/induction silencer in order to meet then current and future sound level legislation. So the space-absorbing spine frame had to go. Despite claims of a need to offer customers an alternative style of frame solely for aesthetic choice, Triumphs adoption of a more orthodox and much simpler twin-spar frame for its third generation, 1999 Sprint ST did not ring true. A second aluminium frame after the first one's expensively convoluted introduction must have cost the makers a fortune.

Be that as it may, in sporting terms the 'curly framed' 455lb (206.5kg) T595 Daytona had been rightfully hailed as one of the great sportsters. Its maximum speed of 150/160mph (241/257km/h) was less than some but its power spread, braking and handling qualities endowed it with an utterly harmonious balance of qualities that at least equalled and usually surpassed anything else on two sporting wheels.

The British press especially went wild with joy, to such a degree in its celebration of a world-class big sportster, that its often somewhat exaggerated praise led more gullible buyers into believing they were to ride nothing less than a miracle on two wheels. Innumerable disappointments led to a temporary flux of second-hand Daytonas.

Triumph has just moved into its new factory. Built on a 10-acre site, within its geometrically unrelieved walls brand-new production plant will provide at least a 60,000 unit annual capacity. The future would appear to be rosy but Triumph is unusual in modern industry inasmuch that it operates without an executive management. There is John Bloor at the company pinnacle and there is middle management under his direct and close control, but if Bloor were to go, so, in all probability, would Triumph, at least in any currently related form.

When Triumph began operations at Hinckley, Bloor made plain his policy of distancing himself from Meriden, because of the old company's old-fashioned products, their notorious unreliability and the ramshackle shape of its retailing network. In some respects Bloor's decision was correct. What he has cast aside, and this may yet prove to be to Triumph's cost, is what Bernd Pischetsrieder, then BMW's managing director, recognised as Europe's car and motorcycle manufacturers' most valuable asset – their heritage. The memory of old Triumph is still cherished by the majority of motorcyclists the world over as a perhaps the greatest of the marques between the late 1930s and the early 1970s, most especially in America, where practically nothing could stand against it. The deliberated trampling of such an icon is at best foolishness of the first order and at worst downright self-destructive.

Without anyone to seriously stand against him, Bloor's decisions are final. Great man and gifted industrialist though he undoubtedly is, his policies are sometimes seriously flawed. For example, the Adventurer which he forced into production in 1995 was rightfully an unloved motorcycle from its inception. The 2000 TT600 sports four, as forecast by a trade less full of hope for a glorious sales future than it was of doubt over the wisdom of tackling the very class the Japanese had made all its own, has enjoyed doubtful commercial success. The 2001 Bonneville, which motorcyclists around the globe had been anticipating with an excitement like kids on Christmas Eve, was so bland it was limp, lacking even the remotest hint of its proud forebear's elemental warrior spirit. The new Bonnie had been born smugly middle aged.

Despite that, Triumph's current range is by any modern criteria secure in its market, universal in its appeal and exciting in its presentation. Materially and dynamically the bikes equal the best of their competitors and considerably exceed a good many, as a comparative cross-country joust between an 885cc Thunderbird Sport and an 880cc (or even 1200) HD Sportster will all-too-quickly reveal.

20

Completion

*A summary of models produced since Triumph moved
to Hinckley*

Trident 750. £5,299. 1991–98, 749cc (76 x 55mm) triple, 89bhp (66kW), 470lb (212kg), 126mph (203km/h). Roadster. This is the smoothest model yet built at Hinckley, which because of its good nature in another guise, would have perfectly qualified as heir to the 1950s Thunderbird's unimpeachable reputation had Hinckley shown more empathy with its past. Undeservedly overlooked in favour of the torquier and rougher, 900. Indiscernibly slower over ordinary roads than the bigger triple, but slightly revvier.

Trident 900. £5,799. 1991–98, 885cc (76 x 65mm) triple, 97bhp (72kW), 470lb (212kg), 132mph (212km/h). Roadster. 900 Trophy stripped to the bare bones in Triumph's budget bargain near-sportster of immensely brawny compulsion.

Trophy 900. £6,448. 1991-on. As Trident. 500lb (227kg) 134mph (216km/h). Sport-tourer. Clad in full fairing with panniers. One of Hinckley's all-time greats and a wholly justified major sales success. A growing reputation for reliability, stamina and longevity. Surprisingly agile. More popular among experienced motorcyclists than the 1200 version.

Trophy 1200. £6,849. 1991-on, 1,180cc (76 x 65mm) four, 540lb (245kg), 105bhp (78kW). Grand Tourer. A motorcycle noted particu-

larly on its introduction for its extraordinary appetite for effortless express inter-city travel when heavily laden. Also its prodigious torque which, at a claimed 141lb/ft (104 Nm) at 5,000rpm, gives not the slightest indication of its effect low down the revband, where in top gear little more than idling revs will return neck-bending acceleration. Its additional weight over the 900 Trophy in practice effects powerful caution during direction changing out of all proportion to the 40lb (18kg) or so involved. If the model has any weaknesses they lay in the puny rear suspension damp-

ing and the final drive chain's vulnerability to stress and weather.

Daytona 1000. £8,789. 1991–92, 998cc four (76 x 55mm), 485lb (216kg), 120bhp (89kW), 140mph (225km/h). Sportster. The one that got away. Barely recognised in its time but probably the most impressive motorcycle to have left Hinckley because it exemplified new Triumph's remarkable technical capabilities. Slightly heavy steering but imperturbable stability and rev-happy, unburstable engine with an excellent power spread. Hard suspension and

Halfway through the 1990s, the Speed Triple had established itself as a peerless sports-roadster . . . Author

'wooden' brakes, but a fierce challenger of Japanese contemporaries.

Daytona 900. £8,199. 1992–96. As Trident. Sportster. Supposed to have replaced the Daytona 1000. The first triple sportster, but a half-hearted attempt relying on little but cosmetics. Uninspiring and uncommon.

Daytona 1200. £8,899. 1992–98. 1,180cc four (76 x 65mm), 512lb (232kg), 147bhp (110kW), 160mph (257km/h). Sportster. A weight lifter trying to be a gymnast, but not quite succeeding. On paper the most exciting sportster of its period but in reality too much useful midrange torque was sacrificed for barely attainable top-end bhp, and its handling was slow and heavy. For all Triumph's brevity, actually a naiveté, and no more than a potentially thrilling motorcycle. Dated on its release, rare yet barely collectable now.

Sprint 900. £7,349. 1992–97. Sport-roadster. As Trident. 134mph (216km/h). Top-faired mainly for people who needed high-speed wind rather than Trophy-type all-weather protection.

Sprint Sports/Exec. £8,299. 1996–98. Successor to the Sprint, but with restyled top-half fairing.

Tiger 900. £7,099. 1992–98. 885cc triple (76 x 65mm), 84bhp (63kW), 470lb (213kg), 120mph (193km/h). Trail-style roadster. A torque curve like bikes used to have back in the good old days when . . . So popular amongst a host of devotees it has become a true cult bike. A wonderful motorcycle if, 1) the owner is long-legged, 2) he, repeat he, never goes off road unless he is young, big and strong, 3) the off road route is dry because in mud the Tiger really does go like a hot knife through butter – downward sans all adhesion! As tough as old boots and utterly indefatigable. A peerless long-haul tourer of supremely undemanding yet fascinating ease. The stuff of legend.

Speed Triple 750. £7,409. 1996–97. Sport-roadster. Trident 750 engine in 900 Speed Triple rolling chassis.

. . . the misbegotten Adventurer was set to become a flop . . . Author

Listed but rarely, if ever, sold. An oddity for collectors of lost causes.

Thunderbird. £7,549. 1995–98. 885cc (76 x 65mm) triple. 65bhp (51kW), 117mph (188km/h), 495lb (225kg). Retro-classic. A case of style over content. Gentle, pleasant, docile suburban cruiser in which all has been subjugated to style. Any two of the five gears would be ample. Eye-catching and harmless.

Thunderbird Sport. £7,939. 1997-on. As Thunderbird. 82bhp (61kW), 120mph (193km/h). Retro-classic. EFi Tiger-like power characteristics, as well as similar tube steel peripheral frame. A huge improvement over its namesake. Deservedly a cult bike of deceptively fast and easy capability. Charm, glamour, fun and practicability in one unique package. Perfect short-legged alternative to the long-legged Tiger.

. . . the Trophies 1200 and 900 had established themselves as a standard by which other sporting tourers were judged . . . Author

. . . the Thunderbird was achieving near-cult status with an adoring public in whose eyes it equalled its post-war namesake . . . Author

Adventurer. £9,169. 1995-on. As T'bird. Retro-classic. Misbegotten spawn of the worst of Seventies half-baked commercial 'customising'. Ghastly. The less said the better.

Speed Triple. 1994–96. £8,299. As 900 Trident. Sport-roadster. One of Hinckley's great bikes but short lived, possibly because company policy decided to kill it prematurely in favour of the brand-new fuel-injected range. By nature a direct descendent of the wicked old 650 ring-road scratchers of the 1960s. Even had its own race formula. Beloved hooligan still sought after by would-be cult-members.

Super 111. £9,699. 1994–96. 885cc (76 x 65mm), 114bhp (85kW), 145mph (233km/h), 480lb (218kg).

. . . the Tiger had achieved high-cult status and found itself identified as the beefy, go-anywhere, do-anything, all-round good guy of motorcycling. Author

Sportster. By far the most potent of the old long-stroke carburettor triples, but probably let down by the ambiguous coupling of the old spine frame to a high price. It actually deserved better than its publicly neglected status because, while on the edge of obsolescence, it returned a magnificent, if slightly raw, performance. For future collectors.

Legend TT. £6,289. 1998-on. Roadster. An oddity born probably of the need for Hinckley to shed a stockpile of old T'bird and Adventurer running gear. Cheap and cheerful.

Daytona T509. 1997–99. 885cc (76 x 65mm) triple, 128bhp, 446lb (202kg), 155mph (249km/h). Sportster. Complete redesign. Brand-new low-mass engine, fuel injection, aluminium frame. Early failures of some frames and gearboxes were corrected quickly to reveal exceptional and well-rounded power delivery, handling and braking placed in perfect balance to return an almost flawless sports performance from a motorcycle of equally inspiring styling. Handsome is as handsome does.

Daytona T955. 1998-on. 955cc (79 x 65mm) triple, 130bhp (97kW), 440lb (197kg), 160mph (257km/h). Sportster. A glorious refinement of the 509 over which Triumph excelled itself. Especially manageable, and therefore quick in capable hands, thanks to a generous torque development further down the scale than any sportster deserves and flawless high speed manners. It's this that makes it so uncatchable. Nicely finished and gratifyingly comfortable, but the high mechanical sound levels of the engine are somewhat retrogressive. A gemstone.

Speed Triples 509 and 955. £8,299. 1997-on. As Daytona. 110bhp (82kW), 441lb (200kg). Sport-roadsters. Lean, mean yet muscle-bound naked brother to the Daytona, sharing all the basics except for the fairing. Engine tweaked for high mid-range torque. Huge popularity far exceeds mere cult status and proves beyond all doubt that most motorcyclists place other than high maximum speed as the prime criterion. Impeccably man-

Meanwhile, the Sprint lay halfway twixt Trophy and Speed Triple . . . Author

nered in all dynamics yet far from bland. If your neck can withstand the blast it's enough of a quick shifter to rival most Dukes. Too exuberant to be a hooligan.

Tiger EFi. 1999-on. 885cc (76 x 65mm), 86bhp (64kW), 490lb (222kg), 120mph (193km/h). Trail-style roadster. No longer the mythical monster of yore, thanks to the sweet-as-silk injected engine's uncanny low-speed tractability in which once the clutch is dropped no gear other than top is needed, and a heavy tube steel frame in place of the old spine-type. But a splendidly rewarding all-rounder handing out entertainment and practicability in uniquely generous measures. Triumph's 'Range Rover'.

Sprint ST. 1999-on. As Speed Triple. 475lb (216kg), 150mph (241km/h). Sport-tourer. High-stepping probable replacement for the 900 Trophy. In fact, the Speed Triple's engine in a new Trophy-style touring fairing *et al* and cradled in a brand-new twin-spar aluminium frame. Despite appearances, the accent is on sport rather than tour but very comfortable on long trips. Immense torque almost rivals Trophy 1200 while high-speed capabilities exceed those of Speed Triple thanks to the fairing. Superb ultra high-speed cornering when heavily laden. Slightly disappointing finish. All things to all men, and women!

Sprint RS. 2000-on. As Sprint ST. Top-half faired. For those who dislike flies on their teeth, preferring them on their legs.

TT600. 1999-on. 599cc (68 x 41mm) four, 108bhp, 380lb (172kg), 160mph (257km/h). Sportster. Sold in haste before properly finished so first year models won a poor and widespread reputation for ragged combustion and insufficient torque at low and medium engine speeds. Despite intense development that has transformed them into the equal of any Japanese 600 four, TT600 sales have never fully

recovered. It may be because Triumph overlooked the fact of indelible brand loyalty to the Big Four in the sharp-elbowed and smokin'-knee world of 600 sport fours. Or, hopefully, it may be because Triumph is commercially courageous and is operating a long-term corporate marketing strategy rather than merely appealing to a popular sales class. In reality, because of the astringent competitiveness of this particular market, Britain has never built such a ferociously competitive motorcycle. In this the TT600 exceeds even its big brother Daytona, which over most roads in most hands it would probably leave behind thanks to its miraculous pickup, handling and braking. Its pioneering fuel injection forced other 600 sport four builders to follow suit. However Bloor's commercial aptitude may be viewed by history, his strength of purpose and Triumph engineers' talents are utterly magnificent – the equal of any – as demonstrated by the TT600's feral nature.

Bonneville. 2001-on. 790cc (86 x 68mm) parallel twin, 485lb (220kg), 105mph (169km/h). Retro-roadster. The name, probably the most famous in motorcycling, is all. The old Bonnie was not an especially good bike but it was indisputably great. It and its close relations live as potent as ever, recalling shining times of desert and

. . . and the Daytona had finally settled into Triumph's recognised and very highly respected flagship as a 900 triple sportster capable of holding its own in any fast company. Author

it any such thing, apart from a common cylinder symmetry. But the new Bonneville is technically related to the W650. Not because Triumph engineers have copied Kawasaki, but because both are representative of their period. As a consequence Bloor's applied policy of adopting unerring mainstream Japanese design methods has resulted in what in effect is a machine alien to the traditional Brit.

There is nothing implicitly wrong about this. From the Honda CB72 on, Japanese influence on British and European design has been wholly beneficial. But, led mainly by Ducati, European design has been one of individualism, despite the commercial follies so often involved. And Japan has recently been forced to follow suit, as witnessed by Yamaha's TDM 850 parallel twins and Suzuki's TLS V twins. It remains to be seen whether Bloor's wholesale digestion of traditional Japanese design philosophy, at a time when Japan is adopting some of Europe's policies, will work with a branded model name steeped in the British/European way of competition origin and potential.

Triumph is now a century old, being founded as a commercial motorcycle manufacturer in 1902. By the author's reckoning this places it among the oldest of the surviving pioneering manufacturers, in which rare company AJS ranks as the chronologically senior (1897), followed by Peugeot, which still makes flyweight utilities (1899), and Harley-Davidson (1903).

If it is to survive it must publicly honour its past. Without intellectual foundation it will decline. John Bloor is a remarkable individual who deserves a place in the history of automotive manufacturing alongside marque saviours Herbert Quandt –

endurance racing, of trials and record breaking, of sidecar moto-cross and drag racing – for that matter of everything two wheeled. Not much else stands comparison, in particular its current namesake, which is benign almost beyond hope.

The new Bonneville's balance-shafted and solidly five-point-mounted engine runs as smoothly as a four but without the ultra-high-frequency vibration, and it finishes long, hard 100mph rides as dry as when it started. It would also run all sorts of other behavioural rings around standard T120s, with a single exception – off road. Tragically the massively constructed, water-cooled, wet sump engine signals alienation from sand and mud founded competition. So does the slow handling, at least in its original spine-type frame, which benightedly replicates Harley-Davidson's Sportster's lazy chassis geometry in its steering's 20° rake, 4.6in (142mm) degree trail and 59in wheelbase.

In irony of the bitterest sort, Hinckley's Bonneville replicates to an uncanny degree Kawasaki's W650 twin. At its launch the new Kawasaki was hailed by schools of teenybopper 'journalists', desperate for a hook on which to hang an entertaining commentary, as a 'Bonneville look-alike'. Only by minimal technical reality was

Top: *The Daytona in T595 form had been given fuel injection, 128bhp (95.4kW) and an improved torque spread, as well as flawless roadholding . . .* Author

Bottom: *The restyled Trophy 1200, ageing after over a decade's production but still one of the great two-wheeled Gran Turismos.* Author

BMW, Lee Iaccoca– Chrysler, Vaughn Beals – Harley-Davidson and, of course, Bloor's predecessor at Triumph and Ariel, Jack Sangster. All these men saved their companies from probable extinction. England, one of the group of nation-states comprising Great Britain, is currently in a time of perceived crisis as it witnesses the final stages of the loss of all its major hot-metal industries, including the automotive. John Bloor stands almost alone as the one of the very few identifiable heroes who have successfully bucked what appeared to be an irreversible trend. He deserves greater recognition than anyone beyond the confines of motorcyling has allowed.

Motorcyclists around the world, and in Britain particularly, are all-too-aware of their debt of gratitude, but it is essential for Triumph's future that he publicly acknowledges a past without which his resurrection of Triumph would have been impossible.

May Triumph triumph for another 100 years!

21

Hinckley's racing

*On the track again, Jack Lilley and Clive Wood wave the flag,
Paul Messenger sets up a TT600*

For all its renown in competition Triumph has no great tradition of factory participation in racing. Not until virtually forced into it by American demand in the 1960s did Meriden finally relent and begin to develop its 500 twins, then 750 triples, into road racers specifically for the Daytona 200. Until then almost all Triumph racing in Britain had been in the hands of its agents' own teams, such as Boyers of Bromley.

Not much has changed. Hinckley maintains the tradition, to the intense chagrin of the world's Triumph enthusiasts. The reason is simple: racing costs a fortune, a winning team costs an unimaginable amount more besides, and Triumph has no alternative but to feature large in any race series, therefore incurring prohibitive expense better used towards directly financing commerce. The marque may well equal HD and Honda as a global icon of motorcycling but in reality Hinckley's brand is little more than a decade old and so far all its energies, and capital, have by necessity been devoted to the business of production and sales. John Bloor closely studies racing and fully appreciates its potential rewards, but prefers to leave it to the enthusiasm and skill of his agents, much as did Edward Turner. To suggest, as some critics have, that Bloor lacks the courage to go racing is a denial of the man's valiant industrial record which, against all Establishment advice and wisdom –

'don't invest in hot metal manufacturing or motorcycles' – is soaring.

However . . . From the day of its launch in 1994 the Speed Triple became the darling of the back road scratchers. It's 900 triple engine developed more torque than the Daytona 1000, and its lower mass gave it a huge handling advantage over the clumsy Daytona 1200. It was probably Hinckley's first cult bike and filled a highway role very similar to Meriden's T120 Bonneville. Why, though, as it was little more than a sporty styled

Trident and identically powered to boot, did it win so many true-blue British hearts? For the simple reason that in the form of Hinckley's Speed Triple Challenge series Triumph went racing. After a break of 20 years or more, triple Trumpets could be seen and heard around the circuits, although as the new triples had to conform to sound level regulations unimaginable in the roaring Seventies they lacked their forebears' nerve-jangling exhaust notes.

Few solus model race formulae sur-

The Clive Wood-managed Jack Lilley racing team, 2001. Left to right: R. Adam Lewis, rider, astride his T955; Paul Messenger, engineer, machinist and race mechanic; Gill Wood, secretary and logistics chief; Clive Wood, director, race and development engineer and administrator, astride the team's TT600. DDS Photographic

Andi Notman at the May 2000 Donington Park round of the World Superbike Championship on the Jack Lilley team T595 production racer. Bryan Turner

vive for more than a handful of years for the simple reasons that that they are formulaic and therefore eventually perceived by a previously adoring public as predictably uneventful. Also, as their models' standard technical specification advances so the governing regulations become increasingly

difficult to administer fairly. To cap it the envy of other manufacturers towards model formula racing encourages them to start their own and thus dilute the unique attraction of the event. With this in mind Hinckley devised a race series to capture the imagination of its major markets. All

rounds would be held at major international meetings on major circuits and the bikes would be Speed Triples conforming to a strictly enforced standard production specification. Its life would be limited to a few years.

A single toe-in-the-water event inaugurated what was to become the

Jim Hodson in the 2000 IoM Junior TT on the Jack Lilley TT600, on which he lapped at a best of 115mph (185.1km/h). Eric Whitehead

Alan Batson won the coveted Joe Craig Trophy for the fastest-lap British bike at 116.9mph (188.1km/h) in the 1998 IoM PR TT, finishing 17th. Island Photographics

series at the British Grand Prix, Donington, 1994. Its popularity exceeded all expectations, by not only exciting British enthusiasts but stimulating similar series in France, German and the USA. As Hinckley forecast, a pack of top riders on more-or-less identical machines provided spectators with some of the closest-fought racing anyone had seen in years.

Regarding the bikes: highway auxiliaries such as lights, mirrors, pillion rests, indicators, stands, speedometers and so forth could be removed. Suspension could be modified as long as it was restricted to mono-shock replacement by one of Triumph's own, and stiffer springs and damping by means of shuttle valve alteration in the tele-forks. A standard Speed Triple engine – Hinckley's regular 885cc three – was claimed to give 97/98bhp at 9,000rpm, which provided a maximum speed of 140mph plus in road trim. For racing purposes entrants were not allowed exceed 100bhp or to remove or tamper with the 10,000rpm rev-limiters. But they could remove the air cleaner, while retaining the air box itself, and they could change the main jet, although all other carburettor settings were enforced as standard. Nor could the cylinder heads be reported, although there were no regulations against meticulous blueprinting. Triumph's own competition exhaust systems were permissible, as was an oil cooler and steering damper, but gearbox modifications were not.

As a consequence of these controls such power tuning as was allowed concentrated on mid-range torque development, which gave the race bikes the kind of performance that most highway enthusiasts dream about. Almost all were capable of 160mph (257km/h) maxima.

To cope with this extra power and speed, full race tyres were permitted. Brake pads could be changed, as could brake hoses, but the discs and callipers had to remain standard.

Hinckley guaranteed to back the venture with £75,000 per annum of prize money and in 1995 the Speed Triple Challenge series of eight races got under way. It ran for three years and won Triumph the kind of credibility among enthusiasts raised on

Japanese machinery it could never have achieved through non-sporting publicity. More than any other factor, the Speed Triple Challenge gave Hinckley the right to adopt Meriden's crown.

One little piece of regulation-bending chicanery that arose from the applied equalising factors of the Challenge concerned the starting grid. Around 30 Speed Triples and riders would be placed on the grid in direct order of their practice times – fastest at the front. This was not simply a matter of fairness but one of safety as well, for with identical power on tap overtaking was difficult enough without the impediment of less-talented racers. Thus entrants devised various methods of quick-change power tuning their rider's practice machines, such as free-flow exhaust and carburation systems. By this means they won themselves high practice times and a better grid position, before returning the model to Challenge specification.

Mark Phillips won the Challenge in 1995, David Jefferies in 1996 and Jason Emmett in 1997. By this time Triumph had built the new T509 Speed Triple and this model, with its Daytona-developed fuel-injected engine, had a much better power/weight ratio at 110bhp and 440lb as well as a top speed of 150mph (240km/h) plus. Hinckley engineers had learned a great deal from their race experience and the new Speed Triple had been especially tuned for torque and, moreover, equipped with a six-speed gearbox. To top it all off the old fabricated spine frame, adopted as an inexpensive means of suiting all models, was dropped in favour of a brand-new aluminium one with dual perimeter 'beams', both lighter and torsionally stiffer. The old and new simply did not, could not in all fairness, mix on the race track. It seemed like a natural break.

One team in particular came to the fore during the Challenge. This was Jack Lilley's which, in turn was, and remains, managed by Clive Wood. Jack Lilley at Shepperton, south west of London, is Britain's largest Triumph agency. With a similar policy to Hinckley, Lilley decided against splintering its intensely focused business of retailing Triumphs by going racing

The 1998 Jack Lilley T595 as campaigned in that year's Power Bike Series, ridden by Francis Williamson. Clive Wood

itself. Clive Wood had been racing Triumphs since 1982, when he campaigned a T120 Bonneville. When, in 1991, Hinckley presented its Triumphs to an excited and fully suspecting world, Wood, almost alone, picked up the new baton and ran with it. He bought a Trident 900 and in similar manner to the Speed Triple Challenge bike, stripped it of all impedimenta and at Mallory Park's 'Plum Pudding' meeting, 1991, raced it. Or he would have done had he not crashed badly at the start and spent the rest of Christmas in Leicester hospital.

From the very start the names Clive Wood and Jack Lilley Racing have been coupled. When Wood began racing his Trident he did so with sponsorship from Jack Lilley and under that company name he has continued to race.

Practice had been enough to convince Wood of the Trident's potential race potency. He thought it was bigger and heavier than he would have liked, but was impressed by the obvious strength and the power of the engine. With a simple Dynojet operation he lifted mid-range torque and put a full 100bhp at his right fist. The weight problem was beaten by the simple yet meticulous application of an angle grinder. 'I lost 22lb (10kg) in the first 20 minutes.'

The following year Wood, again more-or-less the only new Triumph

campaigner, raced his Trident in whatever it was eligible for, mainly in 1,300cc production formula and more often than not finished in the top six. His best event was Snetterton's Six-hour Endurance, in which he came home fourth.

By 1993, he decided to concentrate on the BEARs (British European Racing) and found himself mixing it with Ducatis, HDs, Guzzis, as well as a load of specials like the Britten, and always in the top 10. He raced in the Manx Grand Prix, to which he found the Trident perfectly suited. Then, at Pembrey, on the Trident he won his first event, a BEAR's round. There, in an open 1300 race he found himself beating serious machinery like Yamaha YZ750s. By this time he was persuading 126bhp at 9,000rpm out of his Trident, which was still rich in torque, so one may appreciate the man's talents both in the saddle and on the bench. Yet he still more-or-less rode Triumph lone-handed. Why? Because, as he puts it: 'The (British) punters were cynical and saw me as some sort of a fluke.' They had, after all, been raised on diet of rice.

It seemed as though he had broken a barrier of some sort because by the end of 1994 he had won his first championship, competed in the first-ever Speed Triple Challenge at the British GP and come third in Snetterton's Six-hour Endurance.

The front and rear ends of the Jack Lilley T595 in close-up. Clive Wood

Clive Wood is a pretty untypical racer, insofar that he is the epitome of the well-rounded professional. His on-track racing always has been only a part of the whole. His preparation is faultless of course, but unlike so many, to whom racing is an end to itself, Wood has patiently dedicated himself towards the organisation of a team, never an individual. His methodology is painstaking, his records impeccable, his presentation flawless, the approach to racing is so smoothly integrated it appears seamless. Most of all, his stud-ied commitment to the strategies of team management have given him the wisdom to exploit the politics of road racing, which for all their subtlety can be stunningly profound.

By 1995, Clive was in the top rank of his racing class. His race team was entering many more machine's than his Trident alone, and included a 1200 Daytona and another Spondon-framed Trident 900. He was runner-up in the BEARs Championship and finished second in the Six-hour Endurance race at Snetterton.

So confident had Wood become by 1996, that apart from contesting the four rounds of the British Endurance Championship and winning two of them with a Speed Triple at Pembrey and Snetterton, he contested the final round, also at Snetterton, on Triumph's big traily Tiger. And, sharing the saddle with co-riders Ian Penfold and John Laker, he won both race and championship!

As Meriden Trumpet buffs were only too keen to exploit to the hilt back in the 1950s and '60s, modular construction, in which a variety of models sharing similar components are designed to fulfil quite different roles, holds major advantages. To this end also, Wood's PR Tiger borrowed vital parts from related triples including 12:1 Daytona pistons, Daytona teles with race-improved internals from WP, Daytona footrests and controls, Maxton/Daytona mono-shock, Speed Triple three-spoke 17in wheels shod with full race Dunlop D207GP 120/70 and 180/55 tyres, a rechipped ignition system with a faster advance, gas-flowed cylinder head skimmed to further lift compression by 0.7 atmosphere, balanced and polished conrods, lightened Daytona Mk III cams, balancer shaft lightened by 2.2lb (1kg), restructured free-flow induction system partnered to Yoshimura exhaust pipes, Suzuki GSXR-750 calipers with Ferodo race pads coupled to a big-bore master cylinder, stronger Daytona 1200 clutch springs and finally the removal of the gearbox's backlash mufflers to reduce friction.

All this combined to give the Tiger some real tiger. Hinckley claims its carburetted model delivers 84bhp at the crankshaft. If we drop 10 per cent through transmission loss the gearbox sprocket figure becomes a practical 76bhp. Allow for another five per cent loss through rear chain and tyre and we have 72bhp to play with. This puts Wood's claim of 114bhp at the rear tyre into perspective, because an extra 42bhp equates to a 42 per cent power lift. It was not achieved by sacrificing torque. The standard Tiger is renowned for its beefy 67lb/ft (91Nm) at 4400rpm. The Wood Tiger finalised at 73lb/ft (99Nm) at 6,500rpm without appreciable loss of its standard acceleration

In the 1996 Boxing Day 'Plum Pudding' endurance race at Mallory Park, John Laker campaigned a barely modified Tiger. It is said that following the three-hour event the ruts he made with the big triple can still trap the unwary even today. Clive Wood

Jack Lilley banner Clive Wood's race team thrived. In 1997, Wood gave up his leathers to concentrate on team management and technical development. Adam Lewis took over the Speed Triple Challenge with the new 509 as well as upholding Jack Lilley and Triumph honour in the British PR Championship. It proved more than capable of holding its own in a host of FireBlades, as New Zealander Shaun Harris proved with a 17th place against 88 starters in the IoM PR TT.

Things got even better in 1998 when, in the hands of Francis Williamson, the Jack Lilley 595 contended *Superbike* magazine's National Sports Production Championship. Against mainly FireBlades and Yamaha R1s, Williamson secured third place overall. While in the IoM PR TT Alan Batson took home the coveted Joe Craig trophy, awarded annually to the fastest race speed for a British bike, at 112.39mph (180.84km/h) on his 595, including a pit stop.

The Jack Lilley/Clive Wood race team went from strength to strength, providing Triumph with the kind of publicity it so desperately needs, yet seems incapable of providing itself.

Triumph celebrated the turn of the millennium with the TT600, a sports four bravely, or insanely, designed to challenge the Big Four Japanese marques in the one class that they had originated and made their very own – the 600 super-sportster fours. Alas, combustion problems resulting from a flawed fuel injection system put a 'hole' in its low-to-medium rev power. Combined with a somewhat cynical press reaction it almost killed sales and undeniably injured the model's reputation, from which it has never quite recovered, even though it is currently regarded as one of the best of the 600 sport fours ever made.

In its first year, in the hands of Adam Lewis, the team's TT600 won its first race at Thruxton after a year's campaigning in the MRO National 600 Championship. The big surprise of 2001 was watching the TT600 finish regularly in the top six of most PR events, ahead of such formidable machines as GSXR1000s. Two TT600s are being campaigned in the

to match any super-sportster and a maximum velocity lifted from 125mph (201km/h) to 160mph (257km/h).

Along with most other motorcyclists who have ventured far from familiar highways on a Tiger, after two exhausting ventures in the Cambrian mountains the author freely confesses to having serious doubts about the off road capabilities of Hinckley's massive 500lb (227kg) traily. A man with a robust sense of humour, Wood saw the potential fun to be had by entering two Tigers in Mallory Parks 'Plum Pudding' Christmas meeting, 1996. One was the previously described road racer and the other a lightly

modified Tiger for the three-hour enduro around the circuit's parkland held concurrent with the endurance race on track.

Unlike its road race counterpart the off-roader was lightly modified. A 21in front wheel was employed to facilitate use of a enduro front tyre and all highway equipment was removed, but that was all. It was ridden by John Laker (who deserves a commemoration medal). He did not win but he did finish and he proved a point, which remains an enigma beyond the ken of everyone but Trumpet buffs everywhere.

For the next few years under the

Francis Williamson on the Clive Woods/Jack Lilley 2001 T955 Daytona. It regularly finished in the top six in open PR races against GSXR1000s and R1s and was unbeaten in the 2001 Sound of Thunder series. DDS Photographic

Junior Superstock Championships for 2002, in addition to the team's other commitments.

As these machines must be as stock as the Speed Triple Challenge machines, what is there that can be done to make the Jack Lilley's TT600s more competitive than the rest? Paul Messenger, the race team's leading technician explains about preparation.

'The first thing to do is to remove all surplus road items. These include headlight, rear light, indicators, stand switch, horn, pillion pegs, road silencer, standard fairing.

'Because we have found nothing as efficient as the original brake equip-ment, we leave it alone. But we do monitor pad wear very closely and as soon as combined wear exceeds 1mm we install a new set. This allows us to maintain a minimum of brake fluid without loss of brake power. The front brake lines are modified and are replaced by two separate hoses to each calliper rather than the usual one line feeding both. The rear brake system is left completely untouched because in racing it is really surplus to requirements. But we file the rear pads' leading edges to 45° to assist with fast wheel changes. Both wheels remain stock but are fitted with road legal race tyres. Because the heat build-up during a race is much greater than it is with road riding we set tyre pressure lower to allow for the pressure increase. For wet tyres the initial pressure is set higher than standard race tyres, although their optimum operating temperatures are the same, because wet tyres build up less heat.

'The standard plastic fairing is replaced by a glass-fibre item. It is a two piece rather than the ordinary three piece because it incorporates an oil capture tray in its belly-pan. This is designed to prevent oil spilling on the track in the unlikely event of a cata-strophic failure (break-up) of the engine's bottom end. The racing seat is also a specially built item. To give better clarity at an acute angle the screen is exchanged for a thinner one of superior material. Apart from its team colour, painting the tank is left unchanged. All body work is finished in team colours complete with spon-sors' decals.

'Each machine has more than its fair share of special one-off race items that the Jack Lilley machine shop turns out. Wheel spacers that replace the speedo drive are a good example. And we use the standard clip-on 'bars but machined out for weight reduc-tion. We fit a guard to the underside of the swinging arm to prevent the rider's foot being trapped between chain and sprocket. Interestingly, we replace the standard chain by a nar-rower one which gives a small but measurable power increase, and we use an aluminium sprocket.

'The front forks are standard but equipped with stronger springs and stiffer damping following revalving.

A fine view of T595 PR campaigner Andi Notman at Brands Hatch. Bryan Turner

The rear shock is exchanged for a Penske race unit incorporating high and low speed compression damping, as well as rebound and ride height adjustments. Depending on the circuits we fit a variety of springs and a steering damper is added to maintain stability on the bumpier circuits. Great care is taken to ensure that wheel alignment is correct: on most bikes the chain adjustment marks are too inaccurate for racing.

'Many items have to be lock-wired in place after fastening to ensure fluids cannot escape, also on fasteners that could work loose during a race. These items include: oil filter, sump plug, external oil pipe banjo bolts, coolant fittings.

'Soft race tyres pick up a lot of stones, especially after another rider has returned to the pits from the gravel traps. So we fit an aluminium mesh guard in front of the radiator to prevent stones from penetrating it.

'Race regulations require that every machine uses standard crankshafts, con-rods and pistons. We strip the engine down completely and check that all bearing surfaces are flawless and within the specified tolerances. We also remove all sharp and projecting edges from the inlet tracts. These are vital parts of the blueprinting process. And that's about all we are allowed to do to the engine.

'The chassis involves more work. We have to remove the side stand, as well as grinding away its pivot. This means we have to make provi-

On his T595 Francis Williamson tops the 'Mountain' at Cadwell Park. Clive Wood

sion for front and rear paddock stands. The front fits into the bottom (fork) yoke, which may require slight machining. And at the rear we have to drill the swinging arm so a threaded sleeve can be welded into place. Bobbins are then bolted either side for stand location. Stands are vital for servicing of course, but they are most important so we can remove both wheels for tyre changes or to allow tyre warmers to be used before the race.

'The wiring loom is placed and measured as neatly as possible within the frame to ensure it does not fray, stretch or tangle. Electrical problems could be disastrous.

'Some riders prefer to ride with the gear shift reversed i.e. 1-up 5-down, not the standard 1-down 5-up. Then they can change up while banked hard over on left-handers. This means we have to make special gear linkages. The foot pegs are also changed for lighter, rubber coated items. They have to have an 8 mm radius on their ends to avoid penetrating injuries in a spill.

'We also exchange many low stressed items such as the battery box, instrument fittings and rear 'guard for lightweight aluminium to save weight.

'Because the bikes are not road legal they have to be run-in on the dyno'. This usually involves between two to three hours, continually increasing revs to mimic the road break-in period and 'ease' the engine into higher loads. This is followed by a high-speed run to ascertain the performance datum for every machine's record. Instrument-measured checks are also made to ensure that the correct fuel mixture is being fed into the engine by the fuel injection system or carburettors when the straight through race can is fitted.'

As it always has, Triumph races what it puts into its showrooms.

Twisting the tail of a Tiger. In this case, Clive Wood in one of his last races at Snetterton, 1996. Clive Wood

22

On the road with Hinckley's finest

*Beyond modular design, sportsters progress, 'Lucas' makes good, a
flawed four conquers the world*

When Triumph was reborn at Hinckley it was forced by circumstances dictated by limited investment capital and engineering experience to a policy of modular design and robust over-engineering. This no longer holds true and while the range of eight distinctly different models retain obvious family design and build similarities, a multitude of engine and rolling chassis variables are currently employed to attain specific style and performance types.

The range is grouped into three classes – Touring, Classic and Sports. Contradicting the obvious, in fact the Classic range is the most recent, while only amongst the three tourers may be found evidence of Hinckley's first, foundation model, the Trophy 1200. Beneath a restyled fairing exists the flat-slide carburettor engine and fabricated spine frame that first saw the light of day in 1990. It has continued unchanged in all essentials since then and despite the advances made by rivals from Honda and BMW, this big, heavy, powerful yet gentle giant can still hold its own in any touring company. At the time of writing Triumph admitted that it was working on a brand-new heavyweight touring replacement.

Partnering the Trophy 1200 four, are the Sprint ST and Tiger, with which the Trophy has nothing in common, and apart from their engines, which are prepared to different states of tune, neither have the Sprint or Tiger.

Equally different is the Classic range, which is expanding fast to include such as the parallel twin America and the T100 built around the existing Bonneville design, all at 61bhp, as well as the Thunderbird with its silken-soft tuned 69bhp 900cc triple engine. The Bonneville America is particularly interesting because, unlike the standard Bonny and the T100, its crankshaft has been thrown at 90°. While the practice of imitating the compelling rhythm of a

V-twin originated in large scale commercial production originated with Yamaha for its TDM 850 twins a decade earlier, its use by Triumph has given it a previously missing edge against old-time rival Harley-Davidson's raunchy exhaust note.

Our interest, however, is primarily with the sportster range, and the TT600 and Speed Triple in particular.

When the Speed Triple first appeared in 1994 it won the hearts of British motorcyclists because, by its

Perhaps Hinckley's greatest success, the base model Bonneville. Triumph

brawling, robust nature it filled the vacuum left by Meriden's T120 Bonneville in 1970. Devotees of the model may like to reflect that although the original Bonnie so indelibly imprinted itself on us it seems from a distance to have been with us forever, in fact its life was just one year over the decade. Its successor by type, the Speed Triple, is at the time of writing into its eighth year, and going strong.

As with the T120, *what* the Speed Triple did was of less importance than *how* it did it. A top speed somewhere beyond 130mph (210km/h) even in 1994 may not have been overly impressive because by this time sportsters like Suzuki's GSX-R750 and Yamaha's YZF 750R were mewling into the 150/160mph (244/257km/h) bracket. As that supremo of track and race testing Alan Cathcart wrote at the Speed Triple's launch in *Motor Cycle International*: 'Nothing since Ducati's bevel-drive 900SS more than a decade ago so perfectly captures the minimalist yet meaty appeal (of) the cafe-racer . . . a styling package that has the presence of a Ducati Monster . . . (but) where the Monster is petite the Trident is muscular . . . where the Monster is built to pose, the Speed Triple is an altogether more serious piece of hardware, built to accelerate hard, corner hard and brake hard.'

As the author himself discovered to his delight during a 900-mile (1,500km) round trip into the Highlands of Scotland shortly after that, neither the Yamaha TRX 850 nor the Ducati 888 had quite the mixture of unrelenting stamina and broad spread of torque to match the Triumph over a big mileage. They simply lacked the Triumph's easy, tireless thunder as well as its winning ways with cornering, the Duke feeling a little slow and the Yam' mildly jittery after a few hundred miles in the hands of weary scratchers.

If these first models had a single fault it lay with Triumph's inexplicable decision to remove top gear from the box, leaving the Speed Triple with five. Why Hinckley imagined that its Trophy 900 tourer, aimed at a more mature rider and probably pillion passenger, concerned primarily with highway cruising required more gears than

With its 90° crankshaft throw, the Bonneville America's exhaust note is all. Triumph

its sporty counterpart is imponderable. More to the point, Triumph left the Speed Triple's fifth and top gear on the same ratio as standard. This returned handsome top gear tractability and acceleration of course, but on a long ride the unnecessarily high revs caused by the over-low top fifth on other models was irritating. As an example, the Trophy 900's sixth, top gear ratio was 4.7:1, while the Speed Triple's was 5.05:1. Uniquely, the bike's maximum speed was restricted not by the usual wind resistance, but by running out of revs in top gear at the limiter's 9,700rpm.

Yet this was all from what amounted to a mildly tweaked Trophy package. The Speed Triple demonstrated with crystal clarity the astonishingly high quality of Hinckley's overall first package.

One of the world's great sportsters, a 955i Daytona doing what it does best – fast cornering. Triumph

With good reason, one of Hickley's most popular models, a top sportster, the 955i Daytona. Triumph

Dramatic changes occurred in 1997. Triumph at last got to grips with its top super-sportster, the Daytona, which until then in various guises, had never quite matched anyone's hopes. The Daytona 509 was equipped with the first of Triumph's second generation engines and rolling chassis. Materially no relationship existed between the old Speed Triple and the new. For that matter nor was its pedigree the same. Whereas the original had been a sports modified tourer, the 509 was a sports-roadster sired by a super-sportster, the Daytona 509. Moreover, it was much more of a machine engineered specifically to meet the challenges of its own particular class – the streetfighter. Thankfully it was rewarded with a sixth gear.

Not until 1998 did the Speed Triple and its brothers truly come of age however, because that was when the 955 engine appeared. More perceptive aficionados will appreciate that while the 905 engine was of lower mass thanks to improved, lighter casting methods, its bore and stroke (76 x 65mm) and thus 885cc capacity were identical to the original Trophy 900's. Internally, and significantly, it employed a great many of the older engine's components. For all its fuel injection, the new engine proved on road and track to be slower than the carburettor engine. Despite factory claims very few developed much above 88bhp, whereas the carburettor engines were producing close to their claimed 98bhp and, more to the point in the Speed Triple Challenge, could be more easily persuaded above that without arousing suspicion.

One is forced to assume that Hinckley delayed introducing the 955cc (79 x 65mm) 955 engine in order to exhaust stocks of old engine parts. When it did arrive the 955 proved to the world that Triumph was equal to the best around. It was also technically unrelated to the old Trophy engine. While the Daytona from which it was derived provided 140bhp, the Speed Triple developed 108bhp (80.5kW) and a 70lb/ft (95Nm) torque curve of such muscle that in the hands of most owners over bendy roads it was actually the quicker of the two models. By 2002, power development had been revised upwards again and the Speed Triple was turning out 118bhp, enough for a top speed close to 150mph (233km/h), although their stock naked trim denied all but a select few of the most determined owners the opportunity to keep the wire tight all the way. By this time the streetfighter had actually inherited the super-sport Daytona's engine lock, stock and barrel. The only difference lay in a milder cam form profile and different fuel injection/ignition mapping.

Here is what amounts to the heart and soul of the Triumph triples – its mapping. When Triumph decided to replace the Trophy 900 engine, its engineers wisely decided to choose the best engine management system available, rather than the least expensive.

Aggressive styling and a muscular Torque curve, the scratcher's darling, a 955 Speed Triple. Triumph

Let us for a few brief moments diverse. The British, being a mixed race of some vigour and now without a clear national ideal to pursue, are often cynical, sometimes destructively so. So when the first Hinckley Triumphs appeared in such a remarkably short space of time all manner of killjoy rumours circulated concerning an over-similarity between mainly Kawasaki, but also Yamaha sport fours and Hinckley's engines. Then again, when it seemed that the 905/955 engine's production had been delayed, blame was heaped once more on Lucas's head. After all, more than any other materially identifiable factor, had not the aptly named 'Prince of Darkness' contributed so generously to the British auto-industry's decline and fall? What remained of Lucas's auto-electric division had been bought by Sagem, a French company not unlike Bosch in its diversification of interests. Sagem had developed one of the most advanced and powerful engine management systems available to the car industry.

In reality, Triumph had like any other manufacturer, closely analysed its competitors' products. Not to have done so would have been counterproductive to the point of stupidity. By the time John Bloor had installed his first dozen or so engineers at his new factory in 1988, the pool of the old industry's experienced motorcycle engineers and subcontractors had irretrievably dispersed. In view of the calamity of Hesketh's V-twins perhaps this was all too the good. Hinckley then, in its embryonic period, relied on an unusually wide selection of non-motorcycle design and development experience. Most of this was car-founded. Apart from consultation with production engineers within or catering to the Japanese motorcycle industry, new Triumph relied heavily on the British car industry, hence Cosworth's early involvement.

During long periods of development riding at MIRA Triumph engineers met Lucas (Sagem) engineers. Taking the long view and rather than deciding in favour of the popular Nippon Denso or Magneti Marelli motorcycle engine management packages, Triumph decided in favour of Sagem's.

Shown without its panniers, the Trophy 900's replacement, the sports-tourer Sprint RS. Triumph

As a consequence, the fuel-injected Triumphs now have by far the most refined and powerful system of any motorcycle. The superiority of the Sagem system over others at the time of writing is demonstrated by Triumph's ability to produce the only motorcycles that meet all global emission control levels without a catalytic converter. 'Cats' are fitted to some export market machines, but only to comply with that area's insistence on one for its own sake, and not as a means of emission control.

The first packages used from 1996 to 1998 were Sagem's MC2000, which because they were adapted car units capable of managing the much more rigorously enforced emission controls of car engines, actually greatly exceeded Triumph's requirements. Two years later it had been restructured into a lighter, tailor-made motorcycle system, the MC1000.

Triumph's answer to Honda's VFR 750/800 range, the Sprint ST, is almost the classic V-4's equal. Triumph

Even so, it monitors every millisecond engine rpm, engine temperature, air temperature, barometric (or atmospheric) pressure, combustion load, induction load and gear ratio, and adjusts ignition and injection to suit. More extremely still, it measures air filtration and adjusts mixture to suit the microscopic blocking of the filter during its life.

Apart from the advantages to engine and atmosphere, there are two others with the Sagem systems. The prime one to most users and their dealers is its 'freeze frame' facility which in the case of complete or partial breakdown, registers and records for up to 40 heat cycles (restarts) in its memory of the precise condition of all aspects of engine operation at the moment of breakdown. This may be computer-read and analysed by a Triumph technician prior to rectification. The other, of less importance to most owners but of essential value to racers, is the Sagem system's ability to adjust to altitude changes, constantly maximizing the combustion process. As Clive Woods noted, the world's foremost authority on race-tuning Triumphs, the IoM TT Mountain circuit, with its abrupt climb to nearly 2,000ft (610m) and astonishingly capricious meteorology around those 37 miles, no longer demands the unsettling carburation compromises that once characterised the circuit, often baffling tuners.

That Hinckley's grasp of its rich model name heritage is slippery is demonstrated . . .

. . . is this centenary special model's contradictory identification as the Bonneville (ex-650) T100 (ex-500). Triumph

Whatever the progress Triumph so clearly manifested in its new engine, the most profound change was demonstrated in the Daytona/Speed Triple rolling chassis. There was nothing intrinsically wrong with the original fabricated steel spine frame. In fact this type of frame has been used with every success by a multitude of progressive manufacturers, including Moto Guzzi, Vincent and Egli, all of which were revered in their day as unsurpassed roadholders. Clearly, Triumph engineers recognised along with other equally great designers that the responsibility for torsional stiffness was best left to the comparatively massive block of the power unit, which was designed to cope with far greater internal forces than could be expected from any extraneous force.

The problem was image – marketing. By the time the Hinckley bikes appeared in 1990, the world's sport bike buyers had been seduced by a decade of aluminium twin-spar frames and they, the buyers, knew best. As amply proved by grand prix racing, these complex perimeter frames offered exactly the right balance of stiffness and flexure (frames of total axial rigidity are at best an embarrassment during high-speed direction changing and at worst, downright dangerous) and were light. Structurally they allowed designers to keep the overall height and gravity centre of the gross machine/rider mass low but, and this went against Triumph's grain, they were excruciatingly expensive to manufacturer and almost impossible to repair.

Nevertheless, through feedback from its agents Triumph was aware that its spine frame was perceived as anachronistic by a majority of motorcyclists. So it produced its all-aluminium, duplex tube, perimeter frame. If Hinckley wanted individuality, it got it, because the curlicues of its duplex spars resembled nothing else and, while everyone enthused over the handling and stability of the Daytona and Speed Triple, its material and/or fabrication was suspect.

To a greater degree than any other motorcycle major manufacturer or British distributor, Triumph plays its

Few modern motorcycles enjoy quite the same devotion as the Tiger in any of its variations. This is the Tiger 955i, all-rounder supremo. Triumph

cards very close to it chest. Considering that it is Britain's one and only large scale engine manufacturer its reluctance to openly communicate with the technical or specialist press is curious and, in the long term damaging. While most British journalists are unreservedly proud of their flagship marque, they are resentful of the doors Triumph habitually closes against them. As those employed by Britain's leading journal are primarily newspaper journalists with an eye on headlines, this resentfulness bubbled up when Triumph's new frame began to exhibit flaws. One would have thought from reportage that at least half of the new models sold were cracking up in the hands of owners *en route* twixt dealer and lawyer. In reality, a few dozen frames did crack. Why? There was a weakness, of that there is little doubt, because some early models were recalled and the design was subsequently modified. Amongst Triumph agents however, there is a strong suspicion that most frame failures were probably a consequence of light front-end impacts following a mild mishap and by heavy landings following high wheelies.

The sheer robustness of Triumph gearboxes had always denied them the

micro-slick cog-swaps that had become standard among Ducati, Suzuki and Kawasaki machinery. They were far from bad, equalling most Hondas, and in practice exceeded by miles the all-too common clunky

backlash of Yamaha, but the inertia of their heavy gears resisted harmonious meshing. So Triumph lightened them, too much. In the hands of a few more forceful owners some broke. This was hastily rectified.

The new frame was partnered by improved brakes and, of prime significance, very greatly improved suspension, the dampers in particular. While the teles had always performed well, Triumph's had traditionally been plagued by under-damped mono-shocks, which through an undulating fast curve, especially when incurring a change in velocity, usually provoked a queasiness strangely reflective of pre-unit 650 forebears in the 1950s. This is no longer the case. The old swinging fork has been changed to swinging arm and teles have been changed to inverted 45mm units.

When the Daytona 955 was announced the author found to his delight a British designed and built motorcycle that at very high speed handled direction changes with a lightness exceeding that of the classic standard bearer, the Ducati 991, and with all the imperturbable elegance of a Kawasaki ZX7R at full stretch.

In view of its technical similarity the 955 Speed Triple has become a

The foundation modern 'Trumpet', the immortal Trophy 1200. No longer young but still one of the finest big mileage tourers available. Triumph

Over the TT600's initial flaws John Bloor must have peered into the abyss. Long since perfected, it is now at least the equal of and maybe better than anything comparable. Triumph

distinctly different machine. Constant, thoughtful honing by Hinckley has been devoted to the model's handling characteristics. Where once the Daytonas and Speed Triple were so similar, the 2002 Speed Triple now has a wheelbase of 56.2in (1,429mm), and steering geometry has been changed by reducing rake by 0.5 to 23.5, trail down to 3.3in (84mm) and the adoption of a 17in front wheel taken, it is claimed, from the TT600. For a big, powerful, modern machine, this is unusually short. With the advent of increasingly punitive speed enforcement however, the vital area of handling lies much less with the ultra-high speed stability that is the Daytona's speciality, than with the demand for mercurial mid-range direction changing that is the Speed Triple's. To cap it, Triumph has managed to lighten the dry weight of its streetfighter from 416lb (189kg) to a new 401lb (182kg).

The author can say with his hand on his heart, that in 36 years of road testing he cannot remember riding anything with such a fearfully addictive nip-and-tuck appeal. A Speed Triple's extraordinary easy handling combined with its massive torque, acceptable weight and utterly secure nature, gives it the kind of amenable ferocity probably unique amongst

modern machines. If the ride is in darkness then nothing, but nothing on two wheels has headlamp tops to remotely compare with the Speed Triple's pair.

If the second series Speed Triple suffered from a difficult reception, that of the TT600's was close to terminal. Hinckley, through John Bloor's strictly enforced production and marketing policies, had earned itself an undeserved reputation for copying Japan's big four. A good many pundits, including the author, also mused long and hard over the wisdom of Triumph's apparent determination to tackle the big four head on with designs so very similar to their own. The reality was that Triumph was awake to the market needs of the time, which were that enthusiasts raised on a diet of silky-smooth sports fours would only, could only, want more of the same. Bloor was proved right, those of us who doubted, were proved wrong.

There is, however, one class of bike that beyond all argument is the big four's very own. Kawasaki laid the foundations of the 600 super-sports four in 1982 with its 75bhp (56kW) 135mph (217km/h) GPZ600. Two year later Honda followed with its similarly equipped and performing CB600F and the rest, as they say, is

history, with 600 super-sport four race formula events almost rivalling grand prix status for many a year. No-one else got a look-in. No-one else was mad enough to interfere. British enthusiasts, or all of them in their informative years of two-wheeling, knew instinctively that the finest form of illegal speeding off motorways was to be found flat on the tank of a Dyno-jetted, recanned 600 four. This was more-or-less the way of life for two decades.

Then along came Triumph to celebrated the turn of the millennium with its very own 600 super-sport four. It had been anticipated, but for all that it astonished the nation's enthusiasts. The initial reaction was similar to the introduction of the 955 Daytona, when the press lost all sense of objective analysis and simply went bananas. *Motor Cycle News* headlined its first launch test with: 'How Many Reasons Do You Need? Triumph's four-cylinder 600 is among the lightest, most powerful, sharpest-handling supersports bikes in the world. It happens to be made in Britain – if you need another excuse.' The test continued in a similar paean with but a brief, passing reference to a hole in the power band between 4,000 and 9,000rpm.

Within a couple of month's as the TT600s got into the hands of their new owners this 'hole in the power band' began developing into a black hole apparently capable of swallowing its maker. Buyers familiar with the seamless power style of Japan's sport fours, protested long and loud about their disappointment with their TT600's almost unreadable combustion hesitancy right where it was most needed – mid-range. With 108bhp (80.5kW) and 50.5lb/ft (68.4Nm) of torque on tap, its speed (160mph/257km/h at 14,000rpm) should have equalled its Japanese rivals, while its impeccably designed and fabricated rolling chassis gave it the handling to leave them behind. In fact, trouble with the electronics of its engine management system led to fuel injection problems which in turn depressed combustion. Production TT600s were returning to dealers with fits of the staggers.

Sales fell until in the first year with a bare 300 sold. Triumph had been anticipating 10 times the volume. Unsurprisingly, it made press headlines and Triumph was roundly castigated for the old British industry's tradition of using its public as development riders.

Why was such a farcical, and potentially damaging, hiccup given public airing? Such secrets are locked in Hinckley's bosom but it is known that John Bloor was determined at all cost to launch his new model at the turn of the millennium and, unwisely, he forced the pace too much.

The model was in development for four years, which is the same period as the original Trophys involved. As it was technically unrelated to any other Hinckley model this is actually a surprisingly short time span for such a small company. It may also be seen as the first wholly new Triumph in a decade, machines such as the 905 and 955 being major redevelopments of existing designs.

Its single-spar aluminium perimeter frame closely resembled its popular rivals, which considering its market target, is no surprise, and four rather than three cylinders were chosen because engine power was the goal. The lighter reciprocating masses, the smaller therefore faster burning combustion chambers, the extra combustion stroke per engine revolution and the shorter stroke of a four all contribute to faster acceleration and superior power over a three. In the sensitive world of super-sport 600s, small things count for a lot.

Significantly enough, when the Trophy 900's replacement, the Sprint RS appeared, it was equipped not with the duplex tube perimeter frame of the Speed Triple to which it is related by a shared engine, but with what was plainly a slightly larger edition of the TT600's frame. During TT600 testing a prototype rolling chassis had been equipped with a 130bhp (97kW) 509 engine simply to prove its capabilities.

Another great change involved with the TT600's manufacturing process was over its engine casing's die-casting, where it was previously sand cast. The company's greatest energies were invested two ways. The first was over something Edward Turner would have admired – weight saving. Because the actual amount of material employed to construct a 600cc and a 900cc of the same engine type approximates to a very similar amount, that the 600 should weigh appreciably less is unlikely. So if the 600 is burdened with an extra cylinder, a fairing and all entailed, the likelihood becomes even more remote. So to save the 40lb (18kg) difference between Speed Triple and TT600 Triumph development engineers had to pare weight by mere ounces at a time from such as sprockets, brake discs, fork internals and frame fittings. Most of all, though, engine mass was taken to its practical lower limits. A new, pressure die-cast crankcase was designed, and through its one-piece construction, would be stronger, therefore saving weight through its light fabrication. In fact, the entire engine is ultra-light, with pistons weighing a minimal 5oz (146g) each.

The second important design factor was fuel injection. For all their high performance, all the Japanese 600 fours breathed through carburettors. Triumph beat them to it with fuel injection. For its initial problems, the mid-range power block was overcome through meticulous remapping of its fuel injection management system. By 2002, the TT600's performance was as sweet as honey right through its range, but by this time, of course, the Japanese had taken up the challenge and sharpened their own rivals to the point where they now may just about have the edge on engine power, although their handling still does not quite match Triumph's smallest

motorcycle. Of all the 600s however, Triumph's, while still an undiluted super-sportster, has the edge on long-term comfort. The others without exception demand riders accept a cricked back or aching wrists on a long trip as an unavoidable sacrifice to speed. Not so the TT600 and surprising though it may seem, one can tour comfortably on one.

Despite a major fire at its new factory in the spring of 2002, Triumph's future appears to be assured. No longer bound by its springboard modular assembly strictures, its designs are becoming increasingly varied, as witnessed by pre-production news of a brand-new near-2-litre in-line roadster triple all set to challenge Harley-Davidson. And there are strong hints of a brand-new shaft-drive 1200 Trophy tourer with which to take on BMW. Sales are increasing around the world, but Triumph is beginning to suffer like all Western hot-metal manufacturers from unsustainably high production costs. Will Triumph go under, or move abroad?

In all probability, Triumph will follow the pattern of others in a similar position and subcontract more component and component group manufacturing to less developed, mainly eastern nations, while overall design, development and assembly will remain in Britain.

A more significant query hangs over Triumph management. Sooner or later, its founder and sole owner, John Bloor, will be forced by his expanding company and/or retirement to delegate executive responsibility elsewhere. This is something that his record of hands-on personal management in all departments suggests he will find difficult. Dynamos of his seemingly limitless energy, do not easily run down.

May Triumph continue to thrive for another century, but would we recognise its products as motorcycles then?

Bibliography and acknowledgements

So much has been written and recorded about Triumph at Coventry and Meriden over the past century that original research is unlikely to reveal much new of significance. This does not apply to Triumph at Hinckley, where a treasure trove of information lies secreted in the memories of its management and engineers. As with old Triumph, this will only be made public as retired employees feel the bonds of loyalty that once held them, fall away.

The author of this work makes no bones about his reliance on the information provided by the following publications. As a professional writer himself the author is fully aware of the huge amount of research that has so often been invested into these publications, of which the public is rarely aware. He offers his grateful thanks and full appreciation to the army of dedicated journalists and authors that have gone before.

Periodicals

The VMCC's library of *The Motor Cycle* and *Motorcycling* magazines. Also, *The Motor Cyclist Review, Motor Cycle Mechanics, Motorcyclist Illustrated, Cycle, Cycle World, Classic Bike, Classic Bike Guide, Which Bike?, Motorcycle Mechanics, Motorcycle International, The Classic Motorcycle, Motorcycle Sport (& Leisure), Classic Car,* and *Moto Retro.*

Books

Triumph Tiger100/Daytona by John Nelson
Bonnie – The History of the Bonneville by John Nelson
The Ariel Story by Peter Hartley
Norton by Mick Woollett
Velocette by Ivan Rhodes
The Story of BSA Motorcycles by Bob Holliday
Motorcycle Parade by Bob Holliday
BSA by Don Morley
Triumph in America by Lindsay Brook & David Gaylin
Triumph Motorcycles in America by Lindsay Brook
Triumph Twins from 1937 by Cyril Ayton
A-Z Guide to British Motorcycles by Cyril Ayton

Triumph Motorcycles from 1950 to 1988 by Steve Wilson
Triumph Bonneville by Steve Wilson
American Racer by Stephen Wright
Triumph Motorcycle Buyer's Guide by Roy Bacon
The Story of Triumph Motorcycles by Harry Louis & Bob Currie
The Pictorial History of Triumph Motorcycles by Ivor Davies
The Return of the Legend – Triumph by David Minton
Triumph Bonneville Gold Portfolio by R. M. Clark
The Vincent HRD Story by Roy Harper
Original Vincent Motorcycle by J. P. Bickerstaff
Historic Racing Motorcycles by John Griffiths
British Forces Motorcycles by Chris Orchard & Steve Madden
Motorcycles – A Technical History by C. F. Cauntner
Veteran & Vintage Motorcycles by James Sheldon
The Guinness Book of Motorcycling Facts & Feats by L. J. K. Setright
International Six-Days Trial by Mick Walker & Rob Carrick
Whatever Happened to the British Motorcycle Industry? by Bert Hopwood
Motorcycle Cavalcade by 'Ixion'

Classic Motorcycles by Tim Holmes & Rebekka Smith
The Illustrated Encyclopaedia of Motorcycles by Erwin Tragatsch
Classic Motorcycles by Vic Willoughby
Honda – The Man & His Machines by Sol Sanders
The Pattern of My Life by Sir Harry Ricardo LLD, FRS
Encyclopaedia of Motorcycle Sport by Peter Carrick
Classic British Racing Motorcycles by Mick Walker
Britain's Racing Motorcycles by L. R. Higgins
Motorcycle Engineering, & Rich Mixture by Phil Irving
Study of the 4-stroke Motorcycle Engine by Paul M. Brokaw
Motor Vehicle Calculations & Science by R. C. Champion & E. C. Arnold
The Racing Motorcycle by John Bradley
The Motor Year Book 1956 by Laurence Pomeroy
Modern Motorcycles by Arthur W. Judge
Automotive Handbook by Bosch
Meriden – Historical Summary 1972–1974 by NVT Ltd
Motorcycling Sports Yearbook (various) by R. A. B. Cook

An even greater debt is owed by the author to people and organisations who have given hours of their precious time in assisting with research on Triumph. One in particular stands out. He is John Nelson, Triumph (Meriden's) service manager who supplied what seemed to be days of sound advice and information and a whole file of photographs. And as a continual source of ready reference, his two books on 5T/5TA and 6T-based twins, gave the author more material than he cares to admit. No more valuable factual record of Meriden's twins' history exists than these two books. Their unique text is an elegantly presented, wholly objective weave of technical appraisal and personal comment.

Particular thanks also to Jack Lilley Motorcycles of London and to the company's extraordinary race team manager, Clive Wood and his assistant Paul Messenger for their generous help.

Others who have contributed so usefully have been: Oxford City Public Library, Warwick University records department, Ricardo Engineering, Percy Tait, Stan Shenton, John Anderson, Pat Davey and Annice Colette (VMCC), Tony Page (editor *Triple Echo*), Roger Stokes (Riley Register), Dr David Styles (VMCC editor), Jim Reynolds, Steve Wilson, Frank Westworth, Rowena Hoseason, Bill Crosby (London Motorcycle Museum), Sheila Page, National Motorcycle Museum, Jim Lee (Turner & Page tapes) Hughie Hancox, Peter Glover and Wilf Harrison, Dan Freeze the Triumph Owners Motorcycle Club (GB), Cyril Ayton, Owen Greenwood, and Triumph Motorcycles (Hinckley).

Index